Communications in Computer and Information Science   2851

Series Editors

Gang Li, *School of Information Technology, Deakin University, Burwood, VIC, Australia*

Joaquim Filipe, *Polytechnic Institute of Setúbal, Setúbal, Portugal*

Zhiwei Xu, *Chinese Academy of Sciences, Beijing, China*

Rationale

The CCIS series is devoted to the publication of proceedings of computer science conferences. Its aim is to efficiently disseminate original research results in informatics in printed and electronic form. While the focus is on publication of peer-reviewed full papers presenting mature work, inclusion of reviewed short papers reporting on work in progress is welcome, too. Besides globally relevant meetings with internationally representative program committees guaranteeing a strict peer-reviewing and paper selection process, conferences run by societies or of high regional or national relevance are also considered for publication.

Topics

The topical scope of CCIS spans the entire spectrum of informatics ranging from foundational topics in the theory of computing to information and communications science and technology and a broad variety of interdisciplinary application fields.

Information for Volume Editors and Authors

Publication in CCIS is free of charge. No royalties are paid, however, we offer registered conference participants temporary free access to the online version of the conference proceedings on SpringerLink (http://link.springer.com) by means of an http referrer from the conference website and/or a number of complimentary printed copies, as specified in the official acceptance email of the event.

CCIS proceedings can be published in time for distribution at conferences or as post-proceedings, and delivered in the form of printed books and/or electronically as USBs and/or e-content licenses for accessing proceedings at SpringerLink. Furthermore, CCIS proceedings are included in the CCIS electronic book series hosted in the SpringerLink digital library at http://link.springer.com/bookseries/7899. Conferences publishing in CCIS are allowed to use Online Conference Service (OCS) for managing the whole proceedings lifecycle (from submission and reviewing to preparing for publication) free of charge.

Publication process

The language of publication is exclusively English. Authors publishing in CCIS have to sign the Springer CCIS copyright transfer form, however, they are free to use their material published in CCIS for substantially changed, more elaborate subsequent publications elsewhere. For the preparation of the camera-ready papers/files, authors have to strictly adhere to the Springer CCIS Authors' Instructions and are strongly encouraged to use the CCIS LaTeX style files or templates.

Abstracting/Indexing

CCIS is abstracted/indexed in DBLP, Google Scholar, EI-Compendex, Mathematical Reviews, SCImago, Scopus. CCIS volumes are also submitted for the inclusion in ISI Proceedings.

How to start

To start the evaluation of your proposal for inclusion in the CCIS series, please send an e-mail to ccis@springer.com.

Claus Pahl · Maarten van Steen
Editors

Cloud Computing and Services Science

14th International Conference, CLOSER 2024
Angers, France, May 2–4, 2024
Revised Selected Papers

 Springer

Editors
Claus Pahl
Free University of Bozen-Bolzano
Bolzano, Italy

Maarten van Steen
Digital Society Institute University of Twente
Enschede, The Netherlands

ISSN 1865-0929   ISSN 1865-0937 (electronic)
Communications in Computer and Information Science
ISBN 978-3-032-17285-3   ISBN 978-3-032-17286-0 (eBook)
https://doi.org/10.1007/978-3-032-17286-0

This Springer imprint is published by the registered company Springer Nature Switzerland AG
The registered company address is: Gewerbestrasse 11, 6330 Cham, Switzerland

If disposing of this product, please recycle the paper.

Preface

The present book includes extended and revised versions of selected papers from the 14th International Conference on Cloud Computing and Services Science (CLOSER 2024), held in Angers, France, from 2–4 May.

The International Conference on Cloud Computing and Services Science aims to bring together engineers, researchers and practitioners interested in advances and applications concerning the cloud infrastructure, operations and available services through the global network. Further, the conference considers as essential the link to Services Science, acknowledging the service-orientation in most current IT-driven collaborations, and provides a forum for discussing how Services Science can provide theory, methods and techniques to design, analyze, manage, market and study various aspects of Cloud Computing.

CLOSER 2024 received 48 paper submissions from 20 countries, of which seven (15%) were included in this book.

The papers were selected by the event chairs and their selection was based on a number of criteria that included the classifications and comments provided by the program committee members, the session chairs' assessment and also the program chairs' global view of all papers included in the technical program. The authors of selected papers were invited to submit revised and extended versions of their papers with at least 30% innovative material. The review process was double blind, and submissions received three reviews each on average.

The papers selected to be included in this book contribute to the understanding of relevant trends of current research on Cloud Computing and Services Science, including Microservices and their Management, Container Orchestration, Cloud Quality Management covering Security, Trust and Performance as critical concerns, and Edge Cloud Architectures.

We would like to thank all the authors for their contributions and also the reviewers who helped ensure the quality of this publication.

May 2024

Claus Pahl
Maarten van Steen

Organization

Conference Chair

Claus Pahl   Free University of Bozen-Bolzano, Italy

Program Chair

Maarten van Steen   Digital Society Institute, University of Twente, Netherlands

Program Committee

Luca Abeni	Scuola Superiore Sant'Anna, Italy
Enis Afgan	Johns Hopkins University, USA
Fotis Aisopos	National Center for Scientific Research Demokritos, Greece
Jameela Al-Jaroodi	Robert Morris University, USA
Artur Andrzejak	Heidelberg University, Germany
Marco Anisetti	Università degli Studi di Milano, Italy
Claudio Ardagna	Universita degli Studi di Milano, Italy
Seyed Morteza Babamir	University of Kashan, Iran
André Bauer	Illinois Institute of Technology, USA
Nicola Bena	Università degli Studi di Milano, Italy
Samaresh Bera	IIT Jammu, India
David Bermbach	TU Berlin, Germany
Filippo Berto	University of Milan, Italy
Radhakrishna Bhat	Manipal Institute of Technology, Manipal Academy of Higher Education, India
Luiz F. Bittencourt	State University of Campinas, Brazil
Cristina Boeres	Fluminense Federal University, Brazil
Agustin C. Caminero	Universidad Nacional de Educación a Distancia, Spain
Manuel Capel-Tuñón	University of Granada, Spain
Eddy Caron	École Normale Supérieure de Lyon, France
Adrián Castelló	Universitat Politècnica de València, Spain
Thierry Coupaye	Orange, France

Hermann de Meer	University of Passau, Germany
Francisco Duarte	University of Minho, Portugal
Patricia Takako Endo	Universidade de Pernambuco, Brazil
Paul Ezhilchelvan	Newcastle University, UK
Bernd Freisleben	University of Marburg, Germany
Somchart Fugkeaw	Thammasat University, Thailand
Vinicius Garcia	Federal University of Pernambuco, Brazil
Martin Gilje Jaatun	SINTEF, Norway
Sukhpal Singh Gill	Queen Mary University of London, UK
Lee Gillam	Independent Researcher, UK
Nils Gruschka	University of Oslo, Norway
Marco Guazzone	University of Eastern Piedmont, Italy
Stefan Kehrer	Reutlingen University, Germany
Attila Kertesz	University of Szeged, Hungary
Sunirmal Khatua	University of Calcutta, India
Nane Kratzke	Lübeck University of Applied Sciences, Germany
Adam Krechowicz	Kielce University of Technology, Poland
Giuliano Laccetti	University of Naples "Federico II", Italy
Riccardo Lancellotti	University of Modena and Reggio Emilia, Italy
Shijun Liu	Shandong University, China
Xiaodong Liu	Edinburgh Napier University, UK
Francesco Longo	Università degli Studi di Messina, Italy
Joseph Loyall	BBN Technologies, USA
Ioannis Mavridis	University of Macedonia, Greece
Andre Miede	Hochschule fuer Technik und Wirtschaft des Saarlandes, Germany
Antonio Montieri	University of Naples Federico II, Italy
Kamran Munir	University of the West of England, UK
Juan Murillo Rodríguez	University of Extremadura, Spain
Hidemoto Nakada	Juntendo University, Japan
Philippe Navaux	Federal University of Rio Grande do Sul, Brazil
Michael Palis	Rutgers University, USA
Marcin Paprzycki	Polish Academy of Sciences, Poland
David Paul	University of New England, Australia
Dana Petcu	West University of Timisoara, Romania
Christian Prehofer	DENSO Automotive Germany, Germany
Radu Prodan	University of Klagenfurt, Austria
Antonio Puliafito	Università degli Studi di Messina, Italy
Gleb Radchenko	Silicon Austria Labs, Austria
Christoph Reich	Furtwangen University, Germany
António Rosado da Cruz	Instituto Politécnico de Viana do Castelo, Portugal
Patrizia Scandurra	University of Bergamo, Italy

Yuji Sekiya	University of Tokyo, Japan
Richard Sinnott	University of Melbourne, Australia
Frank Siqueira	Federal University of Santa Catarina, Brazil
Ellis Solaiman	Newcastle University, UK
Jacopo Soldani	Università di Pisa, Italy
Ivor Spence	Queen's University of Belfast, UK
Georgios Stavrinides	University of Cyprus, Cyprus
Luiz Angelo Steffenel	Université de Reims Champagne-Ardenne, France
Yasuyuki Tahara	University of Electro-Communications, Japan
Javid Taheri	Karlstad University, Sweden
William Tärneberg	Lund University, Sweden
Gilbert Tekli	NOBATEK, France; University of Balamand, Lebanon
Guy Tel-Zur	Ben-Gurion University of the Negev, Israel
Orazio Tomarchio	University of Catania, Italy
Robert van Engelen	Independent Researcher, USA
Tullio Vardanega	University of Padua, Italy
Yiannis Verginadis	Athens University of Economics and Business, Greece
Huaming Wu	Independent Researcher, China
Michael Zapf	Georg Simon Ohm University of Applied Sciences, Germany
Chrysostomos Zeginis	ICS-FORTH, Greece
Christian Zirpins	Karlsruhe University of Applied Sciences, Germany

Additional Reviewers

Haleh Dizaji	University of Klagenfurt, Austria
Martin Grambow	TU Berlin, Germany
Fabio Moretti	Independent Researcher, Italy

Invited Speakers

Pascal Felber	Université de Neuchâtel, Switzerland
Lydia Chen	Delft University of Technology, Netherlands
Valeria Cardellini	University of Rome Tor Vergata, Italy

Contents

Towards a General Methodology for the Quantification of Performance and Energy Efficiency Trade-Off in Virtualized Data Centers

Carlos Juiz[1], Belen Bermejo[1(✉)], Alejandro Fernández-Montes[2], and Damián Fernández-Cerero[2]

[1] Department of Computer Science, Universitat de les Illes Balears, Palma, Spain
`{cjuiz,belen.bermejo}@uib.es`
[2] Department of Computer Languages and Systems, University of Seville, Sevilla, Spain
`{afdez,dfernandez6}@us.es`

Abstract. Currently, energy consumption and energy efficiency are some of the concerns of cloud system administrators. In recent years standards such as ISO/IEC 30134-4 and ISO/IEC 21836 have emerged to improve energy efficiency. Both standards are focused on the evaluation of physical servers, considering the power consumed and the maximum peak of performance, under running a SPEC benchmark. Then, server consolidation through virtualization is not considered in these standards. However, the QoS is another point that is important to consider, at the same time, by data centers administrators. In this work, we proposed a standard methodology to quantify the trade-off between the energy efficiency and the QoS of consolidated servers. As a result, it has been demonstrated through real experimentation that the proposed methodology considers the consolidation of servers in any type of virtualization environment. Besides, this methodology helps system administrators to manage cloud data centers and servers more efficiently.

Keywords: Server consolidation · Energy efficiency · Performance · Tradeoff · ISO/IEC 30134-4

1 Introduction

Currently, Information Technology (IT) represents around 15% of the worldwide greenhouse gas emissions. There are many contributors to these emissions, but the main contributors to these emissions are cloud data centers. Besides, the use of IT and data centers is increasing day by day since the population is demanding more services, the performance demand for data centers is increasing too.

Nevertheless, increasing the demand for data centers implies an increment in the power consumption of data centers and, particularly, the servers are the most power-demanding devices, that is, the 50% of the power consumption of the whole cloud data center. On this point, it is important to highlight that the reduction in power consumption

C. Pahl and M. van Steen (Eds.): CLOSER 2024, CCIS 2851, pp. 1–28, 2026.
https://doi.org/10.1007/978-3-032-17286-0_1

in cloud data centers can be achieved by lowering the server's performance. However, if users' services or applications consume more time to be performed due to lowering the server's performance, the servers will consume more energy. Then, cloud data centers aim to maximize energy efficiency without interfering with performance, finding a trade-off between them [1].

1.1 Server Consolidation

Server consolidation (or virtual machine consolidation) is one of the techniques to help system administrators to manage servers (and data centres) flexibly. This technique is based on the reallocation of virtual machines (or containers) among different physical servers. That is, it aims to allocate the maximum workload (virtual machines or containers) in the minimum number of physical servers. Then, the utilization of physical resources increases, and the number of switched-on physical servers decreases [8].

For example, in Fig. 1 we can observe that the virtual machines from servers A and C can be moved to the physical server B (if physical server B has enough resources capacity). In this case, the physical server B increases the number of allocated virtual machines (from 4 to 6), and consequently, the utilization of the server B increases too. Nevertheless, servers A and C can be switched off, experimenting with a power consumption reduction. However, the energy consumption reduction is not clear, since it depends directly on the performance of the server (measured typically in response time).

Moreover, the performance overhead of server consolidation is defined as the extra workload that the physical machine has to perform due to the tasks of managing virtual machines (or containers) and coordinating the access to physical resources from the virtual instances. Therefore, the larger the number of consolidated virtual machines within the same physical machine, the higher the overhead is because the hypervisor is in charge of managing virtual machines that simultaneously demand different resources. Therefore, performance degradation occurs due to the overhead of consolidating virtual machines (or containers) in physical machines.

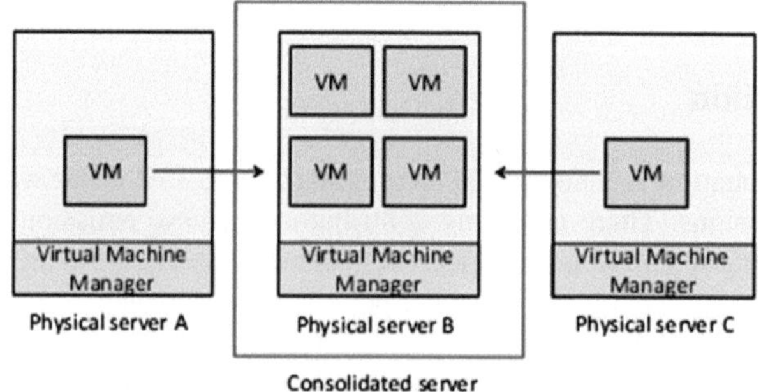

Fig. 1. Server consolidation example based on virtual machines [12].

1.2 ISO/IEC 30134-4

The ISO/IEC 30134 is a standard that specifies data center energy effectiveness KPIs to help cloud data center operators measure and improve specific aspects of energy effectiveness. Specifically, this standard provides a metric, called ITEEsv, reflecting the energy effectiveness capability of servers [4]. ITEEsv defines a method to obtain average energy efficiency for physical servers, where server consolidation is not considered. Moreover, this metric is calculated based on SPEC benchmark. Then, this standard does not consider other current benchmarks or workloads, such as CPU or micro-services-based workloads. Consequently, there is no standard considering server consolidation to balance energy efficiency and performance degradation.

1.3 ISO/IEC 21836

The ISO/IEC 30134 series specifies data center energy efficiency KPIs to help data center administrators measuring and improving specific aspects of data center effectiveness. This standard defines a method to measure the peak capacity and utilization of servers operating in a data center using operator-selected benchmarks. However, it does not provide a method for comparing individual server energy efficiency across data centers, as stated in ISO/IEC 30134-4. The standard ISO/IEC 21836 provides a server energy efficiency metric (SEEM) to measure and report the energy effectiveness of specific server designs and configurations [5].

Since the ISO/IEC 30134-4 does not provide a method for comparing individual server energy efficiency across data centers, the ISO/IEC 21836 appears to fill the mentioned gap. Even though the ISO/IEC 21836 provides a methodology to measure energy efficiency in data centers, it is not devoted to virtualization. Besides, this standard does not consider the server consolidation server. Then, the ISO/IEC 21836 lacks one of the main features of current data centers.

1.4 Contribution and Work Structure

As we depicted in previous sections, ISO/IEC 30134-4 and ISO/IEC 21836 do not consider the trade-off between QoS (or performance) and energy consumption in server consolidation environments (with virtual machines and/or containers). Therefore, the main contribution of this work is the proposal of a standard methodology to quantify the trade-off between the energy efficiency and QoS of consolidated servers. In addition, it is important to highlight that this work is an extension of a previous one, published by [12].

This work is structured in the following sections: Sect. 1 introduces and defines the problem we attempt to solve. Then, in Sect. 2, the metrics regarding the current energy efficiency are depicted. In Sect. 3, we performed a theoretical evaluation of the current energy efficiency metrics. In Sect. 4, the current methodology is evaluated, which is based on the ITEEsv metric. From the obtained results, we proposed a new methodology based on the CiS^2 metric to cover the research gap we found. In the same manner, we performed a set of experiments to demonstrate that our methodology is suitable for solving the problem. The obtained results are discussed in Sect. 6, and we conclude with the more relevant issues and future work in Sect. 7.

2 Server Energy Efficiency Metrics

In [1], authors compared the performance, energy, power, and performance-energy trade-off metrics from the cloud data center and server point of view. Since in this work we attempt to propose a methodology to evaluate the performance and energy consumption trade-off generically, we will consider the generic server's metric [4, 5].

2.1 Energy-Delay Product (EDP)

The Energy-Delay Product considers the total energy consumption of CPUs (or any core processor units) and the time for executing applications [3]. Then, the EDP is calculated as the product of the energy consumption and the response time.

It is important to note that the EDP, originally, was created for microprocessors. But it can also be applied to servers, where the energy consumption corresponds to the energy consumed by the physical server performing a workload, and the response time corresponds to the needed time to execute the workload [1, 3].

2.2 CiS^2 Index

The CiS^2 index is a metric aiming to quantify the "goodness" of a consolidation configuration [7]. That is, it measures the trade-off between the energy consumption and the performance degradation of a physical server which is consolidating a set of virtual machines (or containers) [8]. Since the trade-off is based on the comparison between a physical server and the same physical server with virtual machines consolidated, the CiS^2 index is calculated as Eq. 1 shows:

$$CiS^2 = SP_p \cdot SP_e \tag{1}$$

where SP_p is the speed-up of the performance of consolidating a server, and the SP_e is the ratio of the energy consumption of the physical server and the consolidated one. Considering this definition, the CiS^2 metric can be applied to any type of server, any type of workload nature, and any virtualization platform.

2.3 ITEEsv Index

ITEEsv is a metric that describes the maximum performance per kW of all servers or a group of servers in the data center, based upon a specification or potential performance of these servers [4, 5]. Then, the server energy effectiveness is a combination of the capacity to do work per unit energy (capability), the amount of time the server is doing work (utilization), and the ability of the server to reduce the energy used when the workload is reduced (power management). The ITEEsv metric is calculated as Eq. 2 shows.

$$ITEE_{sv} = \frac{\sum_{i=1}^{n} SMPE_i}{\sum_{i=1}^{n} SMPO_i} \tag{2}$$

where $SMPE_i$ is the maximum performance of a server i, and $SMPO_i$ is the maximum power consumption of a server i. For this metric, the maximum performance is obtained from a specific benchmark execution, which is based on transactional workload, being the throughput of the system the performance metric.

2.4 Relation Between Metrics

As we stated previously, this work aims to determine which metrics are more suitable to measure the trade-off between the performance and the energy consumption in server consolidation. For this reason, some statements should be considered:

- The metric of ITTEsv is to provide the relationship between the maximum performance and the maximum power consumption of a physical server. In any case, the virtualization is not considered in this metric.
- The ITTEsv considers a transactional-based workload. Then, if the server workload has a different nature, the metric calculation should be modified. For example, if the workload is CPU-based and the maximum performance is measured in time units, the maximum performance should be calculated as $\frac{1}{\sum_{i=1}^{n} SMPE_i}$ (time and throughput are inversely related). Besides, for this metric, the maximum power consumption is expressed in kilowatts. Therefore, if a comparison is needed between this metric and another power metric, the power values should be scaled.
- As the ITEEsv shows, it does not consider energy consumption. It just considers the power consumed by a specific scenario of the physical servers. Considering only the maximum power consumption (or the power consumption) is not realistic at all. Having the maximum power consumption occurs in special moments during the system execution. However, out of these special moments, the power consumption is not at its maximum value. For this, considering the energy consumption would be more suitable.
- If we want to use the ITEEsv to compare the physical server and the consolidated one, it is necessary to use the following algebra, where c corresponds to the consolidated server and p corresponds to the physical one.

$$\frac{ITEE_{sv}^{c}}{ITEE_{sv}^{p}} = \frac{\frac{1}{R^c}}{\frac{1}{R^p}} = \frac{\frac{power^c}{R^c}}{\frac{power^p}{R^p}} = \frac{R^p \cdot power^c}{R^c \cdot power^p} \tag{3}$$

- The EDP metric considers energy consumption. Nevertheless, in the same manner, as ITEEsv, the EDP considers the state of the energy consumption and the performance of a system in a specific time and conditions. For this reason, the EDP is not suitable for comparing different scenarios for server consolidation. If we would like to compare different scenarios of server consolidation, the use of the CIS^2 provides the relation with EDP (see Eq. 4).

$$CiS^2 = SP_p \cdot SP_e = \frac{R^c}{R^p} \cdot \frac{E^c}{E^p} = \frac{R^c}{R^p} \cdot \frac{R^c \cdot power^c}{R^p \cdot power^p} = \frac{EDP^c}{EDP^p} \tag{4}$$

3 Theoretical View of the Metrics

To evaluate the EDP, the CiS^2, and the ITEEsv metrics in a theoretical manner, we proceed to consider the index and metrics requirements definitions from [4] and [5], and then, apply them to our set of metrics (see Table 1).

These requirements are: quantifiability, sensitivity, linearity, reliability, efficiency, and improvement oriented. It is important to highlight that in this paper, a change in the system's state is a variation in the number of consolidated virtual machines/containers.

After performing this analysis, we can state that all the metrics meet the requirements for being a suitable metric. Nevertheless, from the semantic point of view, the ITEEsv and EDP metrics do not reflect the reality of performance and energy trade-offs in server consolidation. Consequently, the CiS^2 index is the most suitable metric for this aim.

Table 1. Theoretical analysis of metrics.

Feature/Metric	CiS^2	EDP	ITEEsv
Quantifiability	If performance and energy metrics are not quantitative by nature, they have to be transformed. In this case, the value of the CiS^2 index is a real number resulting from multiplying the speed-up of performance and the energy ratio	The value of the EDP index is a real number, resulting in multiplying the mean response time and the energy consumption	The value of the ITEEsv index is a real number, and it results from the division between the maximum performance and the maximum power consumption of a server
Sensitivity	It expresses how much the performance and energy should change before the system state change can be detected. Therefore, a sensitive metric can detect even minor changes in performance or energy. The CiS^2 value depends on the provision of the underlying measurements. Also, the CiS^2 metric is very sensitive even for minor changes in the server performance or energy	It expresses how much energy consumption and response time should change before the system state change can be detected. The EDP value depends on the precision of the underlying measurements. Also, the EDP metric is very sensitive to even minor changes in performance (response time), power consumption, and the consequent energy consumption	The ITEEsv value depends on the precision of the underlying measurements. Also, the ITEEsv metric is very sensitive to even minor changes in the maximum performance and the maximum power consumption

(continued)

Table 1. (*continued*)

Feature/Metric	CiS^2	EDP	ITEEsv
Linearity	It indicates the extent to which process performance or energy changes are congruent with the value of a certain metric. Or, conversely, a small change in the value of a corresponding performance and energy metric whereas an ample performance and energy metric. The CiS^2 is calculated as the product of the efficiency of performance (seconds) and the efficiency of the energy consumption (W·s). Then, the time has more weight in the CiS^2 value and a small change in this value modifies the CiS^2 quadratically	The EDP is calculated as the product of performance (expressed in time units) and energy consumption (expressed in W·s). Then, the time has more weight in the EDP value, and a small change in this value modifies the EDP quadratically	The ITEEsv is calculated as the division of the maximum performance and the maximum power consumption. Then, a small change in both values modifies the ITEEsv
Reliability	The value of the CiS^2 metric is computed using measurable facts and there are no subjective components included in the measurements	The value of the EDP metric is computed using measurable facts and there are no subjective components included in the measurements	The value of the ITEEsv metric is computed using measurable facts and there are no subjective components included in the measurements

(continued)

Table 1. (*continued*)

Feature/Metric	CiS^2	EDP	ITEEsv
Efficiency	Since the measurement itself requires human, financial, and physical resources it must be worth the effort from a cost/benefit point of view. In this case, computing the CiS^2 value is lightweight and requires little computing power. The response time can be directly read from the workload monitor from OS (software) while the power consumption can be directly read either from the power monitor (hardware) or from software monitors included in servers. Moreover, the calculation of the energy consumption as the product of mean response time and the average power consumption is not a weight computing process	Computing the EDP value is lightweight and requires little computing power. The response time can be directly read from the workload monitor from OS (software) while the power consumption can be directly read either from the power monitor (hardware) or from software monitors included in servers. Moreover, the calculation of the energy consumption as the product of mean response time and the average power consumption is not a weight computing process. As a consequence, the product of the response time and the energy consumption (EDP calculation) is also a lightweight process	Computing the ITEEsv value is lightweight and requires little computing power. The maximum performance can be directly read from the workload monitor from OS (software) while the maximum power consumption can be directly read either from the power monitor (hardware) or from software monitors included in servers. As a consequence, the division of the maximum performance and the maximum power consumption (ITEEsv calculation) is also a lightweight process
Improvement-oriented	The CiS^2 metric measures the performance and energy of the process, even errors or non-optimal behavior of the administrative personnel operating a data center	The EDP metric measures the performance and energy of the process, even errors or non-optimal behavior of the personnel operating a data center	The ITEEsv metric measures the performance and power consumption of the process, even errors or non-optimal behavior of the personnel operating a data center

4 Current Methodology: Evaluation of ITEEsv Metric

In this section, we attempt to demonstrate if the ITEEsv is suitable for server consolidation from the empirical point of view.

4.1 Experimental Setup

The experimental methodology is based on the comparison of CPU-intensive workloads [9]. In this case, the Sysbench v0.4 benchmark [2]. Besides, the workload is distributed balanced over N physical machines against the same workload distributed over N virtual machines or containers consolidated in a single physical machine (see Fig. 2). The comparison is made in terms of the ITEEsv metric. In this work, we consider the system under test (SUT) as a black box, applying benchmarking and monitoring as performance engineering techniques [6, 10]. The SUT executes the workload, and its performance and power consumption are monitored during the workload execution. We selected the response time as a performance metric. Also, the experiment setup is as follows:

- Physical servers: all the physical servers have deployed the Ubuntu 16.04 server as an OS.

    - Dell Power Edge T430 (16 CPUs and 8 GB RAM size).
    - Dell Power Edge T330 (8 CPUs and 16 GB RAM size).
    - Fijitsu RX600S5-1 (48 CPUs and 1024 GB RAM size).
    - Lenovo ST550 (20 CPUs and 96 GB RAM size).

- Power meter: we measured the power consumption of the SUT with a Chroma 66200 device. It is important to mention that the power consumption of the Fijitsu RX600S5-1 server was measured using a software monitor.
- Virtual Machine Monitor: Kernel-based Virtualization (KVM) (Type-I), Virtual Box (Type-II) and Docker (container-based). It is important to highlight that for the Lenovo ST550 server, the deployed hypervisor was only KVM.
- Virtual Machines and containers: Ubuntu 16.04 server as an OS, 1GB of RAM, and the same number of physical CPUs, in any case. The consolidated virtual machines and containers use the space-sharing policy. That is, all the virtual machines and containers use all the available resources from the physical machine.

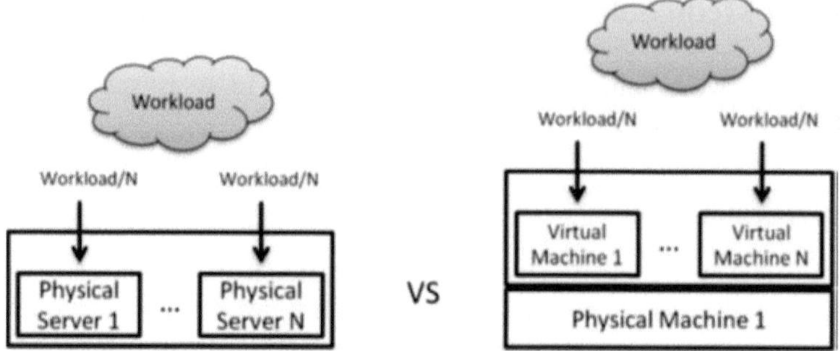

Fig. 2. Workload execution comparison [12].

For the physical servers Dell Power Edge T430, Dell Power Edge T330 and Fijitsu RX600S5-1 execute a Sysbench CPU workload equal to 100.000 prime number. Then, we will compare them. On the contrary, in the Lenovo ST550 server, the workload varies from 50.000, and 200.000 prime numbers. In this case, we can evaluate the workload variation.

4.2   ITEEsv for Physical Machines with a Fixed Amount of Workload

In Table 1, we can observe the behavior of N parallel physical machines executing a workload (100.000 prime numbers) in a distributed manner. The mean response time decreases when the number of distributed physical machines increases. Then, the performance is being improved among the number of physical machines. Besides, when the number of distributed physical machines increases, the power consumption increases similarly.

Since the performance is measured in time units instead of throughput, the ITEEsv metric was calculated considering the maximum as the inverse of the mean response time. Then, when the number of physical machines increases, the performance also increases. As a result, for each type of physical server, the ITEEsv value grows when the number of physical machines increases.

Therefore, the behavior of the ITEEsv does not depend on the hardware features, as Fig. 3 shows. Nevertheless, the values of the ITEEsv change for the different physical servers. As Table 2 shows, for the RX600S5-1 server, the values of this metric are lower than the values of T430 and T330 servers. Moreover, the values for T330 are lower than the ones for T430 server. That means that when the powerful are the computation resources, the lower are the ITEEsv values since more powerful computation resources means a better performance.

Table 2. ITTEsv of physical machines, where 1/R is the maximum performance, the power is measured in kW and the energy consumption is measured in W·s (100.000 prime numbers).

	T430					T330					RX600S5-1				
N	R	1/R	Power	Energy	ITEEsv	R	1/R	Power	Energy	ITEEsv	R	1/R	Power	Energy	ITEEsv
1	24,253	0,041	0,094	2272,622	0,440	48,543	0,021	0,071	3456,387	0,289	80,902	0,012	0,252	20387,228	0,049
2	9,271	0,108	0,187	1735,410	0,576	19,128	0,052	0,143	2727,170	0,367	31,145	0,032	0,504	15697,181	0,064
3	5,297	0,189	0,280	1485,739	0,673	11,198	0,089	0,216	2418,367	0,414	18,264	0,055	0,756	13807,282	0,072
4	3,563	0,281	0,371	1322,572	0,756	7,631	0,131	0,284	2166,709	0,462	12,085	0,083	1,008	12181,277	0,082
5	2,625	0,381	0,464	1216,827	0,822	5,677	0,176	0,354	2008,636	0,498	8,934	0,112	1,260	11256,966	0,089
6	2,039	0,491	0,556	1133,616	0,882	4,474	0,224	0,423	1891,466	0,529	6,973	0,143	1,512	10543,630	0,095
7	1,567	0,638	0,651	1019,921	0,980	3,647	0,274	0,478	1743,966	0,573	5,691	0,176	1,764	10038,571	0,100
8	1,309	0,764	0,744	974,343	1,026	3,068	0,326	0,522	1602,021	0,624	4,787	0,209	2,016	9651,398	0,104
9	1,130	0,885	0,837	945,944	1,057	2,633	0,380	0,566	1489,343	0,671	4,045	0,247	2,268	9173,153	0,109

4.3 ITEEsv for Consolidated Servers with a Fixed Amount of Workload

In this section, we depict the obtained results of the ITEEsv metric from the consolidated servers. That is Type-I hypervisor, Type-II hypervisor and container-based hypervisor.

4.3.1 Type-I Hypervisor

In Table 3, we can observe the ITEEsv metric from the Type-I hypervisor for N parallel virtual machines allocated in a single physical machine. The results are divided into the different physical servers.

For any kind of physical server, the behavior of the response time (performance) and the ITEEsv are the same than the physical server behavior. In this case, when the number of virtual machines increases, the mean response time decreases, having a better performance. In the same manner, this fact is due to the workload division among the different numbers of virtual machines.

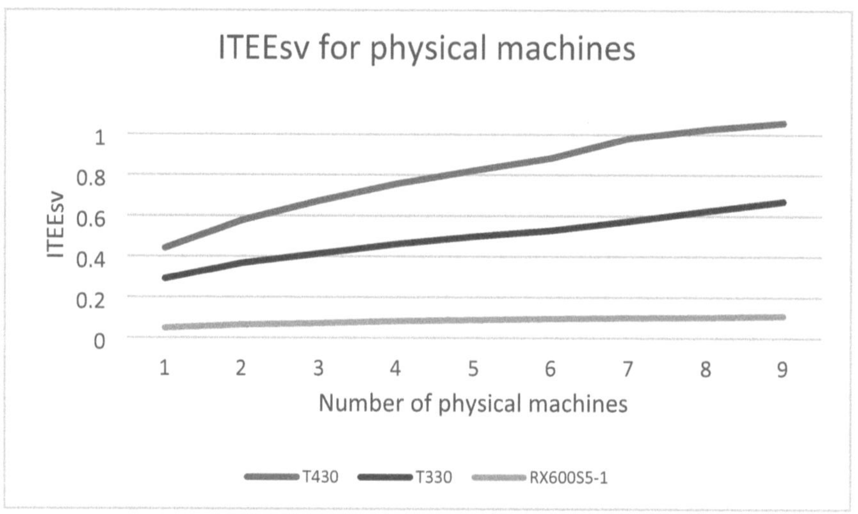

Fig. 3. ITEEsv of physical machines (100.000 prime numbers).

Regarding the power consumption, in this case, it does not increase when the number of virtual machines grows, since the set of virtual machines is allocated in a single physical machine.

As a result, for each type of physical server, the ITEEsv value grows when the number of virtual machines increases, as Fig. 4 represents. Besides, the values of the ITEEsv change for the different physical servers. As Table 3 shows, for the RX600S5-1server, the values of this metric are lower than the values of T430 and T330 servers. Moreover, the values for T330 are lower than the ones for T430 server.

In addition, if we compare the values of the ITEEsv of Type-I hypervisor and physical machines, we can see that for the Type-I hypervisor is lower than for physical machines. This fact is due to the overhead of the virtual machines since they have lesser performance than the physical ones [1]. That is, the virtual machines take more time to execute the same workload than a physical machine due to the hypervisor layer.

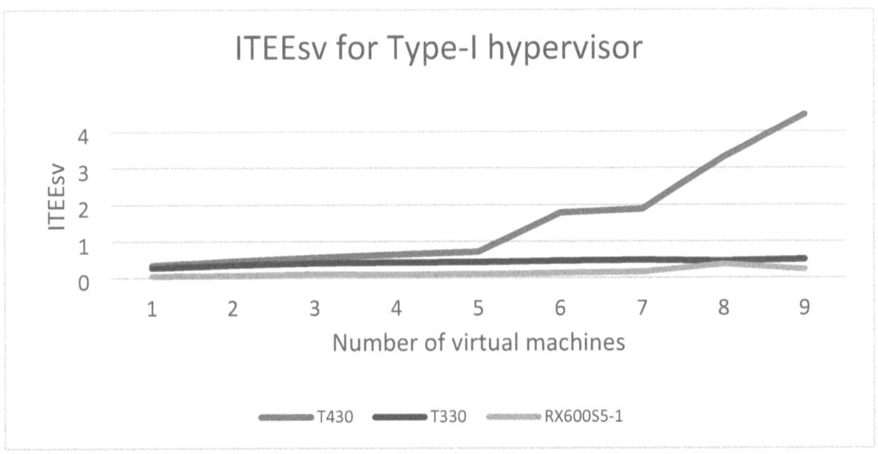

Fig. 4. ITEEsv of consolidated server using Type-I hypervisor (100.000 prime numbers).

Table 3. ITTEsv of consolidated servers using Type-I hypervisor, where 1/R is the maximum performance, the power is measured in kW and the energy consumption is measured in W·s (100.000 prime numbers).

N	T430					T330					RX600S5-1				
	R	1/R	Power	Energy	ITEEsv	R	1/R	Power	Energy	ITEEsv	R	1/R	Power	Energy	ITEEsv
1	25,426	0,039	0,111	2831,414	0,353	50,147	0,020	70,308	3525,749	0,284	83,334	0,012	252,000	21000,092	0,048
2	19,289	0,052	0,112	2156,609	0,464	40,877	0,024	68,057	2781,946	0,359	62,777	0,016	252,000	15819,854	0,063
3	15,838	0,063	0,113	1784,784	0,560	36,020	0,028	67,476	2430,515	0,411	41,863	0,024	252,000	10549,392	0,095
4	13,978	0,072	0,111	1554,018	0,643	33,163	0,030	70,563	2340,111	0,427	45,184	0,022	252,000	11386,374	0,088
5	12,542	0,080	0,111	1395,010	0,717	32,433	0,031	69,920	2267,701	0,441	41,438	0,024	252,000	10442,300	0,096
6	5,156	0,194	0,109	561,849	1,780	31,055	0,032	68,753	2135,132	0,468	30,193	0,033	252,000	7608,560	0,131
7	5,079	0,197	0,105	532,651	1,877	29,736	0,034	68,485	2036,441	0,491	24,656	0,041	252,000	6213,262	0,161
8	2,896	0,345	0,104	302,470	3,306	31,610	0,032	68,539	2166,508	0,462	10,875	0,092	252,000	2740,500	0,365
9	2,293	0,436	0,098	224,030	4,464	29,091	0,034	67,548	1965,012	0,509	17,208	0,058	252,000	4336,391	0,231

4.3.2 Type-Ii Hypervisor

In Table 4, we can observe the ITEEsv metric from the Type-II hypervisor for N parallel virtual machines allocated in a single physical machine. In the same way, the results are divided into the different physical servers.

For any kind of physical server, the behavior of the response time (performance) and the ITEEsv are the same than the physical server and type-I hypervisor behavior. In this case, when the number of virtual machines increases, the mean response time decreases, having a better performance. In the same manner, this fact is due to the workload division among the different numbers of virtual machines.

Regarding power consumption, the behaviour is like type-I hypervisor, since the consolidation architecture is the same.

As a result, for each type of physical server, the ITEEsv value grows when the number of virtual machines increases, as Fig. 5 represents. Besides, the values of the ITEEsv change for the different physical servers. As Table 3 shows, for the RX600S5-1server, the values of this metric are lower than the values of T430 and T330 servers. Moreover, the values for T330 are lower than the ones for T430 server, being the values of T430 server the highest ones. This fact is due to the hardware features and the type-II hypervisor. That is, the T430 is not the most suitable server to consolidate virtual machines with type-II hypervisor.

In addition, if we compare the values of the ITEEsv of Type-II hypervisor and physical machines, we can see that the Type-II hypervisor is lower than for physical machines and Type-I hypervisor. This fact is due to the overhead of the virtual machines since they have lesser performance than the physical ones [1]. The type-II virtual machines take more time to execute the same workload than a type-I hypervisor.

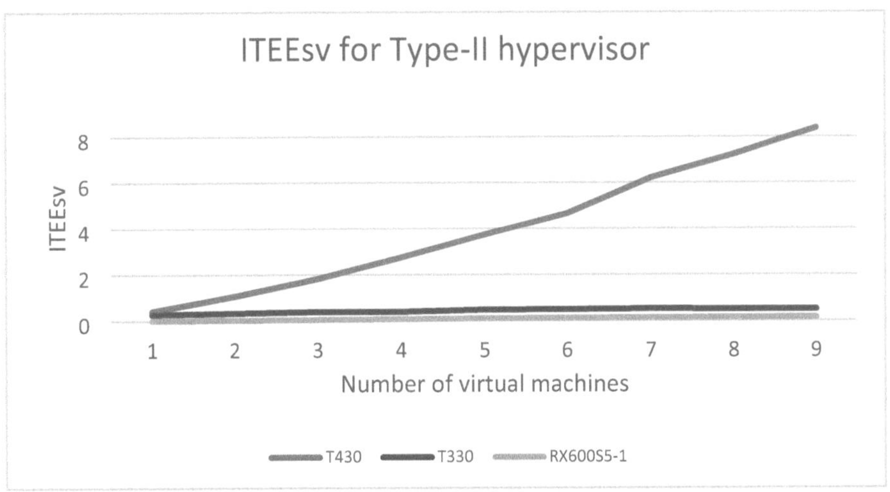

Fig. 5. ITEEsv of consolidated server using Type-I hypervisor (100.000 prime numbers).

Table 4. ITTEsv of consolidated servers using Type-II hypervisor, where 1/R is the maximum performance, the power is measured in kW and the energy consumption is measured in W·s (100.000 prime numbers).

N	T430					T330					RX600S5–1				
	R	1/R	Power	Energy	ITEEsv	R	1/R	Power	Energy	ITEEsv	R	1/R	Power	Energy	ITEEsv
1	26,215	0,038	93,441	2449,556	0,408	57,664	0,017	62,703	3615,725	0,277	412,109	0,002	252,000	103851,443	0,010
2	10,069	0,099	93,858	945,056	1,058	47,988	0,021	63,226	3034,092	0,330	170,554	0,006	252,000	42979,495	0,023
3	5,881	0,170	93,763	551,420	1,813	41,649	0,024	63,072	2626,877	0,381	93,200	0,011	252,000	23486,484	0,043
4	3,904	0,256	93,025	363,170	2,754	41,975	0,024	62,493	2623,125	0,381	62,501	0,016	252,000	15750,189	0,063
5	2,875	0,348	92,984	267,329	3,741	34,922	0,029	60,824	2124,116	0,471	45,397	0,022	252,000	11440,040	0,087
6	2,303	0,434	93,084	214,372	4,665	34,567	0,029	60,518	2091,930	0,478	40,273	0,025	252,000	10148,800	0,099
7	1,733	0,577	92,908	161,010	6,211	31,997	0,031	60,797	1945,342	0,514	33,393	0,030	252,000	8415,000	0,119
8	1,478	0,677	93,543	138,257	7,233	33,726	0,030	60,082	2026,295	0,494	30,447	0,033	252,000	7672,594	0,130
9	1,284	0,779	93,091	119,529	8,366	33,869	0,030	60,259	2040,919	0,490	27,554	0,036	252,000	6943,692	0,144

4.3.3 Container-Based Hypervisor

In Table 5, we can observe the ITEEsv metric from the container-based hypervisor for N parallel containers allocated in a single physical machine. In the same way, the results are divided into the different physical servers.

For any kind of physical server, the behavior of the response time (performance) and the ITEEsv are the same than the physical server, type-I and type-II hypervisor behavior. In this case, when the number of containers increases, the mean response time decreases, having a better performance. In the same manner, this fact is due to the workload division among the different numbers of containers.

As a result, for each type of physical server, the ITEEsv value grows when the number of virtual machines increases, as Fig. 6 represents. As Table 5 shows, for the RX600S5-1server, the values of this metric are lower than the values of T430 and T330 servers. Moreover, the values for T330 are lower than the ones for T430 server, being the values of T430 server the highest ones. This fact is due to the hardware features and the container-based hypervisor. That is, the T430 server is not the most suitable server to consolidate virtual machines with containers hypervisor.

In addition, is we compare the values of the ITEEsv of container-based hypervisor and physical machines, we can see that the container's hypervisor is lower than the rest of the hypervisors and physical machines, due to the different nature of the containers [1].

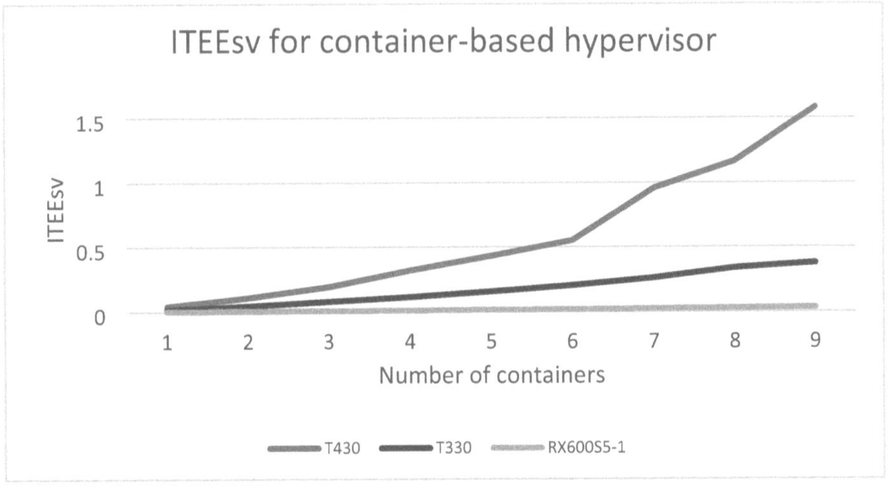

Fig. 6. ITEEsv of consolidated server using Type-I hypervisor (100.000 prime numbers).

Table 5. ITTEsv of consolidated servers using container-based hypervisor, where 1/R is the maximum performance, the power is measured in kW and the energy consumption is measured in W·s (100.000 prime numbers).

	T430					T330					RX600S5-1				
N	R	1/R	Power	Energy	ITEEsv	R	1/R	Power	Energy	ITEEsv	R	1/R	Power	Energy	ITEEsv
1	247,624	0,004	96,597	23919,774	0,042	946,054	0,001	64,004	60551,247	0,017	2646,258	0,000	252,000	666857,092	0,001
2	95,073	0,011	96,393	9164,338	0,109	364,301	0,003	61,037	22235,825	0,045	1017,147	0,001	252,000	256320,918	0,004
3	53,740	0,019	96,519	5186,966	0,193	209,421	0,005	60,981	12770,724	0,078	576,354	0,002	252,000	145241,174	0,007
4	32,627	0,031	96,450	3146,877	0,318	141,691	0,007	62,333	8832,013	0,113	388,115	0,003	252,000	97804,923	0,010
5	23,934	0,042	97,028	2322,313	0,431	103,426	0,010	61,668	6378,086	0,157	273,551	0,004	252,000	68934,892	0,015
6	18,504	0,054	98,037	1814,104	0,551	80,490	0,012	60,979	4908,228	0,204	218,020	0,005	252,000	54941,040	0,018
7	10,625	0,094	98,431	1045,843	0,956	63,148	0,016	61,090	3857,725	0,259	178,311	0,006	252,000	44934,426	0,022
8	8,758	0,114	98,071	858,881	1,164	48,585	0,021	60,999	2963,654	0,337	148,071	0,007	252,000	37313,845	0,027
9	6,518	0,153	97,025	632,416	1,581	43,541	0,023	60,973	2654,847	0,377	124,916	0,008	252,000	31478,922	0,032

At this point, it is important to answer the following question: could we use the ITEEsv metric to compare different consolidation configurations of consolidated servers? Considering the ITEEsv metric definition, it shows the relationship between the maximum performance and the maximum peak power consumed. If the aim is to compare the physical server with the consolidated one, it is necessary to calculate the ratio between the ITEEsv of the consolidated server and the physical one.

Moreover, the ITEEsv does not provide information on whether it is more suitable to consolidate the workload on virtual machines (or containers) or not. This is because the ITEEsv does not consider the energy consumption, and only takes into account the maximum peak power and performance but does not take into account the entire workload execution time.

Therefore, considering the previous results, we can state that the ITEEsv metric is not able to determine the suitability of a server consolidation configuration considering the performance and the energy consumption simultaneously.

4.4 ITEEsv for Consolidated Servers with a Variable Amount of Workload

In this section, we evaluate the ITEEsv metric from the workload variation point of view. In this case, we use the Lenovo ST550 server with Type-I hypervisor, and the workload varies from 50.000, 100.000 and 200.000 prime numbers.

4.4.1 Physical Server

In Fig. 7 and Table 6, we can observe the behavior of the ITEEsv metric when the number of parallel physical machines are increasing for workload variation.

For any amount of workload variation, the ITEEsv value increases when the number of parallel physical machines increases too (see more details in Table 6). This fact is due to the improvement of performance, that is, when the number of parallel machines increases, the amount of workload is divided among the N physical machines.

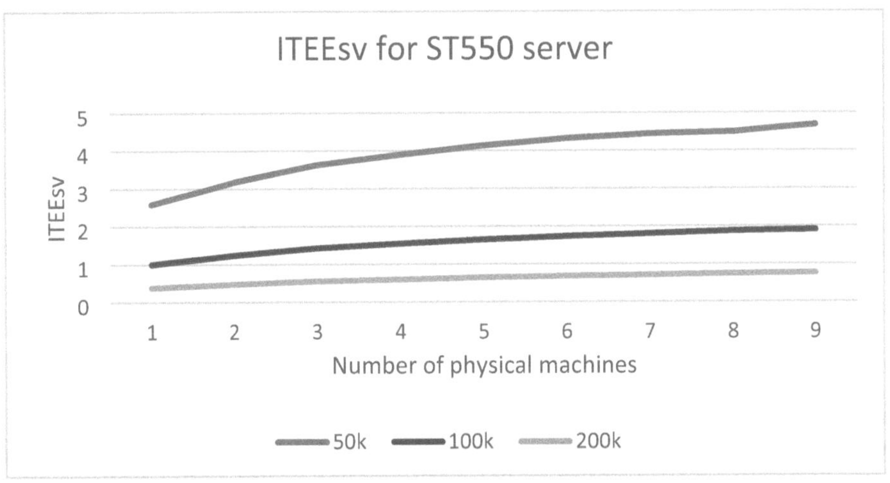

Fig. 7. ITEEsv Lenovo ST550 server for workload variation.

In addition, we can observe that if the amount of workload is higher, the values of ITEEsv metric are lower than the ones for the lower workloads. This fact is due to the nature of the ITEEsv metric since it is calculated considering the maximum peak of performance in terms of the inverse of the mean response time (1/R).

Therefore, it is feasible to compare the physical server under different types of workloads using the ITEEsv metric.

Table 6. ITTEsv of Lenovo ST550.

N	ITEEsv (50k)	ITEEsv (100k)	ITEEsv (200k)
1	2,593	1,000	0,384
2	3,176	1,240	0,478
3	3,625	1,420	0,551
4	3,901	1,539	0,598
5	4,131	1,641	0,642
6	4,322	1,727	0,677
7	4,440	1,795	0,707
8	4,486	1,865	0,735
9	4,673	1,900	0,754

4.4.2 Virtual Machine Consolidation (Type-I)

Regarding the virtual machine consolidation, in Fig. 8 we can observe the behavior of the ITEEsv metric when consolidating virtual machines using Type-I hypervisor and the workload varies.

In this case, we can see that for the higher workloads, the value of ITEEsv is lower, as the case of physical machine. In the same manner, this fact is due to the ITEEsv calculation (maximum peak of performance). Also, for any amount of workload, the ITEEsv value starts decreasing among the number of virtual machines, and then, it starts increasing (see more details in Table 7).

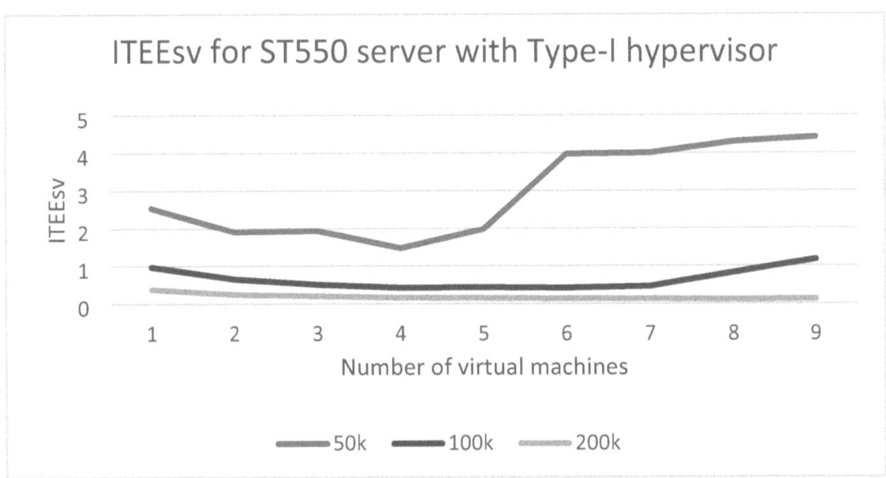

Fig. 8. ITEEsv Lenovo ST550 server consolidation using Type-I hypervisor varying the workload.

Moreover, when the workload amount is 50.000 prime numbers the behavior is different, because the values of ITEEsv metric starts decreasing (from 1 to 5) and then increases in a lower number of virtual machines (from 5 to 9).

It is important to remain that the workload is divided equally among the number of virtual machines. Then, the workload for each virtual machine is decreasing when the number of virtual machines grows. This fact is due to the Type-I hypervisor nature, that is, the virtual machine consolidation overhead [1].

Table 7. ITTEsv of Lenovo ST550 when consolidating virtual machines using Type-I hypervisor and varying the workload.

N	ITEEsv (50k)	ITEEsv (100k)	ITEEsv (200k)
1	2,542	0,971	0,380
2	1,903	0,651	0,243
3	1,928	0,506	0,197
4	1,469	0,420	0,156
5	1,971	0,428	0,144
6	3,971	0,413	0,133
7	4,004	0,451	0,120
8	4,295	0,817	0,104
9	4,420	1,166	0,119

In the same manner, if we want to compare the consolidated server with Type-I consolidation varying the amount of workload, we could only use the ITEEsv metric to compare with the given number of consolidated virtual machines. Then, this comparison would be made without considering energy consumption, disregarding the temporal behavior of power consumption. In this way, we could not determine the suitability of one consolidation configuration or another to consolidate virtual machines under an amount of workload.

As a conclusion, we can say that the ITEEsv metric is not suitable for the comparison between different hypervisors and workload amounts.

5 Proposed Methodology

As we demonstrated in previous sections, the ITEEsv metric is not suitable for the comparison between different server consolidation configurations using different hypervisor types and, under different amount of workloads.

Therefore, in this section, we proposed a generic methodology to measure the energy efficiency in server consolidation based on the CiS^2 metric [7]. As [7] stated, the CiS^2 metric quantifies the performance-energy trade-off of server consolidation, helping system administrators decide the servers' efficiency through benchmarking.

The general methodology is composed of the following phases. It is important to highlight that the workload execution in physical and virtual machines (or containers), was done following the architecture depicted in Fig. 2.

- Phase 1: set up the physical machines. In this stage, the physical machine should be set up with the corresponding workload.
- Phase 2: execution in physical machines with monitoring. After the set-up, the workload division starts with its execution. In parallel, the monitoring system starts to recover data from the performance and power consumption. All of these data should be stored to be used in the last stage of this methodology.
- Phase 3: set up with virtual machines or containers in the same physical machine. At this point, we will use the same physical machine as the previous one. However, deploying a set of virtual machines or containers is necessary to execute the workload.
- Phase 4: execution in virtual machines or containers with monitoring. After the set-up, the workload division starts with its execution in the virtual machines or containers. In parallel, the monitoring system starts to recover data from the performance and the power consumption. It is important to highlight that the performance is measured from the virtual machines or containers, but the power consumption is monitored from the physical machine. All these data should be stored to be used in the last stage of this methodology.
- Phase 5: CiS^2 calculation and comparison. After the workload execution in the physical machines, and the consolidated one, the CiS^2 index is calculated as Eq. 5 shows.

In this stage, the CiS^2 can be calculated using also the EDP metric as Eq. 6 depicts.

$$CiS^2 = S_p \cdot S_e = \frac{R^c}{R^p} \cdot \frac{E^c}{E^p} \tag{5}$$

$$CiS^2 = \frac{EDP^c}{EDP^p} \tag{6}$$

For any number of consolidated virtual machines, a CiS^2 index is obtained. Moreover, the CiS^2 index can be represented graphically as Fig. 9a shows. Also, it is important to note that the CiS^2 index has a reference diagonal aiming to represent the ideal case for consolidation: the linearity of performance and energy. If the CiS^2 value is on the diagonal, the consolidation configuration is the ideal one.

Nevertheless, the values in the green area indicate that the consolidation is efficient. On the contrary, the CiS^2 values in the red area are not efficient for server consolidation. Also, the position in the area influences the efficiency or inefficiency of the CiS^2 value. For example, in Fig. 9b, there are four represented points. Considering the reference diagonal, the point #2 is more efficient than the point #1. However, the point #4 is more inefficient than the point #3.

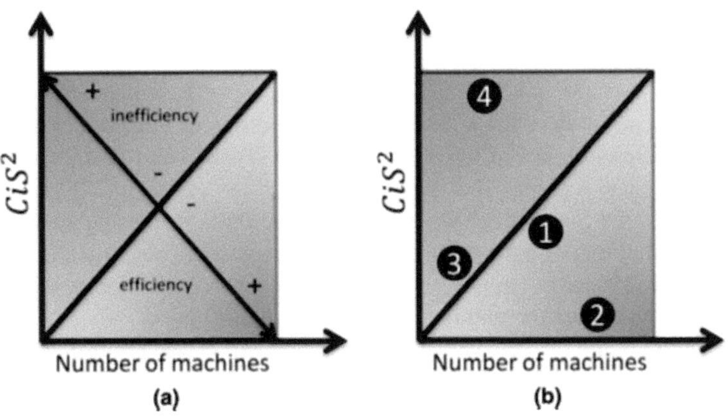

Fig. 9. CiS2 index graphical representation [12].

In addition, the CiS^2 index reference diagonal is represented in Fig. 10. As we can observe, the diagonal points are represented by (1,1), (2,2), ...,(N,N), where the first component of the point is the number of consolidated machines and the second one is the CiS^2 value. Then, a CiS^2 value is determined for each number of consolidated machines (or containers).

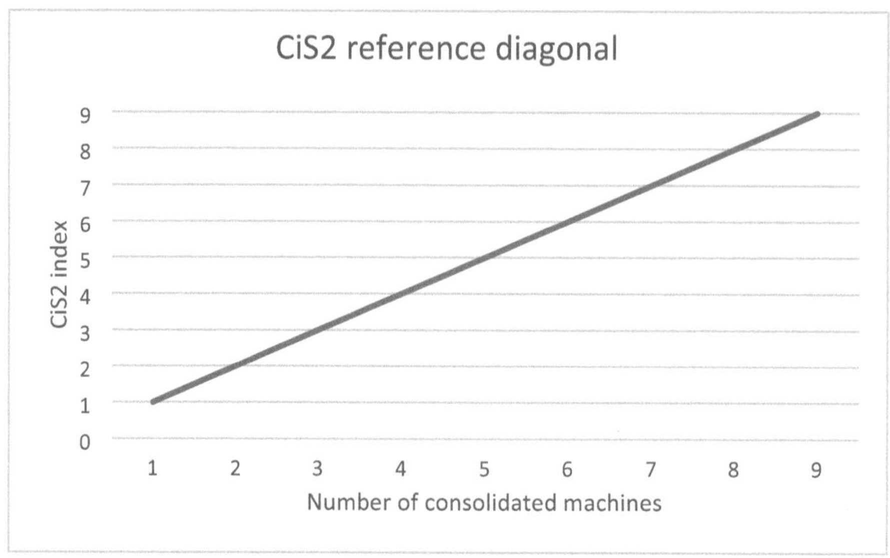

Fig. 10. CiS2 reference diagonal graphical representation.

5.1 CiS2 Metric for Consolidated Servers with a Fixed Amount of Workload

In Table 8, we can observe the CiS^2 index for the different numbers of consolidated machines for different types of hypervisors: Type-I, Type-II and container-based, and for different physical servers.

For any case, we can observe that the CiS^2 value starts increasing and then it goes down when the number of consolidated machines increases. Then, there is an inflexion point with the CiS^2 index. This fact is described in [7] and, it is due to the fact of the workload division among the number of consolidated machines.

Regarding the CiS^2 values, we can observe that the values are different from one physical server to another and from one hypervisor to another. For any physical server, the values of the CiS^2 index for container-based hypervisor are higher than the rest of the hypervisors. This fact is due to the containers' nature, since they are devoted to microservices, and the executed workload for this work is CPU-intensive.

Then, considering the CiS^2 index we can state that it is not efficient to consolidate using containers in terms of performance and energy trade-off. Besides, the T330 server is more efficient for consolidating using Type-I hypervisor and Type-II hypervisor for T430 server. For the T430 server, the consolidation starts to be efficient when N > 5. On the contrary, for the T330, there are no CiS2 values under the diagonal. Then, it is not efficient to consolidate virtual machines in T330 server, despite of Type-II hypervisor is the most efficient.

Table 8. CiS^2 index for the T430, T330 and RX600S5-1 server for a fixed amount of workload considering the number of N consolidated machines (100.000 prime number).

N	T430			T330			RX600S5-1		
	Type-I	Type-II	Containers	Type-I	Type-II	Containers	Type-I	Type-II	Containers
1	1,306	1,165	107,462	1,054	1,243	341,418	1,061	25,948	1069,915
2	2,586	2,297	54,155	2,180	2,791	155,285	2,031	14,994	533,279
3	3,592	3,134	35,418	3,233	4,040	98,761	1,751	8,680	331,959
4	4,610	3,972	21,791	4,693	6,659	75,684	3,495	6,687	257,867
5	5,477	5,483	17,399	6,449	6,505	57,846	4,302	5,164	187,502
6	1,254	3,202	14,526	7,836	8,545	46,686	3,124	5,559	162,916
7	1,693	0,178	6,954	9,521	9,787	38,303	2,682	4,919	140,253
8	0,687	0,163	5,896	13,932	13,903	29,293	0,645	5,056	119,578
9	0,481	0,146	3,858	14,579	17,630	29,482	2,011	5,157	105,985

As we depicted previously, it is possible to compare different consolidation configurations for the same physical server, and the comparison between different physical servers and hypervisors using the CiS^2 index.

5.2   CiS2 Metric for Consolidated Servers with a Variable Amount of Workload

As previous sections, we fixed the amount of workload to obtain the CiS2 index. In Fig. 11, the CiS^2 index is depicted for the different amounts of workloads (50.000, 100.000 and 200.000 prime numbers). Also, the reference diagonal is represented.

In this case, we can observe that for any number of consolidated machines and any amount of workload, the value of the CiS^2 index is under the reference diagonal. Then, all the consolidated configurations are efficient in terms of performance and energy trade-off. Besides, for any amount of workload, the most efficient number of virtual machines are nine (see detailed results in Table 9).

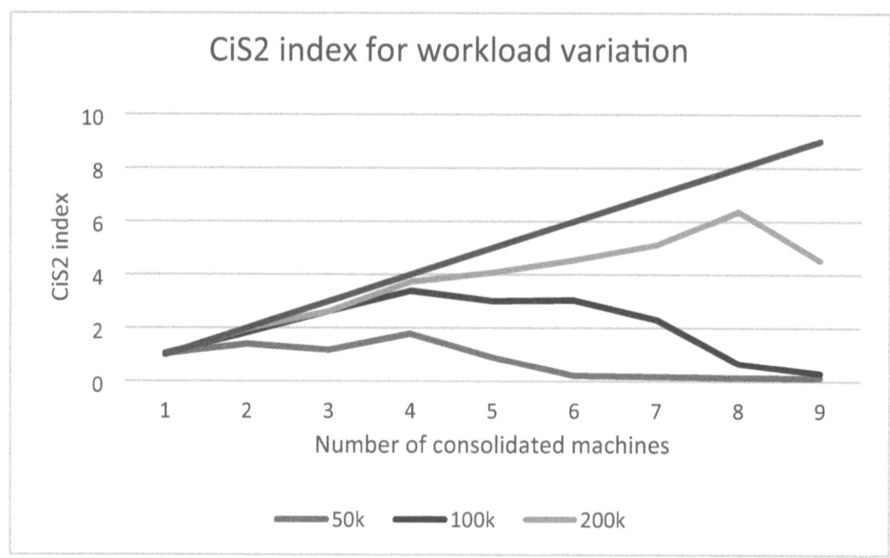

Fig. 11. CiS^2 for ST550 server under different workloads using Type-I hypervisor.

As a results, the CiS^2 index can also be used to compare different consolidated configurations in the same physical server under different amount of workload.

Table 9. CiS^2 index for the Lenovo ST550 server for a variable amount of workload.

N	50k	100k	200k
1	1,034446	1,056047	1,014059
2	1,405335	1,831113	1,953617
3	1,182353	2,63029	2,622791
4	1,785959	3,394539	3,724485
5	0,899285	3,00515	4,071433
6	0,206479	3,048617	4,540486
7	0,179762	2,316884	5,112997
8	0,14012	0,6687	6,370637
9	0,126602	0,300518	4,533869

6 Discussion

Once the evaluation of the ITEEsv metric has been carried out and an alternative methodology has been proposed using the existing CiS^2 metric, we can observe a series of phenomena to consider.

The first is related to the advantages provided by the proposed methodology. This is not restricted using any load (such as those of SPEC) but can be applied to any work scenario. Even the type of virtualization technology used is irrelevant. This is because in this technology the server is considered as a black box.

The second fact is related to the application of the methodology. Deploying virtual machines and containers has a higher cost than just working with physical machines. However, to deploy the scenario required to apply this methodology, it can be easily automated with current tools.

The last refers to the distribution of the load that uses the proposed methodology. As has been seen, it is necessary to use a load than can be distributed among the N physical and virtual servers. However, dividing the load is not a trivial task, and in this case, it would be necessary to correctly select the mentioned workload.

To conclude, we could say that although the deployment of the proposed methodology requires some investment, the truth is that by taking into account the consolidation of virtual machines and containers, a current need would be satisfied.

7 Conclusions and Future Work

Throughout this work, we determined the suitability of the consolidated servers through the current standards: ISO/IEC 30134-4 and ISO/IEC 21836, using real experimentation. It has been proven that both standards are not suitable for server consolidation. As a solution, a generic methodology based on the calculation of the CiS^2 metric has been proposed to cover this knowledge gap. In this way, the proposed methodology could be applied to any server consolidation scenario (any hypervisor and workload type and amount).

As a line of future work, the formal standardization of the proposed methodology stands out. Moreover, it could be interesting to evaluate the suitability of the CiS^2 index using another non-CPU-based type of workload, for example, a transactional or memory workload.

Acknowledgements. This research work is part of the TED2021-132695B-I00 project, financed by MCIN/AEI/10.13039/501100011033 and by the European Union "NextGenerationEU"/PRTR.

This research is part of the project PID2021- 122208OB-I00, PROYEXCEL 00286 funded by MCIN/AEI/10.13039/501100011033 and by Andalusian Regional Government.

References

1. Bermejo, B., Juiz, C.: A general method for evaluating the overhead when consolidating servers: performance degradation in virtual machines and containers. J. Supercomput. **78**(9), 11345–11372 (2022)
2. Casalicchio, E.: A study on performance measures for auto-scaling cpu-intensive containerized applications. Clust. Comput. **22**(3), 995–1006 (2019)
3. Gonzalez, R., Horowitz, M.: Energy dissipation in general purpose microprocessors. IEEE J. Solid-State Circuits **31**(9), 1277–1284 (1996)

4. ISO/IEC (2017). ISO/IEC 30134-4:2017 information technology— data centres — key performance indicators— part 4: IT equipment energy efficiency for servers (iteesv)

5. ISO/IEC (2020). ISO/IEC 21836:2020 information technology– data centres – server energy effectiveness metric

6. Jain, R.: The art of computer systems performance analysis: techniques for experimental design, measurement, simulation, and modeling, volume 1. Wiley New York (1991)

7. Juiz, C., Bermejo, B.: The c i s 2: a new metric for performance and energy trade-off in consolidated servers. Clust. Comput. **23**(4), 2769–2788 (2020)

8. Juiz, C., Bermejo, B.: On the scalability of the speedup considering the overhead of consolidating virtual machines in servers for data centers. J. Supercomput. 1–49 (2024)

9. Juiz, C., Capo, B., Bermejo, B., Fernández-Montes, A., Fernández-Cerero, D.: A case study of transactional workload running in virtual machines: the performance evaluation of a flight seats availability service. IEEE Access (2023)

10. Molero, X., Juiz, C., Rodeño, M.: Evaluación y modelado del rendimiento de los sistemas informáticos. Pearson Educación London (2004)

11. Potts, P.J.: Glossary of analytical and metrological terms from the international vocabulary of metrology (2008). Geostand. Geoanal. Res. **36**(3), 231–246 (2012)

12. Juiz, C., Bermejo, B., Fernández-Montes, A., Fernández-Cerero, D.: Towards a general metric for energy efficiency in cloud computing data centres: a proposal for extending of the ISO/IEC 30134-4. In: CLOSER, pp. 239–247 (2024)

On Dependencies in Microservices: Dependency Management and Maintainability

Tomas Cerny[1(✉)], Md Showkat Hossain Chy[1], Md Arfan Uddin[1],
Amr S. Abdelfattah[1], Jacopo Soldani[2], and Justus Bogner[3]

[1] University of Arizona, 1127 East James E Rogers Way, Tucson, AZ 85721, USA
tcerny@arizona.edu
[2] University of Pisa, Lungarno Antonio Pacinotti, 43, 56126 Pisa, PI, Italy
[3] Vrije Universiteit Amsterdam, De Boelelaan 1105, 1081 HV Amsterdam, Netherlands

Abstract. Rapid evolution characterizes modern software systems, particularly evident with adopting continuous integration and delivery processes. However, while tools for maintaining monolithic architectures are well-established, there is a notable deficiency in methodologies for analyzing and managing changes within decentralized, microservice-based systems. As microservices increasingly become the backbone of cloud-native enterprise solutions, understanding the intricacies of how changes affect these systems becomes crucial. This paper investigates the impact of dependencies on the maintainability of microservice architectures and emphasizes the importance of managing these dependencies to prevent deterioration in system maintainability. We advocate for a systematic approach to dependency management that addresses the actual pathways through which changes propagate, providing a concrete alternative to traditional methods that often focus on symptomatic treatments such as anti-patterns and code smells.

Keywords: Software architecture · Architecture degradation · Micro-services · Maintainability · Dependencies · Service-oriented architecture

1 Introduction

The field of software engineering has experienced a profound shift over the last several decades, motivated by an ongoing quest to achieve higher levels of system maintainability, robustness, and adaptability. This progression has been marked by a significant evolution from traditional approaches like structured programming to more advanced paradigms embracing modular design principles. These changes, which are thoroughly documented in seminal publications by Parnas et al. [34,35] have played a pivotal role in shaping modern software engineering practices. They underscore the importance of structured and modular approaches, which are essential for developing software systems that are maintainable and can evolve with changing technological landscapes.

Alongside these developments, the field has been significantly influenced by the pioneering contributions regarding design patterns by Gamma et al. [20], and the philosophical perspectives on software construction put forth by Dijkstra [18]. These contributions have substantially enriched our understanding and methodologies

C. Pahl and M. van Steen (Eds.): CLOSER 2024, CCIS 2851, pp. 29–52, 2026.
https://doi.org/10.1007/978-3-032-17286-0_2

concerning software maintainability. They have provided a robust framework that has propelled forward the conceptual and practical aspects of software design, focusing on enhancing reusability, understandability, and maintainability. This framework is further supported by the ISO 25010 standard [1], which formally defines software maintainability as the capacity of a system to be efficiently modified to correct faults, improve performance, or adapt to a changing environment. This standard also highlights several critical attributes—modularity, reusability, analysability, modifiability, and testability—that are fundamental to ensuring the long-term health and evolutionary potential of software systems.

The escalating complexity of modern software architectures, coupled with the fast-paced advancements in technology, has necessitated a paradigm shift towards more dynamic and flexible architectural models. This shift is vividly illustrated by the emergence and integration of service-oriented architecture (SOA) [14]. SOA redefines the conceptualization of software, viewing it as a collection of independently deployable services, thus paving the way for systems that exemplify modularization of functionality. This approach allows for systems to be assembled from loosely coupled services that can be individually developed, deployed, and maintained. Embracing SOA not only signifies a leap forward in terms of agility and scalability in software development processes but also aligns with the need for architectures that can readily adapt to new business strategies and rapidly changing market demands.

Taking the robust framework established by SOA even further, the microservice architecture has come into prominence, targeting enhanced granularity in modularity and heightened scalability [32]. This evolution from SOA harnesses the concept of compartmentalized, self-sufficient services tailored to specific business functionalities that can be independently deployed through automated systems [14]. The successful proliferation of microservices [2] highlights their vital role in addressing key demands of contemporary software development, such as seamless integration, scalable frameworks, and robust system resilience.

Despite the advantages, the shift towards microservice architectures introduces several complexities. Notably, the management of microservice dependencies becomes increasingly challenging as the architecture grows more distributed. This growing complexity is magnified by the varied technologies, frameworks, and programming languages that microservices employ, complicating the coordination and implementation of changes across the system. Additionally, the typical microservice environment features distinct teams managing different services independently, adding layers of management complexity.

In this paper, we explore the profound impact that interdependencies have on the maintainability of software architectures, especially when modifications are necessary. By delving into the intricacies of microservice systems, we emphasize the importance of rigorous dependency management to uphold system integrity through evolutionary changes. We challenge traditional approaches to microservice analysis and advocate for innovative methodologies that address the fundamental reasons behind changes. The narrative shifts to spotlighting the meticulous management of microservice dependencies as pivotal in evaluating the ramifications of changes and bolstering the resilience and maintainability of systems. Our goal is to catalyze the creation of advanced tools and methodologies that facilitate precise impact analysis and continuous architectural refinement, equipping developers and architects to navigate microservice ecosystems more effectively and ensure greater system stability and maintainability.

This discussion expands on our previous findings in Cerny et al. [50], where we highlighted issues surrounding microservice dependencies and their impact on system maintainability. In this extension, we provide a more detailed analysis of different types of dependencies, their detection, and practical examples that underscore the complexity of managing these interrelations effectively within microservice architectures. This additional insight fosters a deeper understanding and promotes the development of tools that support robust architectural governance and maintenance practices.

Finally, the remainder of this manuscript is structured to unfold progressively deeper insights into the topic. Section 2 revisits established methods supporting the maintenance of software applications and highlights early signs of architectural degradation. Section 3 explores the pivotal role of dependencies within software architectures, analyzing both their observable effects and fundamental causes. Section 4 examines strategies to mitigate architecture degradation in the context of these dependencies, presenting approaches to manage and counteract their effects. Section 5 delves into various types of dependencies, offering strategies for their effective management to enhance system adaptability and maintainability. Section 6 discusses the challenges of maintainability within the context of microservice dependencies, and Sect. 7 concludes the discussion with a series of open-ended questions that invite further exploration and consideration.

2 Background and Related Work

The evolution of software design has been markedly influenced by principles such as modular design, encapsulation, and the separation of concerns, which are fundamental to enhancing maintainability. The seminal works by Parnas et al. [34] illustrate the benefits of modularization, where clearly defined interfaces and responsibilities significantly ease maintenance efforts and enhance system clarity [35]. Further supported by Dijkstra's principle of separation of concerns [18] and Gamma et al.'s focus on encapsulation [20], these design philosophies collectively foster system maintainability and minimize error propagation during its evolution.

Event-driven coupling, as discussed in resources from enterprise integration patterns, elucidates a facet of microservices that significantly impacts modularity and architectural agility [23, 24]. These insights emphasize the nuanced balancing act between component independence and interdependence, highlighting how event-driven architectures can both enhance and complicate microservice manageability by introducing asynchronous communication patterns that reduce direct dependencies but may obscure data flow and service interaction [23].

Quality assurance in software extends beyond these principles, requiring rigorous adherence to established coding standards [10], the implementation of proven development practices [20], precise role allocation [25], and robust dependency management. This foundation is crucial for exemplary system design and development, supported further by comprehensive documentation, diligent version control, and extensive testing.

The importance of architectural integrity grows as systems increase in complexity. Effective architecture not only facilitates easier modifications but also shields the system against quality erosion. However, the impetus to accelerate feature deployment often risks this integrity, incurring technical and architectural debt [8, 11, 17, 19, 22, 30] that could undermine future maintainability and scalability.

Strategic interventions are necessary to counteract architectural degradation, with systematic literature reviews pointing to various methodologies [9], including the identification of architectural smells, adherence to design rules, and the mitigation of degradation itself. However, most existing research focuses on monolithic systems, often neglecting the distinct complexities introduced by microservices.

Microservices introduce complexities such as multiple moving parts, a disconnected codebase, scattered concerns, and autonomously operating development teams, as highlighted by Conway's law [15]. The loosely coupled nature of these components, though advantageous, also breeds dependencies that can trigger co-changes and ripple effects [12], increasing the system's susceptibility to architectural decay.

In such decentralized microservice architectures, the benefits of modular design are often offset by the challenges in managing the independence and interdependence of components. These challenges make it difficult to track changes and manage dependencies effectively, potentially leading to costly disruptions across teams. While individual microservices may operate very independently, they collectively constitute a cohesive system that demands a unified management approach, revealing complexities that are often only apparent from a holistic viewpoint [12].

The success of microservices hinges on effective Systematic Architecture Reconstruction (SAR), a strategy that provides a focused system analysis approach [12]. Implementing SAR effectively is challenging and demands considerable, continuous effort [37]. Although static analysis [45] can facilitate this reconstruction, a deep understanding of component interconnections is crucial for identifying dependencies and relationships.

Microservices often exhibit distinct architectural smells such as cyclic dependencies, which are indicative of deeper systemic issues [13]. Their detection could use known anti-patterns that could manifest through SAR or through straightforward rule-based analysis of codebases [43]. Despite these methods, metrics specifically designed to evaluate microservices are still underdeveloped. Research in areas such as structural coupling [33], logical coupling [7], and team collaboration dependencies [26] has begun to shed light on these interactions. Yet, it remains a critical question whether these metrics are pinpointing the root causes of issues within microservice architectures or merely highlighting the symptoms.

This paper proposes a reimagined perspective on microservice management, emphasizing the critical role of dependency management in guiding the evolution of microservice architectures. By identifying existing gaps, we aim to encourage further exploration and development of specialized tools and methodologies tailored to meet the unique demands of microservice ecosystems.

3 The Role of Dependencies: Symptoms and Causes

Understanding the interconnectivity of microservices often starts with the most visible elements—"explicit" inter-service calls. These interactions clearly outline dependency pathways, which are immediately recognizable to developers. However, there are less apparent types of dependencies that also play a crucial role. For instance, data dependencies present a subtler form of interconnection that might not be as evident. Walker et al. [46] explore this by developing a canonical data model that spans across microservices, identifying shared data entities by their names or structures. Such dependencies, as shown in Fig. 1, often arise either from shared data exchanges among microservices or as remnants from their origins in monolithic systems. These less visible dependencies require careful consideration, as they can significantly impact the functionality and evolution of microservice architectures.

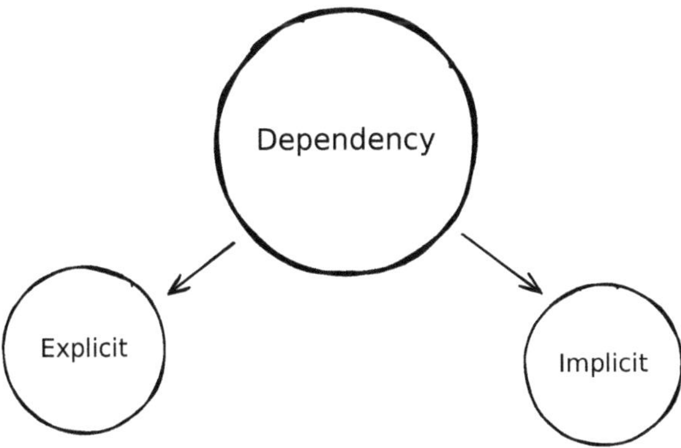

Fig. 1. Types of Dependencies.

However, the realm of "implicit" dependencies often escapes the attention of developers during the assessment of changes. These include dependencies arising from implicit invocations, such as events triggered through messaging systems. Another critical aspect of such dependencies relates to overarching policies and rules that apply system-wide. For example, adherence to regulations like the *General Data Protection Regulation (GDPR)*[1] or specific access rights may not be modularized or reused without breaching the principles of cloud-native architectures and causing potential bottlenecks. Consequently, policies must be individually tailored and applied to each microservice, dispersing the concern across various system components. This dispersion complicates the process when policies need updating, as each modification must be tracked and implemented across the distributed elements. Other types of implicit dependencies also exist and are likely overlooked during the evaluation of change impacts on microservices. Effective dependency management is crucial, as it equips developers

---

[1] https://gdpr-info.eu, accessed on 5 August 2024.

with the insights necessary to anticipate and mitigate potential issues arising from these less visible dependencies.

In the context of microservices, we define dependencies as the reliance of one component on another to function correctly. Dependencies affect how modifications in one microservice can impact other microservices. Such dependencies often precipitate challenges like co-change requirements and ripple effects across the system. These challenges, while significant, are merely symptoms of deeper underlying dependencies. This realization prompts researchers to look beyond conventional dependency models and address these symptomatic issues more directly.

Similarly, understanding the nuances between the causes, the artifacts affected, and the symptoms of dependencies requires a detailed analysis. For instance, version control commits, which are frequently linked to data dependencies between microservices, lead to logical coupling [7], showcasing a symptom of these underlying dependencies. Similarly, team collaboration problems may arise from shared resource dependencies [26].

Software Architecture Reconstruction (SAR) aims to analyze the impact of changes and tends to reveal only control dependencies through dynamic analysis, which are often apparent to developers. While manual SAR can be burdensome and skew towards obvious dependencies, static analysis offers a broader spectrum for discovery. It can reveal code clones across microservices, suggesting potential pathways for changes. These clones, be they syntactic or semantic, underscore the challenge of managing diversity in programming languages within cloud-native systems, despite limited data on the prevalence of such polyglot settings.

Consequently, static analysis extends beyond detecting clones; it is crucial for identifying data dependencies that affect interconnected components. Moreover, it confronts the complexity introduced by overarching policies and rules. The absence of a uniform method for analyzing these elements necessitates the use of strategies like rule annotation or the application of rule engines such as *Drools*[2], to standardize expressions. Furthermore, static analysis is instrumental in spotting technological dependencies, where alterations in one component may require changes in others. A thorough dependency check would encompass shared libraries, configuration files, data sources, and elements of cloud-native infrastructure like API gateways and service discovery tools.

Addressing both functional and non-functional requirements—which dictate component responsibilities and necessitate code modifications—often exceeds the capabilities of traditional automation techniques. However, the model-driven development (MDE) approach offers a promising solution to these challenges, as discussed by Terzić et al. [42]. Despite its potential to streamline development processes, the adoption of MDE has not been widely embraced in the industry, highlighting a disconnect between its theoretical advantages and practical application. This gap underscores the need for further research and development in deploying MDE effectively within microservice architectures. This may be due to the fact that MDE fundamentally goes against the decentralized and lightweight philosophy of

---

[2] https://www.drools.org/, accessed on 5 August 2024.

microservices, suggesting it might remain a situational approach rather than gaining broad support [38].

Comprehending the intricate causes and symptoms of microservice dependencies is pivotal for maintaining the efficiency and reliability of microservice architectures. This paper identifies four key areas where these dependencies manifest: architectural misalignment, resource management issues, performance degradation, and operational complexities. Each area presents unique challenges and impacts on system functionality and maintainability. This analysis delves into the specific symptoms observed, the underlying causes, and the associated artifacts, providing a comprehensive overview of the critical factors influencing microservice dependencies.

3.1 Architectural Misalignment and Design Issues

Architectural misalignment and design issues are significant contributors to microservice dependency problems. Symptoms such as cascading failures, inter-service communication complexity, and functional bottlenecks often indicate underlying architectural flaws. These issues are primarily caused by high coupling, functional centralization, and over-reliance on single endpoints, which create tight interdependencies between services. Key artifacts associated with these causes include HTTP endpoints, client request calls, and source code annotations. Abdelfattah et al. [3] emphasize that addressing these design flaws is crucial for mitigating operational disruptions and enhancing system resilience.

3.2 Resource Management and Quality of Service Issues

Resource management issues and violations of Quality of Service (QoS) present another critical area of concern. Symptoms such as large resource consumption, service conflicts, and QoS violations often stem from differentiated dependencies and challenges in service deployment. These issues are linked to multiple call graphs and service instances that complicate resource allocation and management. Lv et al. [28] highlight the significant impact of these challenges, noting how they lead to substantial resource consumption and QoS violations, necessitating improved resource management strategies to ensure efficient system operations.

3.3 Performance Degradation and Resource Allocation Challenges

Performance degradation and inefficient resource allocation are prevalent symptoms of complex service dependencies. These problems arise from dependencies' dynamic and time-varying nature, which complicate performance monitoring and resource allocation. Key artifacts include affinity matrices, performance monitoring tools, adaptive learning modules, and resource estimators. Meng et al. [31] address these challenges by exploring how service dependencies evolve, highlighting the need for dynamic management tools to mitigate performance degradation and optimize resource allocation.

3.4 Operational and Communication Complexities

Operational and communication complexities significantly impact microservice architectures, leading to symptoms such as service conflicts, uneven communication delays, and uncoordinated transmissions. Non-integrative scaling practices, co-location of microservices, and intricate service function chains cause these complexities. Artifacts such as threshold-based scaling methods, dependency topologies, and interaction relationships are crucial in understanding these issues. Song et al. [41] and Zhou et al. [49] underline the importance of addressing these operational complexities to enhance system performance and reliability.

Thus, the comprehensive analysis of the causes and symptoms of microservice dependencies underscores the need for targeted strategies to manage these challenges effectively. Future research should focus on developing predictive models and integrated management tools to mitigate the impacts of these dependencies, ensuring the robustness and maintainability of microservice architectures.

4 Architecture Degradation Mitigation Strategies in the Context of Dependencies

To counteract architectural degradation effectively, four principal strategies have been delineated [9]: metrics-based detection, smell detection and prioritization, architectural recovery, and addressing architectural rule violations. Illustrated in Fig. 2, these strategies collectively form a robust framework for addressing architectural degradation. Each strategy is designed to provide a nuanced understanding and

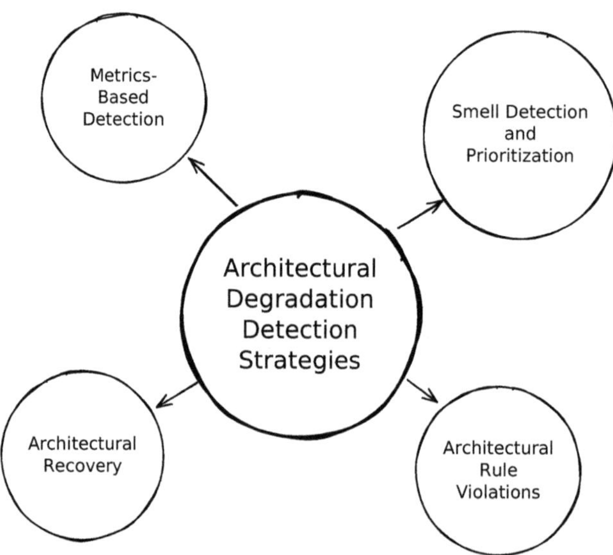

Fig. 2. Microservice architecture degradation detection strategies.

management of system dependencies, which is crucial for maintaining the integrity and performance of the architecture. This holistic approach not only identifies and corrects existing issues but also aims to fortify the architecture against potential future vulnerabilities by deeply understanding and resolving dependency-related challenges.

4.1 Metrics-Based Strategies

Metrics-based detection methods provide critical insights into software quality and maintainability by analyzing source code and assessing architectural stability throughout its development lifecycle. Essential metrics include indicators of instability, modularity, coupling, and cohesion, each providing a lens through which the health of a system can be viewed. For instance, a high code churn rate often signals potential instability and impending architectural concerns. Specific modularity metrics, such as the Average Number of Modified Components per Commit (ANMCC), Index of Package Changing Impact (IPCI), and Index of Package Goal Focus (IPGF), offer predictive insights into the risks of architectural degradation [27]. Similarly, Cyclomatic Complexity (CC) measures the complexity of a codebase and identifies potential maintenance challenges, while metrics that quantify code duplication can reveal issues with modularity that complicate updates and foster inconsistent system behavior.

In the domain of cloud-native systems, where codebases are typically decentralized or segmented into self-contained modules without direct interconnections, traditional metrics may not adequately reflect the system's dynamics. The use of remote procedure calls as indicators of dependencies, for instance, may not provide a complete perspective because of the presence of non-obvious, implicit dependencies that span across microservices. These dependencies can be crucial for system functionality but are often not tracked or visible in the usual metrics frameworks.

Additionally, implicit dependencies pose a significant challenge as they lack direct code connections or clear textual indications, making them difficult to track and manage. Such dependencies often manifest through indirect interactions like message queues, where components communicate asynchronously, enhancing scalability and component reuse but also complicating execution control and dependency management, as highlighted by Garland and Shaw [21].

Addressing the challenge of measuring and managing these implicit dependencies within microservices requires a reevaluation of current metrics applications. A comprehensive approach that includes both explicit and implicit dependencies is necessary to provide a more accurate depiction of a decentralized system's architecture. This approach should not only focus on the immediate impacts of code changes but also consider the broader network effects and the interplay between different microservice components.

Moreover, a detailed analysis of dependency types and their respective impacts on system evolution is critical. This involves both a qualitative assessment of how dependencies interact and a quantitative measure of their effects on system stability and change propagation. By enhancing the depth and breadth of dependency analysis, organizations can better prepare for potential disruptions, plan more effective interventions, and ultimately drive more informed decision-making processes regarding system maintenance and evolution.

> **Highlights:**
>
> – Metrics can guide the evaluation of microservice architectures by highlighting latent dependencies not typically revealed through traditional methods, thus playing a crucial role in identifying potential points of architectural degradation.

4.2   Smell Detection Strategies

The practice of smell detection and the prioritization of code issues have been integral in software maintenance for many years, commonly facilitated by tools like *SonarQube*[3] and other platforms that specialize in identifying anti-patterns. A "smell" in the code usually signals an underlying issue but doesn't specify the cause, making it a symptomatic alert rather than a diagnostic one. Conversely, an anti-pattern represents a more concrete manifestation of a recurring problem.

Traditional smell detection tools are often optimized for monolithic repository systems, which complicates their application in environments characterized by multiple, disjointed repositories. Such environments are typical in microservices architectures, where anti-patterns can extend across various components, challenging their detection [13]. Basic methodologies involving dependency graphs, call graphs, or syntax trees [4,45], along with rule-based matching [43], offer some remedies. These techniques can be thought of as generating an intermediate system representation, which acts as a scaffold for architectural recovery, integrating strategies from established practices [9].

Therefore, this intermediate representation is critical because the more detailed and expansive it is, the more thorough the analysis that can be conducted. This approach not only helps in identifying the dependencies across codebases and artifacts in microservices but also ensures more reliable and actionable insights for developers.

A key question arises regarding the adaptability of these intermediate representations across various frameworks and platforms. Innovations like Oracle's GraalVM suggest possibilities for broader applications, and other developments indicate that similar adaptations are feasible for cloud system development frameworks [39].

However, the reliance on smells and anti-patterns as the primary strategy for identifying architectural issues warrants scrutiny. While established as a useful approach, it's important to recognize that smells often only signal symptoms of deeper problems. Anti-patterns, identified through repeated negative outcomes, offer limited insight unless they are detected afresh in updated system versions.

In contrast, dependencies provide a foundational view of system interrelations and do not require a pre-defined set of rules or visual indicators like graph glyphs to be useful. Proper management and identification of dependencies can reveal systemic issues even without prior knowledge of specific anti-patterns. Comparing different system versions can make the impact of changes more quantifiable than merely relying on a catalog of anti-patterns. By employing techniques like dependency mapping to

---

[3] https://github.com/SonarSource/sonarqube, accessed on 5 August 2024.

visualize service interactions and using change impact analysis to assess the potential effects of modifications, not only can existing anti-patterns be linked to specific dependencies, but new patterns of degradation can also be uncovered. These methods enhance the overall strategy for maintaining and improving software architecture by providing a clearer understanding of how changes in one area can affect the entire system.

> **Highlights:**
>
> – Advancing smell detection strategies with dependency analysis to effectively manage systemic issues and detect degradation patterns in microservice architectures.

4.3 Architecture Reconstruction Strategies

Architecture reconstruction and recovery are essential processes for ensuring the integrity and understanding of the ongoing evolution of microservice architectures. Due to their distributed nature, microservices present a complex landscape where multiple services and infrastructure components interact and depend on each other. The primary goal of architecture reconstruction in such environments is not only to map out the services and their interactions but also to delve deep into the underlying dependencies and the logic behind architectural choices. Recent technological advances have enabled the automation of extracting and analyzing architectural data, integrating both static and dynamic aspects of the codebase and runtime behavior [5].

As discussed earlier in conjunction with smell and anti-pattern detection strategies, architecture reconstruction can also serve as a foundation for resolving queries or documenting the system. This process typically results in multiple system views that allow experts to dissect and understand the architecture more thoroughly. These views or models can be used to extract specific information about the system's structure and operation, effectively answering questions and testing hypotheses about architectural decisions and their impacts.

However, a notable challenge in this process is the focus on explicit dependencies and control flows, which often overlook the subtler, implicit connections between components. This limitation can lead to a superficial understanding that lacks depth in explaining how different parts of the system interact and depend on each other. To address this issue, it is crucial to enrich the reconstructed views or models with detailed information about dependencies. By incorporating a comprehensive mapping of dependencies into the reconstruction process, analysts can perform a more robust and insightful analysis. This enhanced approach helps not only in understanding the current state of the architecture but also in making informed decisions about future modifications and improvements.

> **Highlights:**
>
> – Advanced architecture reconstruction integrates both explicit and implicit dependencies, enhancing understanding and decision-making in microservice architectures.

4.4 Architectural Rule Violation Detection Strategies

Architectural rule violation detection is critical in ensuring that the software development adheres to predefined architectural guidelines. Such rules might dictate that service layers communicate solely through specified interfaces to avoid unauthorized data layer access directly from the UI layer. By categorizing these rules based on their criticality, developers can prioritize efforts to address the most significant threats to architectural integrity.

The effectiveness of these rules largely hinges on their comprehensiveness in encompassing all relevant architectural dependencies. Missed or overlooked dependencies can diminish the rules' effectiveness, leading to unintended breaches in architectural enforcement. Consequently, thorough and ongoing cataloging of all system dependencies is imperative to maintain the efficacy and authority of these rules.

Moreover, the governance of architectural rules demands a proactive approach, akin to the management of the system's codebase. As the architecture evolves, these rules may become obsolete or misaligned with the current system design, necessitating regular updates and maintenance. Establishing a robust maintenance strategy for these rules is essential, ensuring they accurately reflect the latest architectural standards and practices and remain relevant and effective in guiding system development.

> **Highlights:**
>
> - Proper governance and continuous refinement of architectural rules ensure adherence to best practices, enhancing the integrity and relevance of microservice architectures.

4.5 Implications

The strategies currently used to detect architectural degradation often operate at a high level of abstraction, presenting challenges when applied to decentralized systems with independent microservices. For effective architecture reconstruction, it is necessary to individually access and review each microservice's codebase—a task that becomes increasingly complex with the rapid evolution of these systems. Similarly, the enforcement and monitoring of architectural rules require substantial effort. While static analysis provides a preliminary approximation, it often struggles to accommodate the diversity of platforms and the nascent state of supporting toolsets.

In contrast, dependencies represent more granular and fundamental elements within the system's architecture, serving as a foundational layer for developing new analytical tools. These dependencies facilitate the identification of system issues, underlying causes, and potential anti-patterns without needing a pre-existing catalog. When integrated with architectural rules, dependencies offer a more dynamic view of the system's health without imposing the significant maintenance burden typically associated with high-level strategies.

Furthermore, by employing an enhanced system representation that includes meticulously tracked dependencies, it becomes possible to apply existing metrics across the entire system, not just isolated components. This approach allows for a more holistic view of system health and can significantly improve the precision and relevance of diagnostic efforts. Ultimately, recognizing and managing dependencies not only aids in immediate problem resolution but also enhances the adaptability and resilience of the architectural framework, ensuring it can evolve in alignment with emerging needs and technologies.

5 Navigating the Maintainability Challenges of Microservice Dependencies

Effective dependency management is critical to maintaining the integrity and performance of microservice architectures. Furthermore, various benchmarking tools have been developed to detect, analyze, and manage these dependencies, each catering to specific aspects of microservice maintainability. Dependencies can significantly affect system maintainability, leading to increased complexity, higher costs, and longer times for updates and fixes. This section discusses different types of dependencies and the benchmarking tools designed to handle them, highlighting their use cases and the specific challenges they address.

For illustration, a fraud detection system in a financial services context monitors transactions for potential fraudulent activities, as demonstrated in Fig. 3. The system consists of multiple microservices that interact with each other to detect, handle, and log fraudulent transactions. The primary service, Service A (Transaction Monitoring Service), monitors all transactions and communicates with other services to take appropriate actions upon detecting a potential fraud. Service A connects with Service B (Account Service) to fetch and update account information, ensuring the account associated with the flagged transaction is managed appropriately. It also communicates with Service C (Alert Service) to alert customers and internal security teams about fraudulent activity. Finally, Service A logs the details of the flagged transaction by communicating with Service D (Audit Service), ensuring that all activities are recorded for auditing purposes. Different dependencies will be describe from this example in the following section.

5.1 Data Dependencies

Data dependencies arise when microservices share or access the same data entities, leading to maintainability issues as changes in data schemas must be coordinated across services. Tools like the Endpoint Dependency Matrix (EDM) and Data Dependency Matrix (DDM) [3] effectively track and visualize these dependencies, helping to understand how data flows between services. For instance, a company might use EDM and DDM to map how customer data is accessed and modified across various microservices, ensuring changes are synchronized to prevent inconsistencies and system failures. In Fig. 3 highlighted as dashed line, Service A (Transaction Monitoring Service) leans heavily on Service B (Account Service) for account information to evaluate transactions for fraud. At the same time, Service C (Alert Service) and Service D (Audit Service) also bear the weight of transaction and account information. This underscores the significant responsibilities of each service in the system.

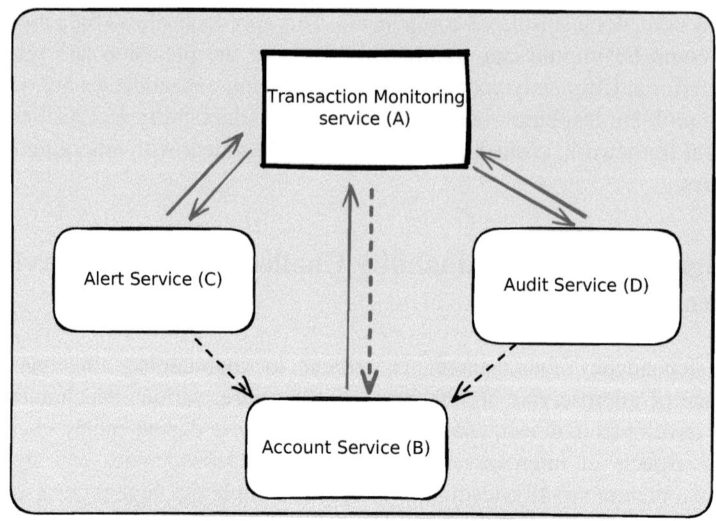

Fig. 3. A Fraud Detection System with Dependencies.

Notably, service design patterns like Tolerant Reader and Request Mapper can be employed to enhance robustness against changes in data formats. According to Daigneau [16], the Tolerant Reader pattern involves designing services that are lenient in what they accept in incoming messages, allowing the service to handle unknown or extra data gracefully without breaking. This pattern increases the resilience of services to changes in data formats and helps maintain compatibility as services evolve.

Similarly, the Request Mapper pattern transforms incoming requests into a format that the service can process effectively. This decouples the internal logic of the service from external data formats, providing a layer of abstraction that simplifies handling data dependencies. By using Request Mapper, services can adapt to changes in data structures more efficiently, reducing the maintenance burden associated with evolving data schemas. These patterns, combined with tools like EDM and DDM, offer a robust approach to managing data dependencies, ensuring services remain flexible and resilient, thus improving overall system maintainability.

5.2   Control Dependencies

Control dependencies arise when the execution of one service is dependent on the control flow or state of another. This type of dependency can complicate maintainability, as it requires a deep understanding of the interaction between services. Figure 3 illustrates that Service A (Transaction Monitoring Service), the pivotal player, controls the workflow by initiating actions in dependent services after flagging a transaction for potential fraud. This underscores the crucial role of Service A in the system.

Furthermore, TraceNet [48] can support the identification of issues in service interactions. By analyzing tracing data, it can pinpoint the root cause of problems, making it easier to visualize the flow of requests across services and locate where failures or performance bottlenecks occur. GDC-DVF [36], on the other hand, focuses on mapping invocation relationships and extracting dependencies, aiding in the decomposition of monolithic applications into microservices. This dual-view fusion approach provides a comprehensive understanding of both the static and dynamic aspects of service interactions, essential for managing complex control dependencies.

For instance, a financial services firm can use TraceNet to trace transaction flows across microservices, identifying exactly where issues arise and understanding the sequence of service calls. GDC-DVF helps visualize and manage the interactions between services, which is particularly useful during their transition from a monolithic to a microservice architecture. This insight is critical for ensuring that the control flows are maintained correctly and that changes in one service do not inadvertently impact others.

5.3 Communication Dependencies

Communication dependencies involve service interactions, such as API calls and message passing. These dependencies are characterized by the exchange of information between services, often through synchronous or asynchronous communication mechanisms. Unlike control dependencies, which influence the execution flow directly, communication dependencies are about the exchange of data or messages between services to achieve a task. As in Fig. 3 highlighted in red lines, Service A (Transaction Monitoring Service) communicates with Service B (Account Service) to fetch account information, with Service C (Alert Service) to send details of flagged transactions, and with Service D (Audit Service) to log transaction details.

ChainsFormer [40] analyzes communication-based interactions among microservices to identify critical chains and nodes, facilitating resource provisioning and dynamic scaling. By understanding the communication patterns and identifying critical paths, ChainsFormer helps optimize the allocation of resources and improve overall system performance.

On the other hand, GSMART [29] creates service dependency graphs (SDGs) to visualize microservice-based systems, aiding in tracing relationships and selecting regression test cases. This visualization helps identify and address potential communication bottlenecks by mapping service interactions. GSMART's ability to trace and visualize these interactions makes it an invaluable tool for understanding the dependencies that arise from service communications and ensuring they are managed effectively.

To illustrate, an e-commerce platform could use ChainsFormer to analyze peak traffic times and ensure critical services are adequately resourced. By identifying the most heavily used service interactions, ChainsFormer enables the proactive scaling of resources to meet demand. GSMART, on the other hand, can be used to identify communication bottlenecks and optimize the flow of information between services, ensuring smooth operation during high-traffic periods.

5.4 Resource Dependencies

Resource dependencies are related to the shared use of computational resources such as CPU, memory, and storage. These dependencies can cause resource contention and performance degradation, making the system harder to maintain. DeepScaler utilizes affinity matrices to scale microservices dynamically based on service affinities and resource usage patterns. This tool continuously monitors resource usage and adjusts the allocation dynamically, ensuring efficient use of resources. The sample microservice described in Fig. 3 demonstrates how all services utilize shared CPU and memory resources to run fraud detection algorithms efficiently.

SYMBIOTE [6] continuously analyzes service coupling metrics to detect potential architectural degradation and optimize resource allocation. By monitoring the degree of coupling between services, SYMBIOTE helps identify areas where resource contention might occur and pre-emptively address these issues. This continuous monitoring and adjustment help maintain optimal performance and resource utilization.

For example, a cloud service provider can use DeepScaler [31] to monitor and adjust resource allocation dynamically based on real-time usage patterns. This not only ensures that services receive the resources they need without over-allocating, but also helps in maintaining efficiency and reducing costs. SYMBIOTE helps maintain optimal service performance by monitoring and adjusting service couplings, ensuring that resource dependencies are managed effectively to prevent performance degradation.

Table 1. Overview of Dependency Types and Their Benchmarking Tools.

Dependency Type	Description	Benchmarking Tools
Data Dependencies	Occur when microservices share or access the same data entities.	Endpoint Dependency Matrix (EDM), Data Dependency Matrix (DDM)
Control Dependencies	Arise when the execution of one service is dependent on the control flow or state of another.	TraceNet, GDC-DVF
Communication Dependencies	Involve interactions between services, such as API calls and message passing.	ChainsFormer, GSMART
Resource Dependencies	Related to the shared use of computational resources like CPU, memory, and storage.	DeepScaler, SYMBIOTE

In summary, each type of dependency introduces unique challenges to the maintainability of microservice architectures where different dependencies overview is presented in Table 1. By leveraging tools like EDM, DDM, TraceNet, GDC-DVF, ChainsFormer, GSMART, DeepScaler, and SYMBIOTE, developers and architects can better manage these dependencies. Each tool offers specific capabilities tailored to different aspects of dependency management, enabling a comprehensive approach to maintaining robust and scalable microservice architectures. Understanding and applying these tools in appropriate use cases ensures that microservice systems remain maintainable, performant, and resilient over time.

6   Maintainability in the Context of Microservice Dependencies

Maintainability in microservice architectures (MSA) is crucial due to the distributed nature of the systems, where services are developed, deployed, and scaled independently. The ease of modifying, extending, or updating software systems in MSA is significantly influenced by the architecture's ability to manage complex and highly intertwined dependencies among services. Effective change impact analysis is paramount in MSA. This process extends beyond simple assessment of modifications; it actively pinpoints and evaluates potential impacts of changes on the system's overall architecture. This is critical in MSA environments, where changes in one service can affect multiple other services, potentially leading to significant system-wide impacts. Such analysis supports maintaining system integrity and minimizing error introduction during updates, ensuring the system remains robust, adaptable, and easier to maintain over time.

In these settings, dependencies act as clear indicators of how changes might affect system maintainability. They provide detailed insights into which specific areas of the system could be impacted by proposed changes. This level of precision is instrumental in pinpointing the root causes of potential issues with maintainability, thereby enabling IT leaders and developers to make informed decisions about the trade-offs involved in implementing changes.

Dependencies offer a more granular understanding than broader metrics or the identification of code smells, which might only hint at potential issues. By clearly outlining the direct relationships between changes and their impacts, dependencies guide strategic planning and the evaluation of alternative solutions or design modifications that could prevent negative outcomes. This focus on dependencies not only enhances the agility and responsiveness of the development process but also ensures that the architecture remains robust and adaptable to new requirements and challenges.

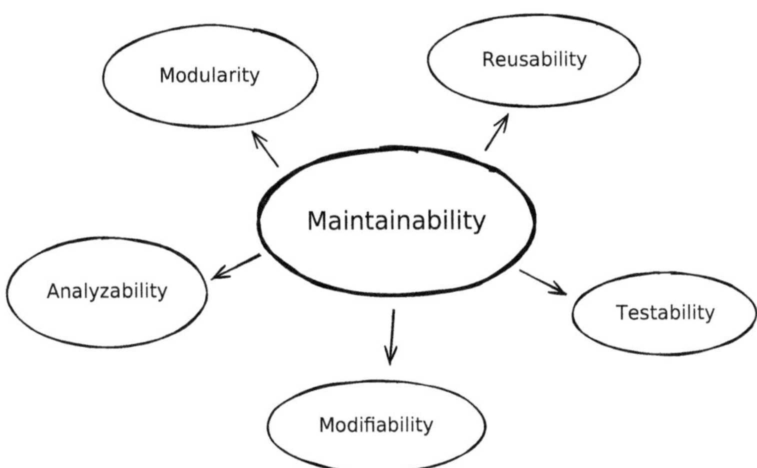

Fig. 4. Quality attribute for maintainability according to ISO 25010.

Maintainability, as characterized by attributes such as *modularity, reusability, analysability, modifiability*, and *testability*, as defined by Bass et al. and the ISO 25010 standard, is crucial in microservices architecture [10]. In this context, managing dependencies refers to the processes involved in identifying, understanding, and controlling the relationships and interactions between different microservices. Effective dependency management ensures that changes in one service minimize disruptions to others, thereby enhancing system integrity and flexibility. This includes using tools and practices such as service registries, automated testing, and continuous integration to handle dependencies proactively. Understanding these quality attributes, as illustrated in Fig. 4, is fundamental to maintaining and improving system performance.

Modularity is one of the cornerstone attributes of maintainability. It involves segmenting a complex system into smaller, independent, and replaceable units, designed to minimize impact on other components when changes occur. In microservices, modularity is achieved by designing each service to perform a distinct function, allowing it to operate independently yet harmoniously within the larger ecosystem. While modularity aims to improve maintainability, reusability, and clarity, realizing this attribute in cloud-native environments presents challenges. The interconnected nature of microservices and the widespread distribution of global policies and knowledge, such as role-based access control (RBAC), complicate the modular design. RBAC can enforce a degree of interdependence among services by requiring them to adhere to shared security protocols and access rules, thereby complicating the modular design by potentially introducing tight coupling based on access controls.

Understanding the dependencies between these modular units is crucial; however, simply identifying these dependencies does not mitigate the impact of changes across the system. While dependency tracking allows for a clearer understanding of potential ripple effects from changes in one service, it does not inherently reduce the broad impact of these changes. Updates to services with many dependencies might still necessitate coordinated updates across multiple consumer services, thus presenting challenges in maintaining true independence and modularity.

To effectively manage the modularity of a microservice-based system, understanding the web of dependencies across services is crucial. While meticulous tracking of these dependencies does not reduce the impact of updates on interconnected services, it does facilitate informed decision-making and strategic planning. When updates are inevitable, this awareness helps prepare for and manage potential cascading effects across the system. A potential strategy to balance modularity with the demands of cloud-native principles, such as those proposed in the Twelve-Factor App methodology [47], involves centralizing shared logic in importable libraries. This approach should be carefully executed to preserve the independence of services and align with cloud-native architectural principles. By doing so, the system not only adheres to microservices best practices but also retains the flexibility to adapt and evolve, ensuring robustness despite the inherent complexities of interconnected services.

> **Modularity:** Dependency tracing is crucial due to complex inter-service interactions and policy dispersion in microservices.

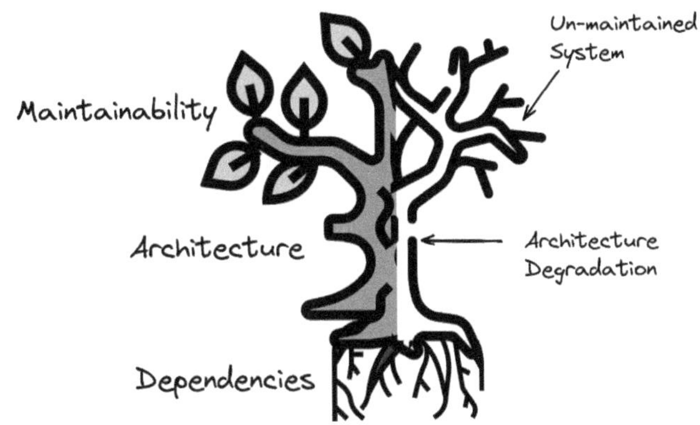

Fig. 5. Visualizing root cause of architectural degradation [50].

Reusability is a core principle of software engineering, traditionally aiming to save development time and resources by allowing components to be used across various parts of a system or in multiple projects. This principle enhances efficiency and reduces redundancy. However, in the context of microservices, excessive reusability can lead to increased dependencies, which is problematic. Microservices advocate a "share-as-little-as-possible" approach to minimize coupling and enhance each service's ability to evolve independently. Excessive reuse of services and shared libraries can complicate this, leading to tight coupling that might hinder the independent scalability and evolution of services [44].

While modularity supports reusability by defining clear, independent units, the transition to microservices often complicates its application due to potential latency and system bottlenecks. To address these challenges, the serverless computing model presents a promising solution. Unlike traditional server-based models, serverless computing executes backend services on-demand without requiring developers to manage server infrastructure. This model facilitates the reuse of functions across different parts of a system or even across projects by removing the overhead of infrastructure management, thus alleviating common challenges associated with microservices and enhancing reusability in modern software development environments.

> **Reusability:** Scalability and independence in microservices challenge reusability, pointing towards serverless solutions.

Analysability measures how easily a software system can be inspected for understanding its structure, diagnosing issues, and implementing improvements. In microservice architectures, where services are decentralized and duties are separated, developers can effectively manage their specific components but often lose sight of the overall system architecture. This decentralization challenges the thorough analysability of the entire system.

Tracing and logging are commonly used to enhance analysability in microservices; however, these methods depend heavily on the consistency of the developers' logging practices and their readiness to potentially compromise performance for better traceability. Static analysis tools, which provide quick insights into the code's structure without execution, often fall short in microservices environments due to their complexity and distributed nature.

To improve analysability in such systems, there is a need for tools and practices specifically tailored to address the unique challenges of distributed architectures. This includes developing more sophisticated tracing mechanisms and encouraging a culture of detailed and consistent logging among developers.

> **Analysability:** The decentralized nature of microservices necessitates improved tracing and static analysis for effective system comprehension.

Modifiability refers to the ease with which a software system can be altered or adapted to meet evolving requirements. This attribute is vital as software must frequently evolve to incorporate new features, fix bugs, and adapt to changing user needs. A system with high modifiability allows developers to implement changes quickly and efficiently, minimizing the risk of errors and reducing the time and effort needed for updates.

In the context of microservices, effective dependency management plays a significant role in enhancing modifiability. Properly managing dependencies enables comprehensive change impact analysis, which helps to mitigate the negative effects of improper design. This analysis identifies how changes in one service affect others, allowing for more informed decision-making and reducing potential disruptions.

However, to conduct effective change impact analysis, a thorough understanding of the system's dependencies is required. This underscores the importance of initially analyzing the system to map out all dependencies. By having a clear picture of these interconnections, developers can better predict the impact of changes, ensure smoother modifications, and maintain the system's overall integrity and performance.

> **Modifiability:** Robust dependency management facilitates efficient and error-minimizing modifications in microservices.

Testability refers to how easily a software system can be tested to ensure it meets its requirements and behaves as intended. A highly testable system simplifies the creation, execution, and maintenance of tests.

In microservice architectures, testability and dependency management intersect significantly. Tests are resource-intensive, and static analysis can sometimes offer insights with fewer resources. However, tests still require maintenance, and changes in the system often impact which tests need to be run or updated.

Proper dependency management can streamline the testing process by pinpointing which specific tests are affected by system changes. This allows for targeted testing, reducing the need for comprehensive system tests and conserving resources. For example, changes in one microservice might only necessitate tests related to that specific service, rather than a full system retest.

Moreover, understanding the dependencies between system components and tests helps identify which tests need modification when changes occur, especially in end-to-end testing scenarios. This ensures that testing efforts remain focused and efficient, maintaining system integrity with optimal resource usage.

> **Testability:** Dependency-aware testing strategies are key to optimizing test maintenance and resource use in microservices.

Figure 5 illustrates the concept of architectural degradation and its impact on system maintainability. In this visual metaphor, the roots symbolize system dependencies, which are crucial for supporting and stabilizing the architecture, represented by the tree's trunk. As the trunk branches out, it signifies the architecture of the system, while the leaves represent maintainability. Barren branches indicate an unmaintained system, suggesting that neglecting the underlying dependencies results in the deterioration of the system's structural integrity. This emphasizes that the health of the system's architecture relies heavily on the careful management of its dependencies. Poor management can lead to architectural degradation and a subsequent decline in maintainability.

7 Conclusions

In this manuscript, we have underscored the critical role of dependency management in enhancing maintainability within microservice systems. As systems evolve, mitigating architectural degradation becomes essential, and while various approaches have been developed for monolithic repository systems, there remains a significant gap in strategies tailored for microservices. We have explored the potential of effective dependency management to support change impact analysis, emphasizing its importance in decentralized systems.

By utilizing managed dependencies as a tool to assess changes, developers can achieve better outcomes more efficiently, ensuring that modifications do not inadvertently compromise system integrity. However, this perspective indicates the need for further research.

Future research should focus on developing scalable and adaptable dependency management strategies for microservices that can keep pace with technological advancements. Addressing these research gaps will not only assist developers in overcoming current challenges but also contribute to the creation of more resilient and maintainable microservice architectures.

Acknowledgements. This work is based upon work supported by the National Science Foundation under Grant No. 2409933.

References

1. ISO 25000 portal (2023). https://iso25000.com/index.php/en/iso-25000-standards/iso-25010/57-maintainability. Accessed 20 Dec 2023
2. Microservices adoption in 2020 (2023). https://www.oreilly.com/radar/microservices-adoption-in-2020/. Accessed 20 Dec 2023

3. Abdelfattah, A.S., Cerny, T.: The microservice dependency matrix. In: European Conference on Service-Oriented and Cloud Computing, pp. 276–288. Springer (2023)

4. Al Maruf, A., Bakhtin, A., Cerny, T., Taibi, D.: Using microservice telemetry data for system dynamic analysis. In: 2022 IEEE International Conference on Service-Oriented System Engineering (SOSE), pp. 29–38. IEEE (2022)

5. Alshuqayran, N., Ali, N., Evans, R.: Towards micro service architecture recovery: an empirical study. In: 2018 IEEE International Conference on Software Architecture (ICSA), pp. 47–4709 (2018). https://doi.org/10.1109/ICSA.2018.00014

6. Apolinário, D.R., de França, B.B.: A method for monitoring the coupling evolution of microservice-based architectures. J. Braz. Comput. Soc. 27(1), 17 (2021)

7. d Aragona, D.A., Pascarella, L., Janes, A., Lenarduzzi, V., Penaloza, R., Taibi, D.: On the empirical evidence of microservice logical coupling. a registered report (2023)

8. Azadi, U., Fontana, F.A., Taibi, D.: Architectural smells detected by tools: a catalogue proposal. In: Proceedings of the Scientific Workshop Proceedings of XP2016. XP 2016 Workshops, IEEE Press (2019). https://doi.org/10.1109/TechDebt.2019.00027

9. Baabad, A., Zulzalil, H.B., Hassan, S., Baharom, S.B.: Software architecture degradation in open source software: a systematic literature review. IEEE Access 8, 173681–173709 (2020). https://doi.org/10.1109/ACCESS.2020.3024671

10. Bass, L., Clements, P., Kazman, R.: Software Architecture in Practice: Software Architect Practice_c4. Addison-Wesley (2021)

11. Besker, T., Martini, A., Bosch, J.: Technical debt cripples software developer productivity: a longitudinal study on developers' daily software development work. In: Proceedings of the 2018 International Conference on Technical Debt, TechDebt 2018, pp. 105–114. Association for Computing Machinery, New York (2018). https://doi.org/10.1145/3194164.3194178

12. Bogner, J., Fritzsch, J., Wagner, S., Zimmermann, A.: Industry practices and challenges for the evolvability assurance of microservices. Empirical Softw. Eng. 26(5), 104 (2021). https://doi.org/10.1007/s10664-021-09999-9

13. Cerny, T., Abdelfattah, A.S., Maruf, A.A., Janes, A., Taibi, D.: Catalog and detection techniques of microservice anti-patterns and bad smells: a tertiary study. J. Syst. Softw. 206, 111829 (2023). https://doi.org/10.1016/j.jss.2023.111829. https://www.sciencedirect.com/science/article/pii/S0164121223002248

14. Cerny, T., Donahoo, M.J., Trnka, M.: Contextual understanding of microservice architecture: current and future directions. ACM SIGAPP Appl. Comput. Rev. 17(4), 29–45 (2018)

15. Conway, M.E.: How do committees invent. Datamation 14(4), 28–31 (1968)

16. Daigneau, R.: Service Design Patterns: fundamental design solutions for SOAP. Addison-Wesley (2012)

17. Das, D., et al.: Technical debt resulting from architectural degradation and code smells: a systematic mapping study. SIGAPP Appl. Comput. Rev. 21(4), 20–36 (2022). https://doi.org/10.1145/3512753.3512755

18. Dijkstra, E.W.: On the Role of Scientific Thought, pp. 60–66. Springer, New York (1982). https://doi.org/10.1007/978-1-4612-5695-3_12

19. Fontana, F.A., Roveda, R., Vittori, S., Metelli, A., Saldarini, S., Mazzei, F.: On evaluating the impact of the refactoring of architectural problems on software quality. In: Proceedings of the Scientific Workshop Proceedings of XP2016. XP 2016 Workshops, Association for Computing Machinery, New York (2016). https://doi.org/10.1145/2962695.2962716

20. Gamma, E., Helm, R., Johnson, R., Vlissides, J.: Design patterns: abstraction and reuse of object-oriented design. In: Nierstrasz, O.M. (ed.) ECOOP 1993. LNCS, vol. 707, pp. 406–431. Springer, Heidelberg (1993). https://doi.org/10.1007/3-540-47910-4_21

21. Garlan, D., Shaw, M.: An introduction to software architecture. In: Advances in Software Engineering and Knowledge Engineering, pp. 1–39. World Scientific (1993)

22. Haendler, T., Sobernig, S., Strembeck, M.: Towards triaging code-smell candidates via runtime scenarios and method-call dependencies. In: Proceedings of the XP2017 Scientific Workshops. XP 2017, Association for Computing Machinery, New York (2017). https://doi.org/10.1145/3120459.3120468
23. Hohpe, G.: Event-driven = loosely coupled? not so fast! In: Enterprise Integration Patterns (2023). https://www.enterpriseintegrationpatterns.com/ramblings/eventdriven_coupling.html
24. Hohpe, G.: The many facets of coupling. Enterprise Integration Patterns (2023). https://www.enterpriseintegrationpatterns.com/ramblings/coupling_facets.html
25. Larman, C., et al.: Applying UML and Patterns, vol. 2. Prentice Hall, Upper Saddle River (1998)
26. Lenarduzzi, V., Sievi-Korte, O.: On the negative impact of team independence in microservices software development. In: Proceedings of the 19th International Conference on Agile Software Development: Companion, pp. 1–4 (2018)
27. Li, Z., Liang, P., Avgeriou, P., Guelfi, N., Ampatzoglou, A.: An empirical investigation of modularity metrics for indicating architectural technical debt. In: Proceedings of the 10th International ACM Sigsoft Conference on Quality of Software Architectures, pp. 119–128. QoSA 2014, Association for Computing Machinery, New York (2014). https://doi.org/10.1145/2602576.2602581
28. Lv, W., et al.: Graph-reinforcement-learning-based dependency-aware microservice deployment in edge computing. IEEE Internet Things J. **11**(1), 1604–1615 (2023)
29. Ma, S.P., Fan, C.Y., Chuang, Y., Liu, I.H., Lan, C.W.: Graph-based and scenario-driven microservice analysis, retrieval, and testing. Futur. Gener. Comput. Syst. **100**, 724–735 (2019)
30. Martini, A., Sikander, E., Madlani, N.: A semi-automated framework for the identification and estimation of architectural technical debt: a comparative case-study on the modularization of a software component. Inf. Softw. Technol. **93**, 264–279 (2018). https://doi.org/10.1016/j.infsof.2017.08.005. https://www.sciencedirect.com/science/article/pii/S095058491630355X
31. Meng, C., Song, S., Tong, H., Pan, M., Yu, Y.: Deepscaler: holistic autoscaling for microservices based on spatiotemporal GNN with adaptive graph learning. In: 2023 38th IEEE/ACM International Conference on Automated Software Engineering (ASE), pp. 53–65. IEEE (2023)
32. Newman, S.: Building Microservices: Designing Fine-Grained Systems, 1st edn. O'Reilly Media, Sebastopol (2015)
33. Panichella, S., Rahman, M.I., Taibi, D.: Structural coupling for microservices. arXiv preprint arXiv:2103.04674 (2021)
34. Parnas, D.L.: On the criteria to be used in decomposing systems into modules. Commun. ACM **15**(12), 1053–1058 (1972). https://doi.org/10.1145/361598.361623
35. Parnas, D., Clements, P., Weiss, D.: The modular structure of complex systems. IEEE Trans. Softw. Eng. **SE-11**(3), 259–266 (1985). https://doi.org/10.1109/TSE.1985.232209
36. Qian, L., Li, J., He, X., Gu, R., Shao, J., Lu, Y.: Microservice extraction using graph deep clustering based on dual view fusion. Inf. Softw. Technol. **158**, 107171 (2023)
37. Rademacher, F., Sachweh, S., Zündorf, A.: A modeling method for systematic architecture reconstruction of microservice-based software systems. In: Enterprise, Business-Process and Information Systems Modeling, pp. 311–326. Springer, Cham (2020)
38. Rademacher, F., Wizenty, P., Sorgalla, J., Sachweh, S., Zündorf, A.: Model-Driven Engineering of Microservice Architectures—The LEMMA Approach, pp. 105–147. Springer, Cham (2024). https://doi.org/10.1007/978-3-031-44412-8_5
39. Schiewe, M., Curtis, J., Bushong, V., Cerny, T.: Advancing static code analysis with language-agnostic component identification. IEEE Access **10**, 30743–30761 (2022)

40. Song, C., et al.: Chainsformer: a chain latency-aware resource provisioning approach for microservices cluster. In: International Conference on Service-Oriented Computing, pp. 197–211. Springer (2023)

41. Song, Y., Li, C., Zhuang, K., Ma, T., Wo, T.: An automatic scaling system for online application with microservices architecture. In: 2022 IEEE International Conference on Joint Cloud Computing (JCC), pp. 73–78. IEEE (2022)

42. Terzić, B., Dimitrieski, V., Kordić (Aleksić), S., Luković, I.: A model-driven approach to microservice software architecture establishment, pp. 73–80 (2018). https://doi.org/10.15439/2018F370

43. Tighilt, R., Abdellatif, M., Trabelsi, I., Madern, L., Moha, N., Guéhéneuc, Y.G.: On the maintenance support for microservice-based systems through the specification and the detection of microservice antipatterns. J. Syst. Softw. **204**, 111755 (2023). https://doi.org/10.1016/j.jss.2023.111755.   https://www.sciencedirect.com/science/article/pii/S0164121223001504

44. de Toledo, S.S., Martini, A., Sjøberg, D.I.K.: Improving agility by managing shared libraries in microservices. In: Paasivaara, M., Kruchten, P. (eds.) Agile Processes in Software Engineering and Extreme Programming - Workshops, pp. 195–202. Springer, Cham (2020)

45. Walker, A., Das, D., Cerny, T.: Automated code-smell detection in microservices through static analysis: a case study. Appl. Sci. **10**(21), 7800 (2020)

46. Walker, A., Laird, I., Cerny, T.: On automatic software architecture reconstruction of microservice applications. In: Information Science and Applications: Proceedings of ICISA 2020, vol. 739, p. 223 (2021)

47. Wurster, M., Breitenbücher, U., Falkenthal, M., Leymann, F.: Developing, deploying, and operating twelve-factor applications with tosca, pp. 519–525 (2017). https://doi.org/10.1145/3151759.3151830

48. Yang, J., Guo, Y., Chen, Y., Zhao, Y.: Tracenet: operation aware root cause localization of microservice system anomalies. In: 2023 IEEE International Conference on Communications Workshops (ICC Workshops), pp. 758–763. IEEE (2023)

49. Zhou, J., Wang, G., Zhou, W.: Dependency-aware microservice deployment and resource allocation in distributed edge networks. In: 2023 International Wireless Communications and Mobile Computing (IWCMC), pp. 568–573. IEEE (2023)

50. Černý, T., Chy, M.S.H., Abdelfattah, A., Soldani, J., Bogner, J.: On maintainability and microservice dependencies: how do changes propagate? pp. 277–286 (2024). https://doi.org/10.5220/0012725200003711

Secure Computation and Trustless Data Intermediaries in Data Spaces

Christoph Fabianek[1] , Stephan Krenn[2] , Thomas Lorünser[2,3]([✉]) ,
and Veronika Siska[4]

[1] Frequentis, Vienna, Austria
`christoph.fabianek@frequentis.at`
[2] AIT Austrian Institute of Technology, Vienna, Austria
`{stephan.krenn,thomas.loruenser}@ait.ac.at`
[3] Digital Factory Vorarlberg GmbH, Dornbirn, Austria
[4] Vienna, Austria

Abstract. This paper explores the integration of advanced cryptographic techniques for secure computation in data spaces to enable secure and trusted data sharing, which is essential for the evolving data economy. In addition, the paper examines the role of data intermediaries, as outlined in the EU Data Governance Act, in data spaces and specifically introduces the idea of trustless intermediaries that do not have access to their users' data. Therefore, we exploit the introduced secure computation methods, i.e. Secure Multi-Party Computation (MPC) and Fully Homomorphic Encryption (FHE), and discuss the security benefits. Overall, we identify and address key challenges for integration, focusing on areas such as identity management, policy enforcement, node selection, and access control, and present solutions through real-world use cases, including air traffic management, manufacturing, and secondary data use. Furthermore, through the analysis of practical applications, this work proposes a comprehensive framework for the implementation and standardization of secure computing technologies in dynamic, trustless data environments, paving the way for future research and development of a secure and interoperable data ecosystem.

Keywords: Secure computing · Data spaces · Data intermediaries · Policy definitions · Decentralized trust

1 Introduction

Data spaces are central to enabling sovereign, interoperable, and trustworthy data-sharing, which is crucial for the emerging data economy. Although certain techniques to support data sovereignty are inherent to data spaces, the use of modern cryptography beyond the state-of-the-art can propel the concept to the next level and unleash collaboration on sensitive data.

In this paper, we focus on privacy-enhancing technologies (PETs) for computing on encrypted data, without the need to trust any third party or particular hardware; namely

V. Siska—Independent Researcher.

C. Pahl and M. van Steen (Eds.): CLOSER 2024, CCIS 2851, pp. 53–81, 2026.
https://doi.org/10.1007/978-3-032-17286-0_3

multiparty computation (MPC) and fully homomorphic encryption (FHE). MPC is a distributed protocol which naturally fits the federated architecture of data spaces and could therefore be an integrated part of it. FHE, on the other hand, enables computations on encrypted data without access to the secret key and thus can also be leveraged directly between two data space participants. FHE has a smaller communication overhead than MPC, but it requires more computations on a single server than MPC.

To the best of our knowledge no comprehensive analysis nor integration concept for MPC and FHE in data spaces exist, except for our preliminary approach presented in [44], especially in support of modern collaborative use cases.

We want to stress that also alternative paradigms for secure computation exist – including, e.g., Trusted Execution Environments (TEEs) or Federated Learning (FL) –, partially offering higher efficiency and lower bandwidth requirements than FHE or MPC. However, the reasons for focusing on those two primitives in this paper are twofold. Firstly, approaches like FL are tailored for specific computations to be carried out, while FHE and MPC are universal in terms of expressiveness. Secondly, especially in the case of hardware-backed TEEs such as Intel SGX[1] or ARM TrustZone[2], additional trust not only into the cryptographic mechanisms but also into the hardware manufacturer is required, which introduces an entire additional dimension for risk assessment, especially in highly regulated domains, e.g., related to patient health data.

1.1 Our Contribution

In this paper we therefore systematically analyze integration challenges for multiparty computation (MPC) and fully homomorphic encryption (FHE) into data spaces, to enable seamless access to secure computation technologies for processing sensitive data in a privacy preserving manner.

Furthermore, we also analyze the potential of data intermediaries facilitating end-to-end secure data sharing and processing within data spaces, therefore addressing critical challenges associated with trust and data integrity for data escrow. The presented approach builds on MPC and FHE techniques to ensure that neither the intermediary nor the compute nodes require trust, thereby eliminating the risk of data loss or compromise. Thus, we significantly extend our previous work in Siska et al. [44] in multiple directions by including FHE and introduction trustless intermediaries.

To holistically approach the problem, we evaluate a representative set of use cases to identify a comprehensive spectrum of challenges. Moreover, we propose a complete approach for the integration, as well as concrete methods and technologies to solve the identified challenges, and identify gaps where further research is required.

1.2 Paper Outline

This paper is structured as follows. Section 2 gives a short review of the concepts of data spaces, MPC and FHE. In Sect. 3 we introduce three use cases and discuss them from

---

[1] https://www.intel.de/content/www/de/de/products/docs/accelerator-engines/software-guard-extensions.html.

[2] https://www.arm.com/technologies/trustzone-for-cortex-m.

a deployment perspective, extracting their key characteristics and challenges. In Sect. 4 we propose a first approach for an ubiquitous and comprehensive integration of MPC and FHE into data spaces. Based on that, potential technical solutions and research gaps for the identified challenges are discussed in Sect. 5. We conclude in Sect. 6.

1.3 Related Work

Related work that considers PETs in the context of data spaces is not extensive, since the latter is relatively young as a research field.

Garrido et al. [22] conduct a systematic review on the application of privacy-enhancing technologies (PETs) for internet-of-things (IoT) data markets, including MPC. They conclude that PETs are not frequently used in this setting, despite relevant use cases; and that there is no consensus on a general architecture, in particular regarding the usage of blockchain.

Agahari et al. [2] and [3] offer a business perspective on MPC for data sharing, building on the business model f or data marketplaces from [45]. They conduct semi-structured interviews in the privacy and security domain to study the perceived value propositions, architecture and financial models [2], as well as control, trust, and perceived risks [3]. They find that the value of MPC is seen in increased privacy, enhanced control and reduced need for trust, but that specific data sharing risks remain since the results may still reveal sensitive information. Different deployment scenarios are also described, such as the distributed, asynchronous setup that we present via data spaces in the current paper.

Müller et al. [37] focus on federated machine learning, with an application for the automotive industry via the project Catena-X[3]. They explore various cryptographic techniques, such as MPC and FHE, and identify usability challenges and efficiency as the primary obstacles. They note that these technologies are lacking in user-friendliness and specialized libraries, and currently necessitate expert knowledge for specific use cases.

Besides the limited research on MPC integration into data spaces, some work on MPC on blockchain exists, with Secret Network[4] and Partisia[5] (described in Sect. 2.3) being the most prominent candidates. One important difference to data space integration is the lack of a registration procedure to establish trust relationships. Contrary to blockchain-based solutions, the MPC node pool in data spaces is open, but nodes and their attributes are certified e.g. via verifiable credentials (VCs). Thus, MPC groups are also not necessarily random subsets, but can be chosen by attributes. Also, there is no need for complex broadcast protocols for arbitration, and contracts can be signed without involving a blockchain. Payment also does not necessarily need to flow through cryptocurrencies.

There is also a blockchain-based integration of FHE for data marketplaces: Serrano and Cuenca [43] describe an architecture based on smart contracts and implement a case study on an Ethereum test chain, with two participants. The resulting system is slower

---

[3] https://catena-x.net/.
[4] https://scrt.network/.
[5] https://partisiablockchain.com/.

and includes approximation errors when compared to a simple computation without any PETs, but improves data privacy.

Furthermore, there are multiple proposals for using trusted execution environments based on blockchain for data marketplaces: Sterling is based on the private blockchain Oasis [26], while PDS2 [24] uses the public Ehereum chain to provide auditability.

To the best of our knowledge, concrete integration of MPC or FHE into data spaces has not been discussed in the literature and we are the first to propose a general and comprehensive treatment. Data spaces require a fundamentally different approach to a pure blockchain based system, and can be more flexible, scalable and energy efficient compared to permissionless systems.

2   Preliminaries

We next outline some fundamental concepts. In particular we explain the concept of data spaces as well as the idea of data intermediaries, which are both novel data governance concepts established in the European Union. Additionally, on the technical side we introduce two important cryptographic methods from the field of privacy enhancing technologies, i.e., secure multiparty computation and fully homomorphic encryption, which substantially matured in research over the last decade and now make its way into first commercial applications.

2.1   Data Spaces

A data space is "a distributed system defined by a governance framework that enables secure and trustworthy data transactions between participants while supporting trust and data sovereignty" [16]. The goal of data spaces is to share data and data-related services via a federated data marketplace [48]. This includes data-based services, such as storage, web servers, or algorithms operating on shared data. The latter is particularly relevant for privacy-preserving and/or distributed computing approaches that respect access and usage restrictions, such as MPC.

Data spaces were introduced in computer science as a shift from a central database to storing data at the source [20]. This new way of data management, where participants retain control over their own data, is now called data sovereignty [38]. Data sovereignty is at the heart of the European data strategy and related regulations, in particular the General Data Protection Regulation (GDPR)[6], the Data Governance Act[7], and the Data Act[8]. The concept is also of international interest: by now, GDPR-like regulations exist in 17 countries and even more on the federal level (e.g. New York Privacy Act[9] and the California Consumer Privacy Act[10]); with some (e.g. South Korea's Personal Information Protection Act[11]) even pre-dating GDPR.

---

[6] https://eur-lex.europa.eu/eli/reg/2016/679/oj.

[7] https://eur-lex.europa.eu/eli/reg/2022/868/oj.

[8] https://eur-lex.europa.eu/eli/reg/2023/2854.

[9] https://nyassembly.gov/leg/?bn=S00365.

[10] https://oag.ca.gov/privacy/ccpa.

[11] https://www.law.go.kr/LSW/lsInfoP.do?lsiSeq=213857&viewCls=engLsInfoR& urlMode=engLsInfoR.

There are many initiatives supporting data space development. The International Data Spaces Association (IDSA) provided the initial concept, including the first reference architecture, the International Data Spaces Reference Architecture Model (IDS RAM). Gaia-X is taking the concept further and considers generic data products, also including services like storage or data analytics, to enable interoperability between different infrastructures. Gaia-X also develops a trust framework: a composition of policies, rules, standards and procedures based on standardized descriptions for participants and services. These are built using W3C Verifiable Credentials: cryptographically signed digital certificates that are thus tamperproof and automatically verifiable.

The Data Spaces Business Alliance (DSBA)[12], formed by BDVA[13], FIWARE Foundation[14], Gaia-X[15], and IDSA[16], aims to harmonize these efforts by providing a common technical framework (DOME) [5]. The Data Spaces Support Centre (DSSC)[17] contributes with coordination efforts, including a glossary and building blocks, whereas simpl[18] focuses on creating reusable data space software. Sector-specific projects like Catena-X in the automotive industry or Manufacturing-X for manufacturing, exemplify the application of these frameworks. Promising open-source software components for data spaces are now also available, such as the Eclipse Dataspace Components (EDC), the Gaia-X cross-federation services or the Pontus-X ecosystem. These collaborative efforts are laying the groundwork for a unified, efficient, and sovereign digital ecosystem, marking significant strides toward the realization of a comprehensive Data Economy.

2.2 Data Intermediaries

Data intermediaries act as important components within data ecosystems, bridging the gap between data providers and data consumers while addressing critical challenges in data processing and security. They play a crucial role in ensuring compliance with regulatory frameworks and enhancing the value extracted from data through various services. These services are essential for maintaining the integrity, usability, and accessibility of data, thereby fostering a robust data economy, and promoting innovation.

Traditionally, data intermediaries have served as brokers, aggregators, and facilitators of data transactions, primarily collecting, standardizing, and cleaning data from diverse sources before providing it to organizations for value extraction. Examples include market research firms, financial data providers, and health information exchanges, which have enabled organizations to access a broader range of data, enhance their analytics capabilities, and make more informed decisions.

The European Union's Data Governance Act (DGA)[19] establishes a framework for the safe and effective sharing of data across sectors and member states. According to

---

[12] https://data-spaces-business-alliance.eu/.

[13] https://bdva.eu/.

[14] https://www.fiware.org/.

[15] https://gaia-x.eu/.

[16] https://internationaldataspaces.org/.

[17] https://dssc.eu/.

[18] https://digital-strategy.ec.europa.eu/en/policies/simpl.

[19] https://eur-lex.europa.eu/eli/reg/2022/868/oj.

the DGA, data intermediaries provide services that facilitate data sharing while ensuring the protection of data subjects' rights and interests.

The DGA outlines a comprehensive framework for data intermediaries, specifying their roles, responsibilities, and operational conditions to ensure trustworthy data sharing. A key requirement is the mandatory notification and registration of data intermediaries with the competent national authority. To further enhance transparency and trust, the Commission has introduced a common logo for data intermediation service providers (cf. Fig. 1), enabling stakeholders to easily identify compliant entities. Additionally, data intermediaries must maintain neutrality and independence, operating as neutral third parties without aggregating, enriching, or transforming data to add value. This structural separation from other services is mandated to prevent conflicts of interest and ensure that their business model does not depend on profiting directly from the data shared through them.

Fig. 1. Logo for EU Recognised Data Intermediary.

Article 10 of the DGA specifies three broad types of data intermediation services that can be seen as enablers of data spaces, including:

- Intermediation services between data holders and potential data users, facilitating bilateral or multilateral exchanges of data;
- Intermediation services between data subjects or individuals and potential data users, primarily dealing with personal or non-personal data sharing; and
- Data cooperatives, organizational structures constituted by data subjects, one-person undertakings, or SMEs to help their members exercise their rights over their data and support collective data management and public interest goals.

These roles highlight the diverse functions of data intermediaries, from facilitating industrial data sharing to personal data management and collective data governance, underscoring their importance in the evolving data economy.

To address the challenges of data security and the risk of data loss, our approach emphasizes the use of zero-trust data intermediaries. These intermediaries leverage advanced cryptographic techniques such as MPC and FHE to facilitate secure data processing without requiring trust in the intermediary or compute nodes. This reduces the risk of data loss and enhances the integrity of the data handling process.

2.3   Secure Multiparty Computation

Multiparty computation (MPC) is a technology for computing on encrypted data in a distributed setting, i.e., with multiple nodes holding only secure fragments of input data not learning anything from them. The concept appeared more than 30 years ago and has been the target of active research over the last 3 decades. For a long time, it was considered only theoretical, but progress in recent years led to many interesting applications which can be realized with practical efficiency, given a suitable deployment.

Basic Model. In principle, MPC can be used to decentralize systems where typically a central trusted authority is needed to execute a function on behalf of the users. With MPC, the function is evaluated jointly between multiple parties such that the correctness of the output is guaranteed and the privacy of the inputs of the individual parties is preserved; only the output of the computation is learned. Furthermore, information-theoretically secure MPC exist which makes it the ideal method if long-term security is needed.

We quickly present the generic model of MPC as introduced in ISO/IEC 4922[20,21]. Different roles are necessary in a generic MPC system in order to qualify as such. **Input parties** hold inputs for the secure computation which must be encoded and then sent to the compute parties. **Compute parties** run the multiparty protocol, which is executed among them as they jointly compute the intended function on the encoded inputs. The **intended function** to be computed is not kept secret and is defined according to the use case. The function is composed of basic operations available to the MPC protocol and typically composed of simple gates from a boolean or arithmetic circuit, depending on the encoding and protocols used. After the computation, the result is held by the compute parties in an encoded form and then sent to the **result parties**, which can reconstruct the result of the computation (Fig. 2).

The main security properties are **correctness** and **input privacy**, and it is the latter which guarantees the confidentiality of the data. Depending on the protocol, the security parameters could hold against different kind of adversaries.

Certain additional, optional security guarantees are also possible, e.g., fairness, guaranteed output delivery or covert security. Fairness means, that malicious parties only receive their output if also the honest parties do so. With guaranteed output delivery the honest parties always receive their output. Contrary, in a covert security model, the protocol aborts in case of error and allows for cheater detection.

In summary, the overall concept is well understood and elaborated, i.e., many computations have been shown practical. However, the security assumptions are very different from traditional secret or public key cryptography. Here, security is mainly governed by the non-collusion assumption, which makes deployment of the technology challenging, especially in dynamic scenarios as we often find in emerging data markets and digital ecosystems with many stakeholders involved.

MPC as a Service. Due to the complexity and deployment challenges, potential users are often reluctant to use MPC. Thus, collaborative use cases are often prevented in data spaces if data privacy cannot be assured.

---

[20] https://www.iso.org/standard/80508.html.
[21] https://www.iso.org/standard/80514.html.

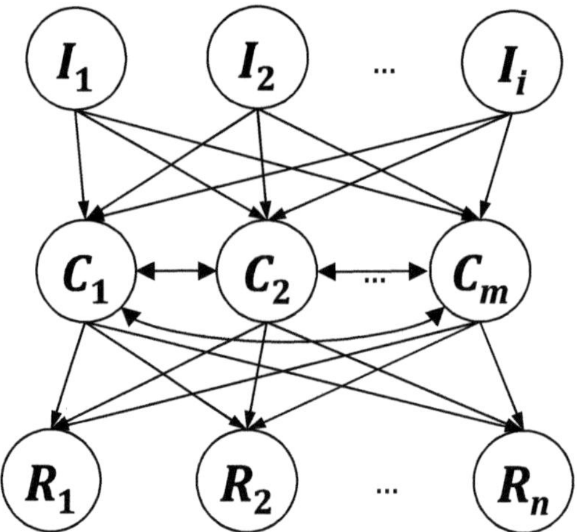

Fig. 2. Generic MPC model: input nodes I_i encode data and send them to compute nodes C_i, which then execute the MPC protocol. After that, compute nodes hold the secret in encoded form, which is finally sent to result nodes R_i that recover the result in plaintext, as also presented in [44].

Leveraging the as-a-service paradigm could be a way out for this problem but requires careful integration of the service to assure high security and prevent data leakage along the data life-cycle.

Moreover, additional integrity guarantees and data leakage prevention methods may be desirable depending on the sensitivity of the data and the use case. In particular, public verifiability could be of additional value for MPC-as-a-service (MPCaaS) and contribute to the trustworthiness of the service.

Publicly verifiable MPC can assure the correctness of computations even if all compute nodes are compromised, and although input privacy does not hold anymore. Typically, this is achieved by combining MPC protocols with compatible zero-knowledge proof (ZKP) systems to provide the best possible security guarantees for the outsourcing scenario of remote MPC, which is the case for the as-a-service usage. Yet, this is only to prevent from corrupt results in the worst case of a fully malicious MPC system, which can be prevented by careful selection of nodes.

The possibility for public audits of computation results have additionally benefits for data spaces because it also allows for high assurance levels of computation results. If even third-party stakeholders are able to verify the results of a computation, this could be used to establish end-to-end authenticity in data spaces. For example, [28] used this concept by combining MPC and zkSNARKS [13] with universal setup to enable flexible verifiability for MPCaaS. The idea has also been shown to be useful in the manufacturing context [36].

Partisia is another example which uses blockchain to persist data and as a broadcast channel in combination with an event driven architecture[22]. Here, MPC node pools are

---

[22] https://medium.com/partisia-blockchain/.

built from available compute nodes, and each MPC service is randomly assigned to a subset of the nodes in the pool. Service buyers pay a pool to run a service, and the whole process is orchestrated via a smart contract, without the secret state appearing on the blockchain.

Although first proposals for MPCaaS exist, it is an open question how generic MPCaaS shall be integrated into data spaces to support a wide range of use cases, but without burdening complex configuration and deployment issues on the users of the system. In our work we systematically analyze this problem and propose relevant technologies to be used to realize the concept.

2.4 Fully Homomorphic Encryption

Besides MPC, fully homomorphic encryption (FHE) constitutes the second main approach for cryptographically secured computation on sensitive data.

The concept of FHE was already introduced in the late 1970s by Rivest et al. [39], but the secure realization was proposed more than thirty years later in a groundbreaking result of Gentry [23], followed by a large body of work focusing on key- and ciphertext sizes, efficiency, etc. The development of FHE has seen significant advancements over the past decade, driven by improvements in both the theoretical foundations and practical implementations. The most notable progress has been in the reduction of computational overhead, which has traditionally been a major barrier to the adoption of FHE. Recent FHE schemes, such as those based on the BGV [8], CKKS [12] and TFHE [14] have significantly reduced the complexity of homomorphic operations. A range of open-source frameworks are available to researchers and developers[23].

Basic Model. Fully homomorphic encryption provides significantly enhanced functionalities compared to classical encryption. Namely, besides solely decrypting the ciphertext, it also allows one to evaluate functions in the encrypted domain. By computing on the ciphertexts, corresponding computations on the underlying plaintext can be realized, without ever requiring access to the plaintext. As a result, data owners can encrypt data, send it to an external (cloud) service together with a specification of the computation to be performed, and retrieve the encrypted computation result, which can be decrypted to receive the results of the computation.

In FHE, three main keys are involved: A **public key** is used to encrypt plaintext data, allowing anyone to perform encryption and homomorphic operations on ciphertexts. The **private key** is used to decrypt the final ciphertext after homomorphic operations, ensuring that only authorized parties can access the plaintext result. In many schemes an additional **evaluation key** facilitates efficient computation on encrypted data without needing the private key, enabling complex operations like multiplication while maintaining encryption. Sometimes a **relinearization key** is used to manage the growth of ciphertext size during operations like multiplication. It helps keeping ciphertexts compact and secure, ensuring efficient computation without excessive increase in size. The main security guarantees are **correctness**, guaranteeing that if all entities

---

[23] https://fhe.org/resources/.

behave honestly, the computation result will be correct, and **data privacy**, guaranteeing that no information about the input data is revealed to the cloud server.

Extended guarantees like verifiability of the performed computation can be achieved by specific schemes, e.g., [47]. Furthermore, when used to analyze data coming from different data sources, also multi-key FHE schemes exist [33], where each participant encrypts their data under their own key; however, despite eased key management, this approach requires all individual secret keys to be involved in the decryption process.

FHE as a Service. The concept of FHE as a Service (FHEaaS) has emerged as a promising approach to making FHE accessible to a broader range of applications and users. Microsoft's SEAL[24] and IBM's HELib[25] are among the most prominent FHE libraries that have been integrated into cloud services. Furthermore, startups like ZAMA[26] and academic projects, e.g., like OpenFHE[27], are also contributing to the development of FHEaaS, focusing on creating more user-friendly interfaces and improving the efficiency of homomorphic computations.

Despite these advancements, several challenges remain in the widespread adoption of FHE as a service. The computational cost of FHE, while reduced, is still significantly higher than traditional encryption methods and will require specific hardware on the server side for high-volume or real-time applications, which is not yet available due to the lack of standardization and interoperability of FHE schemes.

Moreover, key management in FHEaaS is also a critical and complex issue, particularly in scenarios involving multiple parties and long-term data sharing. The challenges include secure key generation, distribution, rotation, and recovery, as well as ensuring interoperability and compliance with regulatory standards.

If used to analyze data coming from different data sources, special attention needs to be paid to the management of the secret key, as it could not only be used to decrypt the computation results, but also the encrypted inputs. Thus, in scenarios where the intended receiver of the computation result – owning the secret key – must not get access to the individual encrypted inputs, it needs to be ensured that the computing server does not leak encrypted input data to the receiver. This has to be achieved on an organization level, i.e., by enforcing strict access policies and assuming non colluding servers similar to MPC.

In general, addressing key management challenges requires not only advanced cryptographic techniques but also robust infrastructure and protocols to manage keys effectively in a way that ensures both security and usability. Threshold versions of various schemes have also been introduced and implemented [4] as well as proxy re-encryption extensions to distribute trust and relax assumptions on individual servers. Switching between schemes is also considered a way to increase agility and flexibility in such scenarios. Furthermore, challenges arise when exploring hybrid approaches, i.e., using FHE in conjunction MPC or other cryptographic protocols. The keys must be managed

---

[24] https://github.com/microsoft/SEAL.

[25] https://github.com/homenc/HElib.

[26] https://www.zama.ai/.

[27] https://www.openfhe.org/.

in such a way that they enable joint computation without revealing the data to any of the participating parties.

A different approach towards outsourcing is the use of FHE on blockchain, which gained substantial attention in recent years. As shown by Dahl et al. [15] the technology can be used to achieve various applications directly on the chain. Among others they support encrypted tokens, blind auctions, privacy-enhancing decentralized autonomous organizations (DAOs) or decentralized identifiers (DID). Despite the progress achieved, work ahead aims at improving the security model potentially invoking trusted hardware, support for flexible sets of validators and reduction of ciphertext size for on-chain storage.

3   Use Cases and Challenges

In the following we explore three complimentary use cares requiring secure computing technologies, and use them to identify and cluster the arising challenges.

3.1   Use Cases

The use cases were selected to be highly complementary, in order to derive representative challenges and requirements.

Air Traffic Management. In air traffic management, the value attributed to individual flights can significantly vary. During peak periods, when demand exceeds available resources (e.g., due to bad weather or strikes), airlines have a vested interest in prioritizing flights that are of higher value to them. This need aligns with the economic interests of airports, which aim for optimal utilization of their infrastructure and a steady flow of passengers. Concurrently, air navigation service providers (ANSPs) are tasked with ensuring the safety of air travel, maintaining fairness and equality among all participants.

This scenario presents a multifaceted set of preferences and constraints, forming an optimization problem: determining the ideal sequence of flights for arrivals and departures. Each stakeholder – airlines, airports, and ANSP – has different needs, which include additional strict confidentiality requirements on which information to keep secret from other stakeholders. In a series of works, [34,41,42] proposed systems to optimize the use of airport capacities while taking all stakeholders' needs into consideration.

Their approach is built on MPC to satisfy the different confidentiality and integrity needs. In particular, verifiability of the computation is required, to minimize the risk of incorrect outputs resulting in a bias for or against a specific airline. More generally, fairness conditions are considered, to ensure that no specific airline is systematically privileged. Performance-wise, slot assignments are periodically computed for larger time intervals and the computation may take several minutes to succeed.

The high confidentiality and integrity needs of all stakeholders directly arise from their economic interests. Furthermore, verifiability of the computation is required, to minimize the risk of incorrect outputs resulting in a bias for or against a specific airline.

More generally, fairness conditions are considered, to ensure that no specific airline is systematically privileged. Performance-wise, slot assignments are periodically computed for larger time intervals and the computation may take several minutes to succeed.

The considered approaches vary slightly: [34] output optimal solutions solving linear assignment problems, while [42] consider genetic algorithms that reach a near-optimal solution with high efficiency. Independent of the precise strategy, the necessary computations are agreed upon in advance by the various stakeholders and remain fixed over a high number of executions.

On the deployment side, air traffic management turns out to be a relatively static scenario, where a steady group of input providers (i.e., airlines) contributes their preferences, and all stakeholders (e.g., compute nodes, inputs providers, output consumers, etc.) are mutually known to each other. The existence of a central trusted entity, such as the local Air Navigation Service Provider (ANSP), EUROCONTROL, or the airport itself, ensures that data integrity and confidentiality are maintained without necessitating the use of a Data Intermediary. These entities inherently manage and optimize air traffic, providing a centralized and trusted framework for the stakeholders involved. Consequently, the implementation of a Data Intermediary for secure data sharing in this sector is redundant, as the established trusted entities fulfill this role effectively.

Manufacturing as a Service. The sharing economy promises environmental benefits, innovation, and reduction of costs, but concerns persist over data sovereignty and trust. Also, centralization in large infrastructures raises economic alarms. Specifically for the manufacturing domain, [36] examine a platform where manufacturing site owners can enlist as producers, registering their machinery along with pertinent meta information such as configurations and quality standards. Customers can place orders, prompting producers to submit bids to secure the order. A high-level architecture and flow is depicted in Fig. 3.

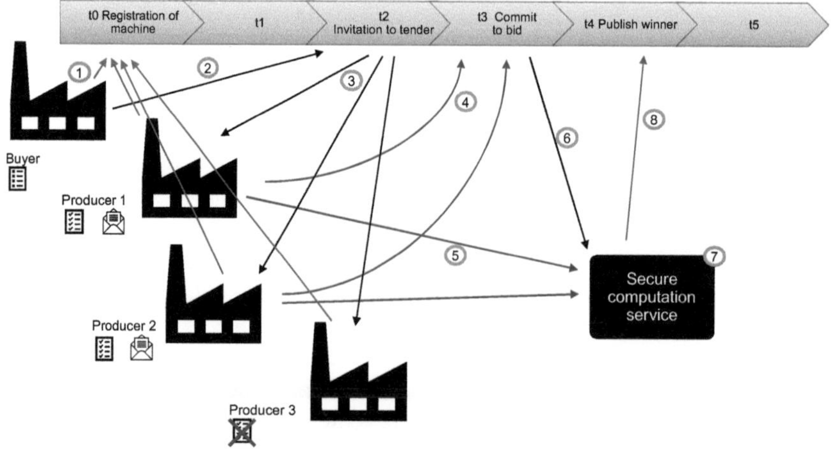

Fig. 3. Manufacturing-as-a-Service Architecture adapted from [36,44].

Regarding requirements, producers need confidentiality to make sure that non-winning bids are not leaked, to avoid exposing internal cost structures or similar information to competitors. Both customers and producers are asking for integrity and verifiability, i.e., it needs to be ensured that the correctness of the computation can be publicly checked. In [36], this is achieved leveraging zero-knowledge proofs in combination with MPC; however, this is not to be misunderstood as a prejudice against FHE for the specific use case, but rather a specific design of the authors. Finally, immutability of bids, to avoid adjustments depending on competing bids, is avoided using blockchain for securely storing encrypted bids and outcomes.

In the scenario of manufacturing as a service, the function to be computed is not entirely static, but may vary depending on the specific tender. For instance, while [36] consider first-price sealed-bid auctions, also alternative options like second-price (= Vickrey) auctions or multi-attribute auctions could be used. The precise model would be defined by the customer when publishing the tender.

From a deployment point of view, the auction platform provider would select any involved compute nodes, so that they can safely be assumed to be known a priori to all stakeholders in the default setting. However, also more dynamic configurations could be imagined, where stakeholders which to be part of the computation to increase data sovereignty. Moreover, as anybody may act as a customer and/or producer, the users cannot be assumed to be static and known to each other, such that a permissioned setting requiring, e.g., a registration phase, need to be introduced in order to overcome challenges with rogue bids and offers.

In this use case, where no central trusted entity exists, the role of a Data Intermediary becomes critical. Manufacturers and consumers engage in collaborative processes without a predefined trust foundation. The Data Intermediary facilitates secure data exchange using advanced cryptographic techniques such as MPC or FHE, ensuring that sensitive data is processed securely with a fixed scope, enabling trustless collaboration while safeguarding proprietary manufacturing data.

Secondary Use of Data. Data is often generated for a specific purpose, e.g., for medical treatment or collecting GPS information for charging road usage. However, often this data would also be highly valuable in other contexts, e.g., medical studies in hospitals or road traffic planning for public authorities. This gives raise to the concept of data marketplaces, which enable selling (computations on) data to customers.

Different approaches based on different cryptographic primitives have been proposed in the literature, e.g., using fully homomorphic encryption [31], or secure multiparty computation [29,30].

According to [29], confidentiality and privacy are paramount, ensuring that (computations on) data cannot be requested without consent. That is, data providers must have fine-grained control over data usage and sales, without relying on a single trusted entity. Furthermore, verifiability and authenticity are crucial: the marketplace operator should not be able to tamper with analysis outputs, and mechanisms are needed to prevent the sale of fake data to increase trustworthiness and value of data, without compromising privacy. Where possible, end-to-end guarantees on data integrity are desirable, spanning from data source (e.g., a sensor) to consumer.

In the context of data markets, it is also crucial to support high flexibility in the computation to be carried out. This is necessary to protect privacy and address the asynchronous nature of these ecosystems, where data providers may not be available at computation time. Therefore, data subjects must have the ability to define precise usage policies linked to their data, specifying constraints on computations, compute nodes, and the number of inputs involved. It is imperative that compliance with these policies is immutably documented for auditing purposes for each computation. Additionally, contractual agreements must be in place, e.g., to prevent the acquisition of previously independent compute nodes by the same entity before data deletion. Moreover, the trade-offs between transparency and auditability on the one hand, and customer needs on the other hand, must be carefully considered. For instance, the mere interest of a customer in certain data may inadvertently disclose information about their business strategy.

In terms of deployment, data markets require a high level of flexibility. Data may be stored in various locations, and users may define different types of policies, such as geographical constraints on nodes. Particularly within the health domain, a Data Intermediary is essential due to the sensitivity and legal constraints surrounding data sharing. National laws or public opinion may restrict the direct sharing of health data with supranational organizations (e.g., UN or EU). To address this, data is encoded using MPC or encrypted with FHE at the national level before being processed by a trustless intermediary. This intermediary could be setup dynamically with a pre-defined scope (e.g., addressing a rare disease) and facilitates secure and compliant data sharing while maintaining the confidentiality and sovereignty of the original data sources.

Additionally, in contrast to the previous use case domains, node selection becomes a complex task. It is also uncertain which nodes will require access to which shares during data creation and storage, necessitating the deployment of advanced encryption mechanisms and related key management procedures to support this dynamism. Furthermore, since data providers and consumers are typically unknown to each other, strong identity management mechanisms are essential. These mechanisms not only ensure that users' policies (e.g., "only medical research institutes may request computations on my data") are adhered to, but also mitigate the risks associated with rogue data. Finally, potential payments for data usage must be executed in a manner that preserves privacy.

3.2   Challenges

As illustrated by the application scenarios above, integrating MPC into complex federated scenarios such as data spaces comes with practical challenges that may directly influence system design. In the following we cluster the lessons learned from the considered use cases to obtain a set of challenge categories to be considered, which are also summarized in Table 1.

C1. Global System Parameters. In case that the protocols to be executed require global system parameters – such as a common reference string (CRS) – the security and trustworthiness of these parameters needs to be guaranteed. This may for instance apply when leveraging zkSNARKs to obtain public verifiability of the computation output.

Table 1. Comparison of challenges affected by different use cases.

	UC1: Air traffic	UC2: Industry 4.0	UC3: Secondary Use
C1. Global system parameters	CRS for end-to-end verifiability and integrity		
C2. Authentication and identity management	static, permissioned	semi-static, permissioned	dynamic, permissionless
C3. Data usage policies	static, fully defined from beginning		dynamic, meta-level specifications
C4. Node selection	static	dynamic	
C5. Access control	online input provisioning; early encoding	synchronous input; early encoding; audit info	asynchronous input; late encoding
C6. Trustless intermediaries	not relevant	fixed scope	dynamic deployment

C2. Authentication and Identity Management. Identity management is at the core of any security architecture: any confidentiality concerns are vacuous if the communication partner is not genuine. In the context of MPC, not only compute nodes that handle the data, but also data providers and receivers need to be authenticated. The former is required to increase trust in the input data and potentially achieve accountability, while the latter is needed to ensure that only eligible parties may request computations.

However, out-of-the-box authentication methods are not always applicable in certain scenarios, as the identity of data sources and data receivers may subject to data protection requirements. For example, it may be desired to determine only the eligibility to request a computation, but not the actual identity. Yet, in case of misuse, methods for accountability may be needed.

The situation is further complicated when the data is managed on behalf of the owner by a third party (data custodian); when the owner is not able or willing to manage their own data. In this case, authentication would also be handled by the data custodian, with the owner first granting the right to do so.

To support large scale adoption, compatibility with governmental identities such as the upcoming European eIDAS 2.0 regulation is also necessary.

C3. Data Usage Policies. Precise data usage policies play a critical role in increasing trust and achieving acceptance by end users, particularly when personal or confidential data is involved.

Such policies describe the permissible ways in which data can be utilized, encompassing aspects such as eligible groups of receivers, temporal restrictions, requirements on the MPC or FHE setup (e.g., threshold, geographical distribution of nodes or preferred provider respective technology to use), the computation to be carried out (e.g., certain statistics including the required sample size or validation mechanisms), or data retention.

However, formulating and enforcing effective data usage policies presents several challenges. These include striking a balance between maximizing data utility for innovation and safeguarding privacy rights, achieving high usability also for end users, addressing evolving technological advancements and data-sharing practices, and ensuring transparency and accountability. Additionally, changing legal and market situations need to be addressable, potentially without re-involving data subjects in asynchronous scenarios.

C4. Node Selection. The security of any MPC deployment crucially depends on the involved compute nodes, as well as the selected parameters (i.e., threshold and number of nodes). Interestingly, although FHE is a completely different approach it shares many similarities when it comes to the requirements for the deployment, if more stakeholders are involved, e.g. decryption threshold and number of nodes for multi-party secret key generation. However, the big difference is in the compute nodes needed to perform the actual computation. For FHE the computation on the ciphertext can be done on a single server and without interaction, contrary to MPC which requires communication between compute nodes. Nevertheless, the computational power needed on the compute nodes to run MPC protocols is less for communication intensive protocols and in general far less than for executing FHE. Therefore, in the future hardware support is envisioned for FHE to accelerate computations and reduce power consumption, contrary to MPC, which does not require special purpose hardware.

Besides the general requirements on the node selection for MPC and FHE, also the time dependence plays a crucial role in the complexity of system management. In certain (mainly static) scenarios, the selection of these nodes can be done once and (almost) forever. However, the situation is very different in highly dynamic scenarios where data from many data sources is used as input, as each of them pose certain constraints on node selection. Furthermore, compute nodes may be offered on an "as-a-service" basis by market players, such that their availability may have temporal variety. Therefore, any mechanism for node selection needs to take these requirements into consideration.

In combination with the identity management challenges mentioned before, it further needs to be guaranteed that the involved nodes are not (potentially indirectly) controlled by a single legal entity.

This immediately also poses the question who decides, which nodes to involve. If this process relies on a central entity, appropriate measures to minimize the required trust should be taken, e.g., by aiming for transparency of performed computations, or by having compute nodes verify usage policies without compromising privacy. On the other hand, if this process is performed in a federated way, a circular argument (who chooses the participants of this set of entities) should be avoided.

C5. Access Control. In static situations characterized by fixed computations and entities, it is often predetermined which inputs and outputs must be accessible to each party. In this case, data providers may, e.g., encrypt input shares directly for designated compute nodes, which in turn encrypt the output for the specified data recipient.

Yet, in dynamic environments, this predictability may not always hold true. Thus, if it is unknown upfront which (or how many) MPC nodes will execute a given computation – and nodes might engage in computations on the same data across different sessions – appropriate technologies must be implemented to ensure that the shares for these nodes can be derived as needed without compromising privacy.

A fundamental challenge lies in avoiding dependence on a single trusted entity or a single point of failure, necessitating careful design of key management procedures. Moreover, it is essential to guarantee that nodes cannot receive multiple consistent shares when the same input data is utilized in multiple computations involving the same node.

C6. Trustless Intermediaries. Advancements in cryptographic techniques such as presented MPC and FHE methods are essential for enabling trustless data intermediaries. These techniques ensure that data remains private and secure throughout the processing lifecycle, even in environments where trust cannot be assumed.

If integrated properly, data intermediaries can directly benefit for the secure computation capabilities in the data space and only store encrypted data locally. However, for regulatory reasons, data intermediaries must meet several stringent requirements. These include robust authentication and identity management systems to ensure that only authorized parties participate in computations, as well as precise definitions and enforcement mechanisms for data usage policies. Furthermore, the selection of compute nodes must also be carefully managed accordingly to keep data encrypted over the whole life-cycle.

Thus, clear protocols must be established regarding who can access what data and with which keys. This includes defining roles and permissions within the intermediary framework to ensure that access to both data and keys is tightly controlled and monitored. The challenge of key management is especially pronounced in trustless environments, where no single entity is trusted with full control over the keys. Innovative solutions, such as distributed key management systems, may be necessary to mitigate these risks, ensuring that no single point of failure can lead to a security breach. Moreover, the access control systems must be designed to enforce these restrictions rigorously, allowing only authorized entities to perform decryption or initiate computations. By meeting these requirements, data intermediaries can securely manage and process sensitive data, maintaining privacy and security in complex and distributed environments.

4   Integration into Data Spaces

We propose using data spaces as a basis to deploy secure multiparty computing in a dynamic scenario; that is, where some or all elements (stakeholders, input data, algorithm) are not known in advance. Our goal is to create an ecosystem where participants can offer MPC-related assets under well-defined conditions ("policies"): input datasets, compute nodes or algorithms (intended function to be computed). Other participants may consume these offers by running a computation on a chosen set of input datasets and compute nodes, while respecting the conditions set by the providers of these assets. We divide the deployment of such a system in three phases: onboarding (participants), (asset) setup, and the transaction phase, where a single computation is executed. The overall architecture is shown in Fig. 4.

4.1   Onboarding and Setup Phase

First, participants need to be onboarded to the system (data space), which includes checking their identity and issuing some form of a proof of membership. At this phase, the identity of participants may be checked, possibly connecting to external trust anchors (TAs), see also challenge C2.

Second, onboarded participants may publish assets in the data space, potentially through the data intermediary representing them. For the computation resource providers (i.e., for MPC or FHE), these include input data, compute nodes or even intended functions, each described by asset-specific metadata and associated with an individual policy that describes how they can be used, cf. C3. Note that in a fully dynamic setting, both steps of the setup are also dynamic: participants and offers may be added, modified or removed during the lifetime of the data space.

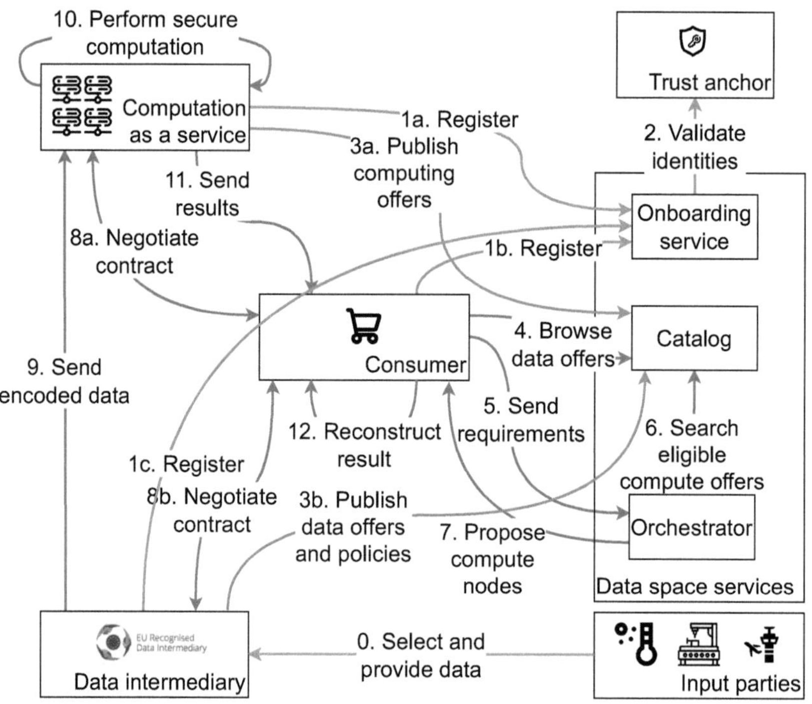

Fig. 4. Components of the proposed data space-based deployment. **Blue**: onboarding phase; **green**: setup phase; **red**: transaction phase. Based on initial ideas from [44] but extended for additional stakeholders and technologies. (Color figure online)

4.2 Transaction Phase

In the last phase, the actual transaction may occur.

Offer Selection and Contract Negotiation. First, participants (potential consumers) may browse available offers and select a combination of input data, compute nodes and a function they would like to evaluate. When selecting compute nodes, the consumer may pick offers explicitly or define conditions that nodes need to satisfy, depending on the selected computing paradigm. For instance, for MPC, they might define that not all nodes should be hosted on the same server, or that all nodes have to be hosted in Europe. From a usability point of view, it could also be desirable to offer some preconfigured choices relevant in different domains [19] and from a performance standpoint also network or performance requirements could be included in the node selection, e.g., latency <30 ms between nodes. However, if the MPC nodes are not concretely defined, the orchestrator service may pick a random selection of compute nodes on offer, to satisfy such criteria. Similar choices and configurations might be done for FHE-based services, e.g., regarding computation resources or location of the server to avoid the transfer of (encrypted) data, e.g., outside the EU.

In either case, the request is sent to data intermediary representing the owner of the respective offers as a contract request, after which an automatic contract negotiation process takes place to validate that all requirements with regards to the policies are met. If this is the case, a contract between all parties is signed and the computation can be triggered. Validation of conditions may happen via a service ("MPC/FHE orchestrator") offered by the data space authority, which can be the same service orchestrating MPC computation, cf. also C4.

Input Provisioning. After all parties agreed to the transaction, the actual computation is started. Therefore, the input data has to be read by the compute parties in encoded form. Depending on the configuration, this step can be done either synchronously by the input parties sending the inputs to the compute nodes, but also asynchronously, if the data have been stored at a data custodian. In this case, for security reasons and following the zero-trust principle, the data should only be stored in encrypted form. However, this is not trivial, if the receiving compute nodes are not known in advance, cf. also C5.

Furthermore, to be more flexible, it is also desirable to delay the time of encoding if possible. Thus, we distinguish immediate and late encoding.

Immediate encoding is the naive way to generate input data by encoding the data prior to encrypting it for storage at the data custodian in the case of MPC. Then each compute node only has to decrypt his received data fragment during input processing. This is easier from a technological point of view, but less flexible and produces more overhead: as each share is encrypted individually, the total amount of data to be stored is large. Additionally, MPC system parameters and encoding scheme have to be defined in advance.

In the case of FHE, immediate encoding means, that the secret key is already defined, and input can be already decrypted under the corresponding public key before storing it in the corresponding system.

In *late encoding*, the plaintext is directly encrypted and stored at the data custodian, also for MPC. This significantly reduces the storage overhead and increases flexibility, as MPC parameters are decided during the transaction phase and not the setup phase. However, it is also technically more challenging, because some form of flexible threshold decryption is needed. A compromise would be to symmetrically encrypt the input data and then only encrypt the key with a threshold method. This would also save storage space but require the compute nodes to first decrypt the data obliviously [35].

Similar questions arise for FHE based late decoding. For FHE data could be encrypted under a user-controlled key and upon request, a re-encryption policy can be shared with the system which allows to transform the ciphertext to be used in a FHE computation under a dedicated key different to the user key.

Protocol Execution. During computation the agreed MPC protocol is executed among the agreed nodes to compute the intended function on the data. For FHE a single compute node is sufficient to compute the intended function, eventually by also receiving an additional evaluation key. Although the step is rather straightforward, from a data space perspective it is important that the protocols available are standardized. Policies can only be practically enforced, if wide interoperability among MPC/FHE nodes available in the ecosystem is guaranteed and enough stakeholders publish offers. Additionally, to executing the MPC protocols or specific FHE schemes, plugins may also be of use. If verifiability is a requirement, an additional zero-knowledge proof has to be generated by the system, posing additional challenges for policy definition, the capabilities of the MPC or FHE nodes, and the trustworthiness of required parameters, cf. also C1, C3, and C4.

Additionally, managing the leakage budget for secure computations which are intrinsic to the compute function by methods from differential privacy could also require for a plugin.

Post-processing. Finally, after the computation the results are held by the compute nodes in encrypted form. To recover the plaintext output the ciphertexts have to be communicated (synchronously or asynchronously) to one or more result parties, which are allowed to learn the outcome of the computation. For MPC the result is typically reconstructed from fragments received from compute nodes, especially for secret sharing based protocols. In the case of FHE, if a single result party was used and FHE computation was done under her respective keys, then she can directly decrypt the ciphertext from the compute node. However, if threshold decryption was defined in the policy, the plaintext can only be decrypted by multiple parties together, which closely resembles the MPC setting.

Finally, after the reconstruction of the result succeeded additional post-computation validation, logging, and payment could take place to finalize the transaction.

In summary, by our comprehensive integration proposal of secure computing methods, i.e., MPC and FHE, into data spaces, we have shown the complexity we are facing when we go beyond the naive approach where dedicated parties with profound technology knowledge run a specific instance of a protocol. However, this extra effort is necessary to make the system interoperable, being compatible with data spaces, and to leverage the MPC-as-a-service approach to lower the barriers for adoption.

5 Technical Solutions

In this section technical methods to solve the identified challenges are discussed. We identify gaps in the state-of-the-art, present potential avenues to address the challenges and highlight where additional research is needed.

5.1 Global Parameters

To minimize the necessary trust, global parameters should be setup in a way that does not give any sufficiently small set of entities the possibility to control the choice of parameters. Different approaches for this can be found in the literature.

One option are so-called *setup ceremonies*, where a group of entities jointly generates parameters that are later needed for cryptographic protocols, thus ensuring the trustworthiness of the outcome. Such ceremonies have been implemented for a variety of applications, including, e.g., the ZCash crypto currency[28].

Another active research field in cryptography is focusing on so-called subversion resilience, where at least partial security guarantees can also be achieved if, e.g., a common reference string (CRS) cannot be trusted, e.g., [1].

Other works, e.g., [6], consider the updatable CRS model, where users can update the CRS at any time, provided they demonstrate the correctness of the update. The new CRS can then be deemed trustworthy (i.e., uncorrupted) as long as either the previous CRS or the updater was honest. If multiple users partake in this process, it's possible to obtain a sequence of updates by different individuals over time. If any update in the sequence is honest, the scheme remains sound.

5.2 Authentication and Identity Management

Authentication and identity management can differ between data spaces and may rely on traditional centralized (e.g. via a user database based on LDAP or Active Directory) or decentralized (e.g. using Decentralized Identifiers and Verifiable Credentials (VCs)) approaches. In any case, an onboarding process needs to be defined as part of data space governance, where the identity of participants is validated before granting them membership. The validation step normally relies on external trust anchors (e.g., eIDAS, DV SSL, GLEIF), with accepted trust anchors defined by the given data space's governance framework. As part of the onboarding process, participants may also record their public key and prove their control over it, providing a basis for a secure communication channel.

For instance, for Gaia-X [21], aspiring participants would submit their data as defined in the Trust Framework (e.g., ID, public key, address) to one of the Gaia-X Digital Clearing Houses (GXDCH) and receive a VC that they can use as proof. Internally, the GXDCH applies multiple validation checks, such as compatibility with the required metadata schema and validation via accepted trust anchors.

When a data custodian (ensuring data accessibility and security for a data owner) is also part of the system, the data owner first needs to authorize the custodian to act

---

[28] https://zkproof.org/2021/06/30/setup-ceremonies/.

on their behalf. This can happen outside the data space context, via a separate contract between these parties, or is part of a data space service offering. The custodian then participates in the data space on behalf of the data owner. A more formalized and regulated instance of a data custodian is a Data Intermediary as defined in the Data Governance Act[29] - while a data custodian focus on the technical and security aspects of data management the data intermediary facilitates data sharing and usage in compliance with legal and regulatory frameworks.

While strong authentication may be required in many application cases, some scenarios require a delicate balance between privacy and authenticity, e.g., when an entity needs to fulfill a data usage policy but does not want to reveal its identity. This can be achieved, e.g., using attribute-based credentials [10,11,46] letting parties prove statements about their attributes without revealing them in the plain. In particular, this also covers selective disclosure as considered by W3C[30] or EBSI[31].

Furthermore, somewhat similar to direct anonymous attestation (DAA) [9] or Intel's Enhanced Privacy ID (EPID)[32], in order to increase reliability in data without compromising security, concepts like privacy-enhancing group signatures [17,32] could be used. These let data sources such as sensors sign data to prove that it was generated using a genuine device, while keeping the precise identity of the device confidential. MPC over authenticated inputs is also considered by [18].

5.3   Data Usage Policies

Usage Control [27] plays an important role in the enforcement of data policies, particularly in complex data environments. One of the significant challenges for MPC and FHE in data spaces is ensuring that data policies are effectively enforced throughout the data processing lifecycle. While the Open Digital Rights Language (ODRL)[33] offers a flexible mechanism for defining permissions, prohibitions, and duties concerning digital content and services, its effectiveness is limited in the context of MPC where data processing involves complex computations across multiple data owners. The enforceability of these policies becomes even more complicated when considering the simpler, yet enforceable, nature of Rego[34] within the Open Policy Agent (OPA) framework, which may not fully cater to the legal nuances required in MPC scenarios.

Moreover, the integration of secure computation as a service within data spaces necessitates a high degree of interoperability between different policy standards and legislative frameworks, no matter if MPC or FHE is considered. The diverse landscape of standards like the Data Privacy Vocabulary (DPV)[35] for expressing policies related to personal data processing, and international standards such as ISO/IEC 29184 and

---

[29] https://eur-lex.europa.eu/legal-content/EN/TXT/HTML/?uri=CELEX:32022R0868.

[30] https://w3c-ccg.github.io/data-minimization/.

[31] https://ec.europa.eu/digital-building-blocks/sites/display/EBSI/Selective+Disclosure %3A+An+EBSI+Improvement+Proposal.

[32] https://www.intel.com/content/www/us/en/developer/articles/technical/intel-enhanced-privacy-id-epid-security-technology.html.

[33] https://www.w3.org/TR/odrl-model/.

[34] https://www.openpolicyagent.org/docs/latest/.

[35] https://w3c.github.io/dpv/dpv/.

ISO/IEC 27560 for online privacy and data sharing, must be seamlessly aligned to support the complex operations of MPC and FHE respectively.

Compliance poses another challenge, especially with the introduction of legislative frameworks such as the Data Governance Act and the Data Act. These acts introduce new concepts like data intermediaries and data altruism, which, while enriching the data ecosystem, also add layers of complexity in ensuring that MPC services adhere to these regulations. Additionally, the empowerment of individuals through platforms like SOLID[36], granting them control over their data, intersects with the operational dynamics of cryptographically protected computations, requiring robust mechanisms to ensure that user consent and data usage terms are respected in a multi-stakeholder environment.

Incorporating also the Data Catalog Vocabulary (DCAT)[37] into the ecosystem of data spaces, to facilitate the discovery and interoperability of datasets, makes integrating usage polices even more challenging but also leads to a convergence of standards and practices for the participating stakeholders. By establishing a common framework, DCAT can serve as a tool in bridging the gap between different data policy standards. This convergence simplifies the process of managing and enforcing data usage policies across multiple platforms and jurisdictions, promoting a more unified and efficient approach to data sharing and processing.

5.4 Node Selection

In contrast to the permissionless systems prevalent in the blockchain world (e.g., Enigma, Partisia), data space services require registration, meaning they operate within a permissioned environment, thereby providing significant benefits with regards to node selection.

Nodes or node operators must be registered, and each node will be assigned with attributes describing its abilities. Besides standards capabilities, like supported protocols, connection parameters like bandwidth, compute capabilities and other functional parameters, nodes must also be assigned with trust parameters. Every node must be assigned to an identity, geo location, and trust zones, to enable automatic matching of compute task policies and nodes. Despite the common attributes required for secure computation in general, we also have specific ones for the different technologies, MPC and FHE in our case.

For MPC we must support flexible definitions on the composition of a computing environment from multiple nodes which fulfil the non-collusion assumption best but still provide enough connectivity (network bandwidth and latency) to ensure efficient performance. The following sample settings illustrate policies that shall be supported in an MPC-ready data space:

– Nodes must be from 3 different entities in three different countries
– All nodes must be from the same country but from three different institutions or trust boundaries

---

– Nodes must have latency ≤ 10 ms but be from different trust zones

It is also of interest to combine basic attribute-based matching with random assignment capabilities for additional robustness. Given the policy settings above, it should be possible to randomly assign nodes from all available combinations for different functions or even sub-functions, thereby also preventing sybil attacks.

In the case of FHE typically only a single node has to be agreed on to run the actual computation, except for the case of partitioning and parallelization of a task onto multiple nodes. Here, hardware support could be essential and also support for more advanced methods for data input and output encoding. However, when support for multi-key FHE or threshold decryption is needed, additional nodes need to be also defined to be part of the input encoding or decryption process which makes the configuration similarly challenging as for the MPC case.

In essence, node selection introduces many aspects which are interesting to support to make the infrastructure more trustworthy but also open and flexible. It enables users to define their deployment requirements and enables participants to contribute compute resources to be used by others in a seamless way.

5.5   Access Control

An integral aspect of data usage policies is the delineation of authorized users' access to specific datasets. While contractual enforcement suffices in numerous practical scenarios, there's a growing preference for technical solutions. This approach, e.g., obviates the need for a data custodian to possess plaintext access to users' sensitive data.

In the following we sketch two options that realize this goal by leveraging advanced cryptographic methods beyond what was already discussed before.

One option following the late encoding approach could be to let data owners encrypt their data under their own public key using a so-called proxy re-encryption scheme [7,49]. This allows the data custodian to transform ciphertexts under the user's public key into ciphertexts under a compute node's public key, provided that the user previously handed a so-called re-encryption key to the data custodian. In case that the encryption scheme supports a homomorphic operation on ciphertexts consistent with the secret sharing scheme, the data custodian could now derive the shares for the selected compute nodes ad-hoc, without ever requiring to access the plaintext. One drawback of this approach is, however, that the user has to derive individual re-encryption keys for all possible compute nodes, which may exclude nodes joining the ecosystem after the user making their data offer.

An alternative option based on early encoding leverages attribute-based encryption (ABE) [25,40]. In an ABE scheme, each participant receives a secret key linked to some attributes (e.g., geographical location), while ciphertexts are linked to policies. A secret key can now only decrypt a ciphertext if the attributes of the secret key satisfy the policy of the ciphertext. For instance, users could encrypt their shares according to their requirements (e.g., each share with a specific country); while each compute node would receive a secret key linked to the country of its location. Assuming proper identity management, doing so could cryptographically enforce that only compute nodes located in specific countries could decrypt certain shares, thereby enforcing that nodes from different legislations participate in a computation. The main limitation of this approach is, that the master secret key, from which the individual secret keys are derived, needs to be administered securely and trustworthy within the MPCaaS ecosystem, e.g., by distributing it among several nodes which engage in an MPC protocol to derive novel keys for joining nodes. Furthermore, the encoding scheme required for the computations need to be known in advance.

5.6   Trustless Intermediaries

A trustless data intermediary is a solution that facilitates data sharing and processing between parties without the need for mutual trust. By leveraging advanced cryptographic techniques such as Multi-Party Computation (MPC) and Fully Homomorphic Encryption (FHE), these intermediaries ensure data privacy and security even when the intermediary itself is not trusted by the involved parties. This approach is particularly valuable in scenarios where sensitive data must be processed or shared across organizational boundaries, and where traditional trust models are insufficient or undesirable.

Multi-Party Computation (MPC) maintains the privacy of each party's data, as only the final result of the computation is revealed, with no individual data points being exposed. The security and effectiveness of MPC relies heavily on the trustworthiness and reliability of the selection of compute nodes. In a static setting, where the computational environment is predefined, this process is streamlined, enabling asynchronous processing and reducing complexity.

Fully Homomorphic Encryption (FHE) ensures that data remains encrypted throughout the computation process, providing robust privacy protection even during processing. This technique is particularly advantageous in scenarios involving highly sensitive data, such as healthcare or financial services, where preventing data exposure at all stages is critical. FHE's capability to securely process data in both fixed and dynamic deployment scenarios makes it highly adaptable. In a static setting, where participants and computational environments are predefined, the secure management of evaluation keys becomes more straightforward, enabling trustless intermediaries to efficiently handle asynchronous data processing.

The challenge of key management is central to the successful deployment of trustless data intermediaries. It is essential to establish clear protocols that dictate who can access what data and which keys. In static deployment scenarios, the intermediary's ability to securely manage and access evaluation keys simplifies asynchronous processing and enhances overall system security. This controlled environment ensures that sensitive data is processed and shared without compromising privacy or security.

In conclusion, trustless intermediaries using cryptographic techniques such as MPC and FHE, offer a robust solution for secure data sharing and processing in contexts where traditional trust models fall short. By focusing on the secure management of nodes/keys and considering the static or dynamic nature of the deployment, organizations can effectively leverage these technologies to protect sensitive data while enabling valuable data-driven collaboration.

6 Conclusion

This paper presents a comprehensive approach for integrating secure multiparty computation (MPC) and fully homomorphic encryption (FHE) into data spaces, laying the groundwork for secure and trustworthy data sharing in the future Data Economy. The authors address various challenges and their potential solutions, namely global parameters, authentication and identity management, data usage policies, node selection, trustless data intermediaries, and access control. By adopting these solutions, organizations can enhance privacy and security while facilitating data sharing in dynamic environments.

Moreover, we also discuss the impact of data intermediaries, which will play an important role in this framework by bridging the gap between data providers and consumers. They enable secure data processing even in scenarios where trust is minimal or non-existent. Through the application of MPC and FHE, these intermediaries ensure that sensitive data can be shared and processed without compromising privacy or security, making them indispensable in cross-organizational collaborations. Their function is vital for maintaining compliance with regulatory frameworks and ensuring that data transactions are both secure and efficient, thus fostering innovation and collaboration within the data economy.

However, several research gaps remain. There is a pressing need for more efficient and scalable MPC protocols that can handle large-scale datasets effectively. For FHE, protocol hardware support will be needed to support practically relevant performance for computation, however, this is on the horizon. Additionally, dynamic and flexible access control mechanisms in distributed environments are essential to address the evolving needs of data usage. Privacy concerns related to potential information leakage during protocol execution also require further exploration. Moreover, the development of standardized and interoperable frameworks will be critical to support MPC- and FHE-enabled data spaces across various domains and applications. By overcoming these challenges and fully leveraging the capabilities of data intermediaries, the potential for secure, privacy-preserving data sharing in the Data Economy can be realized. Further research and development efforts are needed to overcome these challenges and ensure the successful adoption of this approach in practice.

Acknowledgments. This work was in part funded by the European Union under the HORIZON SESAR JU Grant Agreement No. 101114675 (HARMONIC), where UK participants received funding from UK Research and Innovation (UKRI) under funding guarantee grant No. 10091990, and swiss partner from the Swiss State Secretariat for Education, Research and Innovation (SERI). Additionally, it was supported by the Austrian Research Promotion Agency FFG within the PRESENT project. Views and opinions expressed are however those of the author(s) only and do not necessarily reflect those of the funding agencies. Neither the European Union, FFG, nor the granting authority can be held responsible for them.

References

1. Abdolmaleki, B., Lipmaa, H., Siim, J., Zajac, M.: On subversion-resistant snarks. J. Cryptol. **34**(3), 17 (2021). https://doi.org/10.1007/S00145-021-09379-Y

2. Agahari, W., Dolci, R., de Reuver, M.: Business model implications of privacy-preserving technologies in data marketplaces: the case of multi-party computation (2021). https://aisel. aisnet.org/ecis2021_rp/59
3. Agahari, W., Ofe, H., de Reuver, M.: It is not (only) about privacy: how multi-party computation redefines control, trust, and risk in data sharing. Electron. Markets **32**(3), 1577–1602 (2022). https://doi.org/10.1007/s12525-022-00572-w
4. Al Badawi, A., et al.: Openfhe: open-source fully homomorphic encryption library. In: Proceedings of the 10th Workshop on Encrypted Computing & Applied Homomorphic Cryptography, pp. 53–63. WAHC 2022, Association for Computing Machinery, New York (2022). https://doi.org/10.1145/3560827.3563379
5. Alliance, D.S.B.: Technical convergence. Technical report, Data Space Business Alliance (2023)
6. Baghery, K., Sedaghat, M.: TIRAMISU: black-box simulation extractable NIZKs in the updatable CRS model. In: Conti, M., Stevens, M., Krenn, S. (eds.) CANS 2021. LNCS, vol. 13099, pp. 531–551. Springer, Cham (2021). https://doi.org/10.1007/978-3-030-92548-2_28
7. Blaze, M., Bleumer, G., Strauss, M.: Divertible protocols and atomic proxy cryptography. In: EUROCRYPT. LNCS, vol. 1403, pp. 127–144. Springer (1998). https://doi.org/10.1007/BFB0054122
8. Brakerski, Z.: Fully homomorphic encryption without modulus switching from classical GapSVP. In: Safavi-Naini, R., Canetti, R. (eds.) CRYPTO 2012. LNCS, vol. 7417, pp. 868–886. Springer, Heidelberg (2012). https://doi.org/10.1007/978-3-642-32009-5_50
9. Brickell, E.F., Camenisch, J., Chen, L.: Direct anonymous attestation. In: ACM CCS, pp. 132–145. ACM (2004). https://doi.org/10.1145/1030083.1030103
10. Camenisch, J., Krenn, S., Lehmann, A., Mikkelsen, G.L., Neven, G., Pedersen, M.Ø.: Formal treatment of privacy-enhancing credential systems. In: Dunkelman, O., Keliher, L. (eds.) SAC 2015. LNCS, vol. 9566, pp. 3–24. Springer, Cham (2016). https://doi.org/10.1007/978-3-319-31301-6_1
11. Camenisch, J., Lysyanskaya, A.: A signature scheme with efficient protocols. In: Cimato, S., Persiano, G., Galdi, C. (eds.) SCN 2002. LNCS, vol. 2576, pp. 268–289. Springer, Heidelberg (2003). https://doi.org/10.1007/3-540-36413-7_20
12. Cheon, J.H., Kim, A., Kim, M., Song, Y.: Homomorphic encryption for arithmetic of approximate numbers. In: Takagi, T., Peyrin, T. (eds.) ASIACRYPT 2017. LNCS, vol. 10624, pp. 409–437. Springer, Cham (2017). https://doi.org/10.1007/978-3-319-70694-8_15
13. Chiesa, A., Hu, Y., Maller, M., Mishra, P., Vesely, N., Ward, N.: Marlin: preprocessing zkSNARKS with universal and updatable SRS. In: Canteaut, A., Ishai, Y. (eds.) EUROCRYPT 2020. LNCS, vol. 12105, pp. 738–768. Springer, Cham (2020). https://doi.org/10.1007/978-3-030-45721-1_26
14. Chillotti, I., Gama, N., Georgieva, M., Izabachène, M.: Tfhe: fast fully homomorphic encryption over the torus. J. Cryptol. **33**(1), 34–91 (2020). https://doi.org/10.1007/s00145-019-09319-x
15. Dahl, M., et al.: Confidential EVM smart contracts using fully homomorphic encryption. Technical report, Zama (2023)
16. Data Spaces Support Centre (DSSC): DSSC Glossary Version 2.0 (2023). https://dssc.eu/space/Glossary/176553985/DSSC+Glossary+%7C+Version+2.0+%7C+September+2023
17. Diaz, J., Lehmann, A.: Group signatures with user-controlled and sequential linkability. In: Garay, J.A. (ed.) PKC 2021. LNCS, vol. 12710, pp. 360–388. Springer, Cham (2021). https://doi.org/10.1007/978-3-030-75245-3_14
18. Dutta, M., Ganesh, C., Patranabis, S., Singh, N.: Compute, but verify: efficient multiparty computation over authenticated inputs. Cryptology ePrint Archive, Paper 2022/1648 (2022)

19. Framner, E., Fischer-Huebner, S., Loruenser, T., Alaqra, A.S., Pettersson, J.S.: Making secret sharing based cloud storage usable. Inf. Comput. Secur. **27**(5), 647–667 (2019). https://doi.org/10.1108/ICS-01-2019-0016

20. Franklin, M., Halevy, A., Maier, D.: From databases to dataspaces: a new abstraction for information management. ACM SIGMOD Record **34**(4), 27–33 (2005). https://doi.org/10.1145/1107499.1107502

21. Gaia-X European Association for Data and Cloud AISBL: Gaia-X Framework (2023). https://docs.gaia-x.eu/framework/

22. Garrido, G.M., Sedlmeir, J., Uludağ, O., Alaoui, I.S., Luckow, A., Matthes, F.: Revealing the landscape of privacy-enhancing technologies in the context of data markets for the IoT: a systematic literature review. J. Netw. Comput. Appl. **207**, 103465 (2022). https://doi.org/10.1016/j.jnca.2022.103465. https://www.sciencedirect.com/science/article/pii/S1084804522001126

23. Gentry, C.: Fully homomorphic encryption using ideal lattices. In: Mitzenmacher, M. (ed.) Proceedings of the 41st Annual ACM Symposium on Theory of Computing, STOC 2009, Bethesda, MD, USA, May 31 - June 2 2009, pp. 169–178. ACM (2009). https://doi.org/10.1145/1536414.1536440

24. Giaretta, L., et al.: PDS2: a user-centered decentralized marketplace for privacy preserving data processing. In: 2021 IEEE 37th International Conference on Data Engineering Workshops (ICDEW), pp. 92–99 (2021). https://doi.org/10.1109/ICDEW53142.2021.00024

25. Hohenberger, S., Lu, G., Waters, B., Wu, D.J.: Registered attribute-based encryption. In: EUROCRYPT, Part III. LNCS, vol. 14006, pp. 511–542. Springer (2023). https://doi.org/10.1007/978-3-031-30620-4_17

26. Hynes, N., Dao, D., Yan, D., Cheng, R., Song, D.: A demonstration of sterling: a privacy-preserving data marketplace. Proc. VLDB Endow. **11**(12), 2086–2089 (2018). https://doi.org/10.14778/3229863.3236266

27. Jung, C., Dörr, J.: Data Usage Control, pp. 129–146. Springer, Cham (2022). https://doi.org/10.1007/978-3-030-93975-5_8

28. Kanjalkar, S., Zhang, Y., Gandlur, S., Miller, A.: Publicly auditable MPC-as-a-service with succinct verification and universal setup. In: IEEE EuroS&PW, pp. 386–411 (2021). https://doi.org/10.1109/EuroSPW54576.2021.00048

29. Koch, K., Krenn, S., Marc, T., More, S., Ramacher, S.: KRAKEN: a privacy-preserving data market for authentic data. In: Data Economy, pp. 15–20. ACM (2022). https://doi.org/10.1145/3565011.3569057

30. Koch, K., Krenn, S., Pellegrino, D., Ramacher, S.: Privacy-preserving analytics for data markets using MPC. In: Friedewald, M., Schiffner, S., Krenn, S. (eds.) Privacy and Identity 2020. IAICT, vol. 619, pp. 226–246. Springer, Cham (2021). https://doi.org/10.1007/978-3-030-72465-8_13

31. Koutsos, V., Papadopoulos, D., Chatzopoulos, D., Tarkoma, S., Hui, P.: Agora: a privacy-aware data marketplace. IEEE TDSC **19**(6), 3728–3740 (2022). https://doi.org/10.1109/TDSC.2021.3105099

32. Krenn, S., Samelin, K., Striecks, C.: Practical group-signatures with privacy-friendly openings. In: ARES, pp. 10:1–10:10. ACM (2019). https://doi.org/10.1145/3339252.3339256

33. López-Alt, A., Tromer, E., Vaikuntanathan, V.: On-the-fly multiparty computation on the cloud via multikey fully homomorphic encryption. In: Karloff, H.J., Pitassi, T. (eds.) STOC 2012, pp. 1219–1234. ACM (2012). https://doi.org/10.1145/2213977.2214086

34. Lorünser, T., Wohner, F., Krenn, S.: A verifiable multiparty computation solver for the linear assignment problem: and applications to air traffic management. In: CCSW, pp. 41–51. ACM (2022). https://doi.org/10.1145/3560810.3564263

35. Lorünser, T., Wohner, F.: Performance comparison of two generic MPC-frameworks with symmetric ciphers. In: ICETE 2020, pp. 587–594. France (2020). https://doi.org/10.5220/0009831705870594

36. Lorünser, T., Wohner, F., Krenn, S.: A privacy-preserving auction platform with public verifiability for smart manufacturing. In: ICISSP, pp. 637–647. SciTePress (2022). https://doi.org/10.5220/0011006700003120

37. Müller, T., Gärtner, N., Verzano, N., Matthes, F.: Barriers to the practical adoption of federated machine learning in cross-company collaborations. In: ICAART (3), pp. 581–588 (2022)

38. Otto, B., ten Hompel, M., Wrobel, S.: Designing Data Spaces: The Ecosystem Approach to Competitive Advantage. Springer (2022)

39. Rivest, R.L., Adleman, L., Dertouzos, M.L.: On data banks and privacy homomorphisms. In: Foundations on Secure Computation, pp. 169–179. Academia Press (1978)

40. Sahai, A., Waters, B.: Fuzzy identity-based encryption. In: Cramer, R. (ed.) EUROCRYPT 2005. LNCS, vol. 3494, pp. 457–473. Springer, Heidelberg (2005). https://doi.org/10.1007/11426639_27

41. Schuetz, C.G., Gringinger, E., Pilon, N., Lorünser, T.: A privacy-preserving marketplace for air traffic flow management slot configuration. In: IEEE/AIAA DASC, pp. 1–9 (2021). https://doi.org/10.1109/DASC52595.2021.9594401

42. Schuetz, C.G., et al.: A distributed architecture for privacy-preserving optimization using genetic algorithms and multi-party computation. In: CoopIS. LNCS, vol. 13591, pp. 168–185. Springer (2022). https://doi.org/10.1007/978-3-031-17834-4_10

43. Serrano, N., Cuenca, F.: A peer-to-peer ownership-preserving data marketplace. In: 2021 IEEE International Conference on Blockchain (Blockchain), pp. 394–400 (2021). https://doi.org/10.1109/Blockchain53845.2021.00062

44. Siska, V., Lorünser, T., Krenn, S., Fabianek, C.: Integrating secure multiparty computation into data spaces. In: Proceedings of the 14th International Conference on Cloud Computing and Services Science, pp. 346–357. SCITEPRESS - Science and Technology Publications, Angers, France (2024). https://doi.org/10.5220/0012734600003711. https://www.scitepress.org/DigitalLibrary/Link.aspx?doi=10.5220/0012734600003711

45. Spiekermann, M.: Data marketplaces: trends and monetisation of data goods. Intereconomics **54**(4), 208–216 (2019). https://doi.org/10.1007/s10272-019-0826-z

46. Tessaro, S., Zhu, C.: Revisiting BBS signatures. In: EUROCRYPT, Part V. LNCS, vol. 14008, pp. 691–721. Springer (2023). https://doi.org/10.1007/978-3-031-30589-4_24

47. Viand, A., Knabenhans, C., Hithnawi, A.: Verifiable fully homomorphic encryption. CoRR abs/2301.07041 (2023). https://doi.org/10.48550/ARXIV.2301.07041

48. Zappa, A., Le, C.H., Serrano, M., Curry, E.: Connecting data spaces and data marketplaces and the progress toward the European single digital market with open-source software. In: Data Spaces: Design, Deployment and Future Directions, pp. 131–146. Springer (2022). https://doi.org/10.1007/978-3-030-98636-0_7

49. Zhou, Y., Liu, S., Han, S., Zhang, H.: Fine-grained proxy re-encryption: definitions and constructions from LWE. In: ASIACRYPT, Part VI. LNCS, vol. 14443, pp. 199–231. Springer (2023). https://doi.org/10.1007/978-981-99-8736-8_7

Prompt-Driven Container Orchestration

Niklas Beuter[ID], André Drews[ID], and Nane Kratzke[✉][ID]

Lübeck University of Applied Sciences, Lübeck, Germany
`{niklas.beuter,andre.drews,nane.kratzke}@th-luebeck.de`

Abstract. Background: Container orchestration systems such as Kubernetes rely heavily on declarative manifest files that serve as blueprints for orchestration. However, managing these manifest files often presents significant challenges and requires considerable expertise in DevOps. **Methodology.** This study explores the use of Large Language Models (LLMs) to automate the generation of Kubernetes manifest files using natural language specifications and prompt engineering techniques. We evaluate the effectiveness of these LLMs through Zero-Shot, Few-Shot, Prompt-Chaining, and Self-Refine methods to fulfill DevOps requirements and facilitate fully automated deployment pipelines. **Results.** The results indicate that LLMs can produce Kubernetes manifests with varying degrees of manual input, with GPT-4 and GPT-3.5 demonstrating potential for fully automated deployments. Interestingly, smaller models sometimes outperform larger ones, challenging the assumption that larger models are always superior. **Conclusion:** The research highlights the critical role of prompt engineering in enhancing LLM outputs for Kubernetes and suggests further research into prompt strategies and LLM performance comparisons, presenting a promising direction for integrating LLMs into automated deployment workflows.

Keywords: Prompt engineering · Large language model · Cloud-native · Container · Orchestration · Automation · Intelligent service management · Kubernetes · LLM · GPT-3.5 · GPT-4 · Llama3 · DevOps

1 Introduction

In the dynamic field of cloud-native computing, Kubernetes has emerged as a crucial tool for transforming the deployment, scaling, and management of containerized applications. Despite its advantages, the intricate architecture of Kubernetes and similar platforms heavily relies on manifest files, which are used to define the desired operational state declaratively. These manifest files serve as essential blueprints for orchestrating containers; however, managing them can be challenging and often demands high expertise [14]. This situation highlights a potential for automation and optimization. We are particularly interested in whether and how to define non-fine-tuned models for generating descriptive operating states (intended states) of resources such as deployments, services, or pods to be provided and operated in a Kubernetes cluster. If this could be done in a natural language way, it would drastically reduce Kubernetes's somewhat steep learning curve for DevOps engineers.

Concurrently, there has been notable growth in Large Language Models (LLMs) [3,10], showcasing their ability to generate human-like text [23]. As these models

C. Pahl and M. van Steen (Eds.): CLOSER 2024, CCIS 2851, pp. 82–97, 2026.
https://doi.org/10.1007/978-3-032-17286-0_4

advance in complexity and capability, they offer new possibilities for programming in high-level languages. A pertinent question arises: Can LLMs generate declarative deployment instructions for Kubernetes or similar systems [40]? If so, this could simplify the creation of Kubernetes manifests, making them more accessible to DevOps engineers and potentially reducing the need for deployment-specific languages [27].

An underexplored connection between Kubernetes and LLMs lies in prompt engineering. Utilizing LLMs in this way could address many of the challenges Kubernetes faces, particularly in manifest management. As demonstrated in [15], prompt engineering could transform cloud computing and Kubernetes management, leading to more intelligent and efficient systems.

Our earlier work [15] established that systematic refinement, prompt engineering, and prompt chaining could enhance the output of less powerful, smaller language models. However, it also revealed that unexpected 'disasters' could occur in such prompt chains during the refinement stage, degrading the manifest files despite well-intentioned refinement prompts. Notably, our study showed that the refinement stage produced worse outcomes than the initial zero-shot generation in nearly all instances. This shortcoming was primarily due to sequential refinement steps overwriting the outputs of preceding steps.

This paper explores optimizing this iterative refinement process by implementing tool-supported self-feedback, following the concepts proposed by [22]. Specifically, we utilize error messages as feedback generated by the Kubernetes command-line tool `kubectl` if a manifest file were deployed. For clarity and better understanding, we also present the essential parts and results of our initial study [15] in this extended paper. The reader is recommended to consult the original research [15] for further details.

Overall, our research contributes to the technical field of container orchestration and expands the growing body of knowledge on the practical applications of LLMs and prompt engineering in technology and cloud-native computing.

2   Background and Related Work

In Kubernetes, manifest files, typically written in YAML or JSON, define the desired state of operations, such as pods, services, and controllers. These files are essential for deploying and managing applications within Kubernetes. However, as systems scale, managing these files becomes increasingly difficult. Challenges include maintaining configuration consistency, updating features, and ensuring security compliance. The complexity is further amplified by the proliferation of microservices [28,30]. Integrating AI and machine learning, particularly through large language models, offers significant potential to improve the management and generation of these manifests. By automating tasks and optimizing configurations, these technologies promise to simplify management and enhance the efficiency and reliability of container orchestration.

Large Language Models: Large Language Models (LLMs), such as OpenAI's GPT series, have significantly advanced natural language processing by understanding, generating, and manipulating written text. These models have evolved from simple origins to complex systems with impressive linguistic capabilities, transitioning from rule-based systems to neural network architectures that learn from vast datasets to produce contextually rich text [26]. Their expanding role in automation and data processing enables the automation of complex language tasks, including document summarization, code generation, language translation, and content creation [7]. LLMs can analyze text to extract insights and trends, supporting business and technology strategies. Their precise language processing capabilities hold promise in various domains such as healthcare, finance, customer service, and system management, including Kubernetes. In these areas, they can streamline tasks like manifest file generation, error diagnosis, and configuration optimization, thereby reducing manual work and enhancing efficiency.

Prompt Engineering: Training LLMs for domain-specific applications typically involves an extensive pre-training phase for general language comprehension, followed by a specialized fine-tuning phase. Recently, there has been a shift towards a "pre-train, prompt, predict" methodology, which reduces computational demands and utilizes specialized datasets through prompt engineering [4,20]. Prompt engineering entails crafting strategic inputs (prompts) to direct LLMs in producing the desired outputs. In the Kubernetes context, prompt engineering could markedly enhance LLMs' capability to manage technical tasks, such as generating or optimizing manifest files, diagnosing deployment problems, and recommending configuration best practices without needing task-specific fine-tuning. While not extensively studied, prompt engineering presents a promising approach to making Kubernetes management more intuitive and efficient, potentially lowering technical barriers and improving system reliability.

Related Work: Current research on integrating LLMs with Kubernetes highlights several promising but limited approaches. Lanciano et al. propose utilizing specialized LLMs to analyze Kubernetes deployment files, assisting non-experts in design and quality assurance [16]. Xu et al. introduce CloudEval-YAML, a benchmark designed to evaluate LLMs in generating cloud-native application code, with a focus on YAML and a dataset supplemented by unit tests [36]. Kowal et al. suggest a pipeline leveraging LLMs for anomaly detection and auto-remediation in microservices, aiming to improve system stability [13]. These methods generally depend on training specialized LLMs. In contrast, our research explores the use of standard LLMs combined with straightforward prompt engineering to automate Kubernetes configurations for security and compliance, setting it apart from the reliance on specialized models.

3   Methodology

Advanced prompt engineering can guide LLMs to understand the intricacies of Kubernetes manifests better, ensuring best practices in container security and operations. This research intends to connect the advanced language capabilities of LLMs with the technical requirements of Kubernetes management, aiming to improve DevOps efficiency and security in Kubernetes operations. Our objective is to utilize the inherent knowledge base of these LLMs [26] to create accurate Kubernetes configurations. We explored different LLMs and prompt engineering techniques to assess their suitability for this task. We aim to leverage standard LLMs without specific fine-tuning.

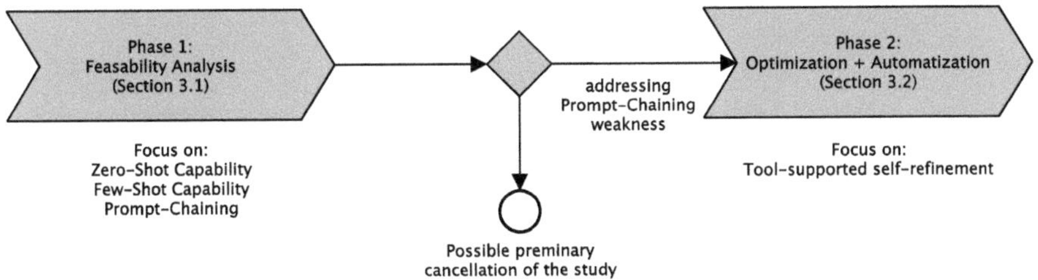

Fig. 1. Methodology pursued to investigate the applicability of LLMs to generate container orchestration manifest files.

Our approach to the analysis was divided into two phases (see Fig. 1). In the first applicability analysis phase [15] (see Sect. 3.1), we analyzed the general applicability of LLMs for generating Kubernetes manifest files. We were interested in how well LLMs can generate Kubernetes manifest files (zero-shot capability) and whether the generation can be optimized with simple examples (few-shot capability). In the first phase, we were also interested in whether it makes sense to refine more complex deployment scenarios step by step or to generate them all at once. The first phase was heavily manual, particularly in evaluation, and depended on DevOps experts and their assessment of generated results. The aim was to determine the strengths and limitations of LLMs for the specific purpose and to obtain a more reliable assessment of whether LLMs are suitable for container orchestration and DevOps use cases.

In the second optimization and automation phase (see Sect. 3.2), we addressed the weaknesses recognized in the first phase. These related, in particular, to increasing the automated evaluation of the generated manifest files and optimizing the iterative refinement process, which proved to be a weak point in the first phase.

3.1 Phase 1: Feasibility Analysis

Although prompt engineering is still very young and dynamic, several distinct approaches exist to different prompting techniques that can be derived from existing prompt engineering overviews [20]. The following methods seem very promising from the current state of knowledge and were used to derive our research questions.

Large LLMs are tuned to follow instructions and are pre-trained on large amounts of data to perform some tasks out of the box (**zero-shot**). For example, an LLM can generate text with a single prompt without any required specifications as input. This works astonishingly well for simple tasks like categorization [34].

RQ 1 (Zero-Shot Capability): *We want to determine how well LLMs can generate Kubernetes manifests out-of-the-box.*

Although LLMs demonstrate remarkable zero-shot capabilities, they fall short on more complex tasks when using the zero-shot setting. In these cases, prompting can enable in-context learning where we provide a guess of expected output text within a prompt, so-called demonstrations (e.g., Kubernetes manifest files) to steer the model to better

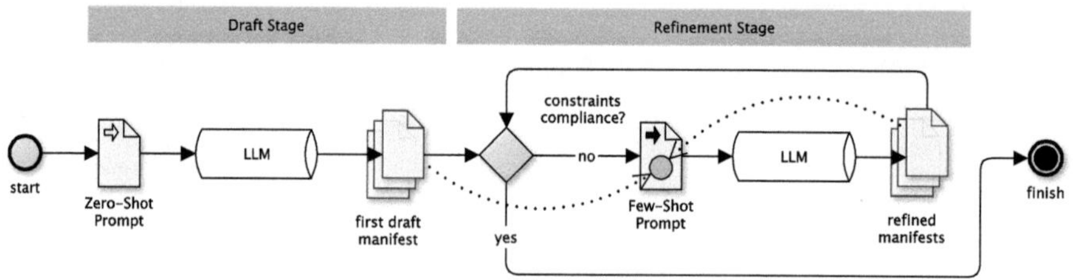

Fig. 2. Phase 1: Analyzed prompt chain composed of a drafting Zero-Shot and an iteratively refining Few-Shot stage (taken from [15]).

performance. The demonstrations serve as conditioning for subsequent examples where we would like the model to generate a response. According to [31], **few-shot** prompting requires models of sufficient size [11].

RQ 2 (Few-Shot Capability): *We are therefore interested in seeing whether larger LLMs produce better results in few-shot settings.*

To enhance the performance and reliability of LLMs, an essential prompt engineering technique involves breaking down complex tasks into smaller, manageable subtasks. This approach starts by prompting the LLM with one subtask at a time. The response generated from each subtask becomes the sequence's input for the following prompt. This method of sequentially linking prompts allows the LLM to tackle complex tasks that might be challenging to address in a single, comprehensive prompt. **Prompt chaining** not only improves the LLM's ability to handle intricate tasks but also increases the transparency and controllability of LLM applications. This approach makes debugging and analyzing the model's responses at each stage easier, facilitating targeted improvements where needed. A frequently used framework in this context is LangChain [29].

RQ 3 (Prompt-Chaining Capability): *We want to determine whether Kubernetes manifests can be gradually refined with prompt chaining in order to add capabilities that LLMs do not "retrieve from their memory" by default in zero-shot settings.*

The techniques mentioned above seem the most promising for an initial explorative analysis based on the current state of knowledge. Nevertheless, techniques such as Chain-of-Thought [12,35], Self-Consistency [33], Generated Knowledge Prompting [19], Tree of Thoughts [8,21,37], Automatic Reasoning and Tool-use [25], Program-Aided Language Models [6], ReACT Prompting [38], and Retrieval Augmented Generation [17] should also be investigated in a systematic screening in the future. In particular, it turned out that problems arose in the refinement stage of our approach. We, therefore, investigated a prompting strategy called Iterative Refinement with Self-Feedback [22] in the second phase of our study.

Analyzed Use Case (NoSQL DB) Considering Real-World Constraints: We examine basic prompt engineering methods like Zero-/Few-Shot and Prompt-Chaining to assess if non-fine-tuned LLMs (e.g., GPT-3.5, GPT-4, Llama2/3, Mistral) can efficiently generate Kubernetes manifest files. Our goal is to determine the effectiveness of these

LLMs and identify which prompt engineering techniques, as discussed in Sect. 3.1, are most effective for designing and optimizing manifest generation.

Our exploratory approach centers on deploying and operating a NoSQL database (such as MongoDB or similar systems) within Kubernetes. Although this may not seem like a particularly complex use case, it allows us to look at all relevant aspects and cross-resource relationships between concepts such as Ingress, Service, Deployment, StatefulSet and Persistent Volume Claim. We also consider aspects such as security and operational aspects (such as security contexts, network policies, avoidance of resource monopolisation), which are often not included in the standard Kubernetes examples found on the web, which are presumably used when training the language models. For such real-world constraints, we have orientated ourselves on the recommendations of the 'Kubernetes Security Hardening Guide' [2].

- The database or application containers should not run with elevated privileges (`securityContext.privileged: false`).
- The database/application should be accessible only within its namespace, necessitating the correct generation of a `NetworkPolicy`.
- The database/application containers should not monopolize resources, requiring the generation of memory and CPU resource limits.

Furthermore, we expect the LLM to derive the necessary manifests even if they are not explicitly requested in the prompt. An experienced DevOps engineer would have developed manifests for the above-mentioned setting. We use this DevOps experience as a benchmark for our expectations of the LLMs.

- Deployment (or `StatefulSet` including a `PersistentVolumeClaim` `Template`)
- Correct Volume mounts in `Deployment/StatefulSets`
- `PersistentVolumeClaim` (unless the LLM opts for a `StatefulSet`)
- `Service`

Generation and Evaluation Strategy: Our evaluation utilized a prompt chain (as depicted in Fig. 2) that starts with a zero-shot prompt to generate initial manifests. This is followed by a second phase involving iterative refinement to ensure operational constraints are met, using a specific check and refinement prompt template.

The following check and refinement prompts[1] were applied in the refinement stage in the following sequence:

1. Verify that a Deployment manifest has been generated for the database.
2. Verify that a PersistentVolumeClaim manifest has been generated for the database.
3. Ensure that the PersistentVolumeClaim manifest is mounted within the database container.
4. Ensure that the container's securityContext is set to privileged false.
5. Ensure that the containers have appropriate resource/limit settings.
6. Verify that a service manifest addressing the database port has been generated.

---

[1] Slightly shortened for presentation.

7. Ensure that a Network Policy restricts database port access within the namespace.

The resulting manifest files from the draft and refinement stages were analyzed by Kubernetes experts and tools (`kubectl apply -dry-run`) to assess whether the generated manifests adequately described the situation and were valid and deployable on Kubernetes (`kubectl apply`).

A DevOps expert identified and corrected errors found by the tool, making the minimum necessary changes to achieve a deployable result. In the second phase of this research, we automated these manual analysis steps to increase assessment objectivity and evaluate larger deployments and datasets. However, this semi-automated approach was adequate for our initial analysis to derive a research position and direction.

This evaluation was conducted for the following manifest generation strategies, based on Fig. 2.

1. **Zero-Shot.** The prompt did not explicitly specify the constraints to be met. Consequently, the refinement stage depicted in Fig. 2 was not executed.
2. **Zero-Shot+Constraints.** The prompt explicitly specified the constraints to be met. However, no incremental refinement was carried out for each constraint individually. Therefore, the refinement stage shown in Fig. 2 was not executed in this case either.
3. **Few-Shot+Refinement.** The prompt did not specify the constraints to be met. However, the draft stage results were explicitly refined iteratively for each constraint during the refinement stage illustrated in Fig. 2.

The main difference between **Zero-Shot+Constraints** and **Few-Shot+ Refinement** is that in the former, an LLM must consider all constraints simultaneously, while in the latter, it can process and improve upon each constraint one at a time.

3.2   Phase 2: Optimization and Automatization

It turned out in phase 1 that the Few-Shot+Refinement approach, in particular, led to significant losses (or, at best, showed no significant effect) and was, therefore, not worth the runtime and token expenditure involved. This surprised us, as we had expected a lot from this approach in particular. We extended this approach to a tool-based refinement approach in the second phase. We used our prompt chain from Fig. 2 with a tool-based self-refinement approach. This approach, seen in Fig. 3, has the advantage that generated manifest files can be checked automatically and tool-based, and the result can, in turn, influence the generation process. As tool to check manifest files we utilize a kubernetes python package, which offers a function named *kubectl* to load the manifest files with a dry-run on kubernetes. The returned message delivers feedback about the success or failure status of the call.

The concept of "self-refinement" refers to an iterative approach where a large language model (LLM) generates an initial output and then uses its own or elsewhere generated feedback (e.g., from a compiler or alike) to improve this output progressively [22]. This process, termed "SELF-REFINE," involves two main steps: feedback and refinement. The model generates an output and then provides feedback on its output, identifying areas needing improvement. The model then uses the feedback to refine the output, and this cycle is repeated until the desired quality is achieved. This method

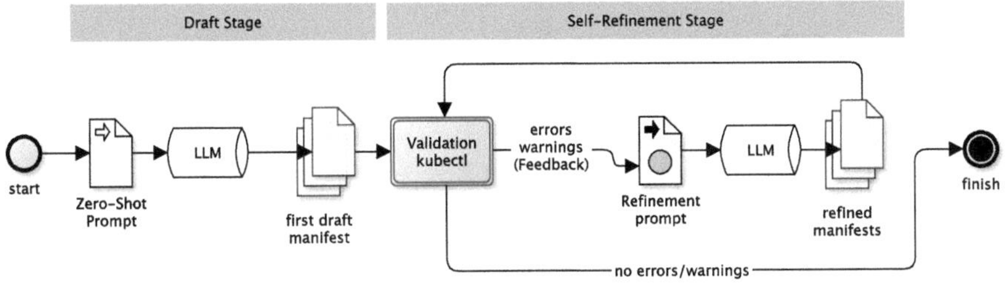

Fig. 3. Phase 2: An evolved prompt chain consisting of a design zero-shot and an iterative self refining stage.

does not require supervised training data or additional training but instead leverages the model's existing capabilities to enhance its performance across diverse tasks [22].

The concept was introduced by [22] and the authors report that a "SELF-REFINE" approach leads to significant improvements across various tasks. For instance, when applied to the GPT-4 model, SELF-REFINE resulted in an 8.7% absolute increase in code optimization performance. The most significant gains were observed in preference-based tasks such as Dialogue Response Generation, where the GPT-4 model's preference score improved by 49.2%.

This led us to the following research question, further analyzed in phase 2.

RQ 4 (Self-Refinement Capability): *Is it possible to increase the quality of generated container orchestration manifest files with tool-based self-refinement?*

4   Results

Table 1 shows the language models that were selected for evaluation based on their current popularity (OpenAI) or reported performance for self-hosting (Llama2/3, Mistral) at the time of each phase.

Table 1. Analysed large language models (self-hosted services were operated using AWQ quantification on mentioned Nvidia GPUs).

LLM	Service	GPU	VRAM	Phase	Remarks
GPT-4	Managed	?	?	1+2	OpenAI (details unknown, [1])
GPT-4o	Managed	?	?	1	OpenAI (details unknown, [24])
GPT-3.5-turbo	Managed	?	?	1+2	OpenAI (details unknown, [39])
Llama2 13B	Self-host	A6000	46.8Gi	1	Chat model [32]
Llama2 7B	Self-host	A2 or A4000	14.7Gi	1	Chat model [32]
Mistral 7B	Self-host	A2 or A4000	10.8Gi	1	Fine-tuned for coding [9]
Llama3 70B	Self-host	A6000	47.8Gi	2	Instruct model [5]
Llama3 13B	Self-host	A6000	23.3Gi	2	Instruct model [5]
Llama3 8B	Self-host	A2 or A4000	14.3Gi	2	Instruct model [5]

All self-hosted machine learning models were run via HuggingFace's Text Generation Inference Interface, enabling AWQ quantization [18]. We worked with the non-fine-tuned base models from HuggingFace, except for the Mistral model. For Mistral, we specifically used a model fine-tuned for coding assistance to evaluate the potential effects of fine-tuning better. The models were used programmatically with the LangChain library[2] and OpenAI[3] or the Text Generation Inference Interface from HuggingFace[4]. We used LangChain's default values and set the temperature parameter to 0.

4.1 Explanation of Phase 1 Results

The big question of phase #1 was which strategy best fulfills all the required constraints and whether there are differences between the LLMs. And does the approach work at all? The results are displayed in Fig. 4. All models succeeded in generating a functional deployment, but their adherence to operational constraints varied.

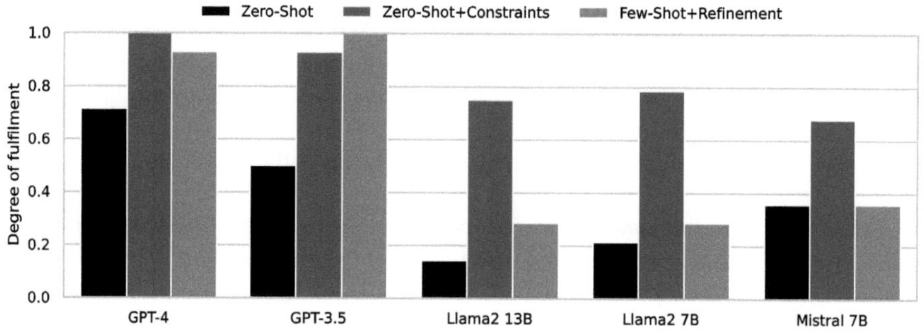

Fig. 4. Which degrees of fulfilment were achieved with which LLM and prompt strategies? For more details, see [15]. It can be seen that the refinement did not significantly influence the results for good models but led to losses compared to the simpler constraint-based approach for smaller or less-performing models.

Fulfilment was evaluated on a scale from 0.0 (no requirements met) to 1.0 (all requirements met), where a score of 1.0 indicates the potential for a fully automatic, error-free deployment in Kubernetes. Scores below 1.0 necessitated manual corrections, detailed in the original study [15].

GPT-4 and GPT-3.5 achieved the highest fulfilment scores, demonstrating their capability for fully automatic deployment. The free models, Llama2 and Mistral, had lower fulfilment levels, with simpler Zero-Shot approaches outperforming iterative refinement strategies. Interestingly, the smaller 7B Llama2 model performed as well as or slightly better than the 13B version. The smallest Mistral model outperformed Llama2 in Zero-Shot tasks but not when operational constraints were included in the prompt.

---

[2] https://pypi.org/project/langchain.

[3] https://pypi.org/project/langchain-openai.

[4] https://pypi.org/project/text-generation.

4.2 Explanation of Phase 2 Results

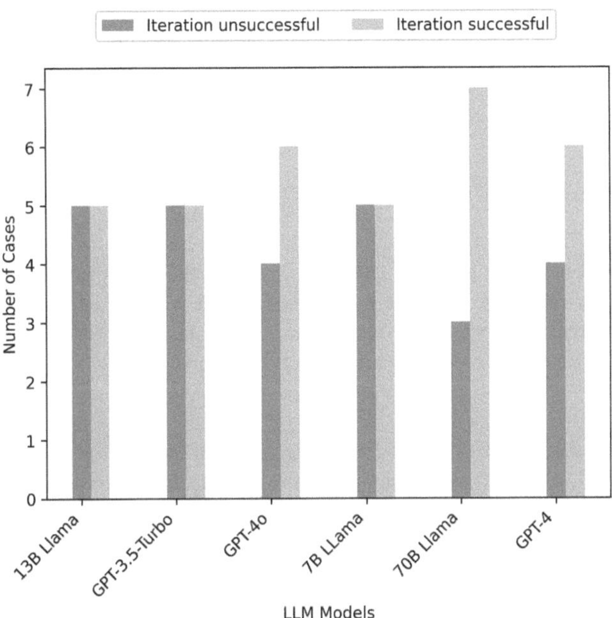

Fig. 5. Which levels of fulfillment were achieved by each LLM? All models successfully recover at least 5 out of 10 use cases. Notably, Llama 70B and GPT versions demonstrate even higher performance, recovering 6 to 7 cases.

Based on the results from Phase 1, it is evident that all models require some degree of refinement or correction for many of the generated manifest files. So far, we focused on a NoSQL use case for manifest file creation. In Phase 2, we expanded the scope to include five use cases (NoSQL, Redis, PostgreSQL, MySQL, NGINX) to validate the results across a broader range of scenarios. As demonstrated in Fig. 3, the tool-based correction iteration is supposed to effectively support the automated generation of correct manifest files.

Of the 30 generated use cases, 20 immediately successfully used the Large Language Models (LLMs). Our focus, therefore, shifts to the remaining 10 cases where corrections were needed to ensure the manifest files ran successfully. Figure 5 illustrates the number of corrected versus uncorrectable files for each LLM. Notably, all models could repair five use cases across the board, but only one or two models successfully handled three cases. LLaMA3 70B and GPT-4(o) stood out as the only models capable of restoring all but two to three original manifest files. Overall, Phase 2 resolved 8 out of 10 failed cases without user intervention, leaving just two unresolved. The LLaMA3 70B model achieved the best performance, with a standard deviation of only 3.39 iterations across all manifest files.

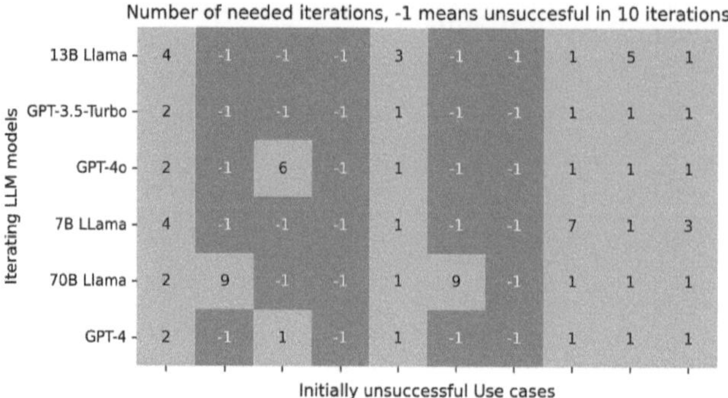

Fig. 6. Details for Phase 2: All initially failed use cases and the iterations needed to correct these files are plotted for each large language model. Failing files are denoted with a '−1'. Three use cases are only corrected by one or two models each. 70B Llama and GPT4 variants outperform the others in these cases. However, two use cases remain unrecoverable by any of the models.

The comparison plot Fig. 6 illustrates the performance of various LLMs in generating manifest files for different use cases and the required iterations to repair them if the initial version fails. The X-axis represents different initially failing use cases without naming them explicitly. The Y-axis displays the iterations each model requires to achieve a successful run. A value of '−1' indicates that at least one manifest file was not successfully repaired after all iterations for that specific use case. For other cases, the Y-axis shows the number of iterations required to get the use case running.

The variation in use cases revealed that certain failures could not be resolved even with the automated approach. These failures typically involved missing information, such as the correct namespace or values represented by placeholders, necessitating manual intervention by the user or more initial information provided for the LLM (e.g., the namespace).

4.3   Discussion of Results

So, what conclusions can be drawn?

RQ1: *How well can LLMs generate Kubernetes manifests out-of-the-box?* All LLMs successfully generated Kubernetes manifest files, correctly recognizing the semantic relationships between components such as Deployment, PersistentVolumeClaim, Service, and NetworkPolicy. However, most cases required some manual adjustments. The two commercial GPT models showed the potential for fully automated database deployment without user intervention. Coding-optimized models like Mistral performed better on simple Zero-Shot prompts than Llama2 but did not surpass the GPT models. Further investigation is needed to assess the generalizability of these findings.

RQ2: *Do larger LLMs generate better results in Zero-/Few-Shot settings?* Commercial LLMs like GPT-4 and GPT-3.5 outperform free models such as Llama2 and Mistral, although larger models (13B) do not necessarily produce better results than smaller ones (7B). Our results indicate that the quality of results depends on both model size and training data; for example, Mistral, optimized for coding tasks, performs better in Zero-Shot tasks than Llama2. Similarly, the superior performance of GPT-3.5 and GPT-4 is likely due to more extensive training data. Prompt engineering is crucial, as proper techniques can enable free models to nearly match GPT-4's performance, suggesting that further research should explore the role of prompt engineering in enhancing LLM outcomes.

RQ3: *Is it worthwhile to gradually refine Kubernetes manifests with prompt chaining?* Our initial hypothesis was that iterative refinement would improve the quality of Kubernetes manifests across various LLMs by addressing specific optimization aspects. Contrary to expectations, the results varied significantly. Incremental refinement showed minimal benefits for commercial models like GPT-4 and GPT-3.5, which already performed well with basic prompt engineering. Conversely, this approach negatively impacted the performance of free models like Llama2 and Mistral, possibly due to the overwriting of earlier optimizations over seven iterations. This suggests that the predefined structure of manifest files limits the effectiveness of iterative refinements due to their low complexity. Interestingly, the final refinement stage focusing on Security-Policy yielded effective policies, raising questions about the optimality of the iterative strategy and the organization of result integration. This discrepancy highlights a potential area for future research, particularly the impact of increasing complexity on the effectiveness of refinement prompts. These findings can be used to optimize the refinement stage, ensuring that later steps do not "overwrite" previous ones.

RQ4: *Is it possible to increase the quality of generated container orchestration manifest files with tool-based self-refinement?* The integration of tools and the iterative process of automatic correction validate our assumption, as many syntactic errors and missing attributes in the manifest files were successfully addressed. However, the overall iterative process proved to be more complex than initially anticipated. Since large language models (LLMs) generate responses based on statistical patterns, we observed significant variation in their iterative outputs. This required extensive parsing, exception handling, and prompt engineering to manage the wide range of responses produced by different LLMs. Notably, LLMs often included extraneous information around or even within the manifest files, such as Python comments, necessitating the extraction of the improved manifest file from the output. In some cases, the model's response did not contain a corrected manifest file at all, which also had to be detected and accounted for during the iteration process.

Interestingly, we found that while some models were unable to correct the manifest file in a single iteration, they succeeded after several iterations. This indicates that even when the model fails to provide the correct improvement initially, it may recover in subsequent iterations. Once the setup was established, we maintained consistent general prompts, and no manual intervention was required, aside from the automatic inclusion of dynamically generated failure information. This suggests that integrating tools with LLMs offers a promising approach to automating pipelines.

For future projects, our experience highlights that applying LLMs to product-centric tasks requires a deeper understanding and fine-tuning of structured outputs. This will help minimize the effort needed later to parse the LLM-generated content for the desired manifest file.

4.4 Limitations to Consider

This study investigates prompt engineering in Kubernetes, specifically assessing Large Language Models' (LLMs) capabilities in expressing Kubernetes operational states via YAML. Our findings, which focus on single-component and typical database deployments, are preliminary and context-specific, cautioning against their generalization for broader LLM performance assessments. Acknowledging the exploratory nature of our work, we emphasize its role in laying foundational knowledge for future, more complex studies. Although our initial research aligns with existing literature, highlighting the utility of LLMs in DevOps, it deliberately avoids the challenges of multi-service, interconnected deployments to ensure a solid baseline for subsequent investigation. Our phased research approach is designed to enhance our systematic understanding of LLMs and Kubernetes deployments, setting the stage for a comprehensive exploration of these technologies' interplay in future studies.

5 Conclusion and Outlook

This extended study reinforces again the potential of large language models (LLMs), such as GPT-4 and GPT-3.5, for automating Kubernetes deployments by generating manifest files from natural language inputs. Notably, performance did not always correlate with model size; smaller models like LLaMA2 and Mistral 7B sometimes outperformed larger ones, highlighting the importance of optimization and prompt-engineering strategies.

We introduced a tool-based self-refinement approach to address limitations observed in our initial study, where the refinement stage often failed to yield significant improvements. This enhanced iterative process employed a Python-based Kubernetes toolchain to automatically validate and refine manifest files through feedback from dry-run outputs. Results show that this approach significantly improved manifest file accuracy by automating much of the error detection and correction, particularly in more complex deployment scenarios. However, the process proved more complex than anticipated due to variations in LLM outputs, necessitating robust parsing, exception handling, and prompt engineering.

The study found that while many errors were successfully corrected through multiple iterations, some, particularly those involving missing information, still required manual intervention. However, using a standardized prompt chain with integrated tool feedback proved effective across various and typical deployment scenarios (NoSQL, Redis, PostgreSQL, MySQL, NGINX).

These findings confirm that challenges remain while tool-based self-refinement strategies improve the quality of generated manifest files. These include handling the variability of LLM outputs and integrating models into deployment pipelines. Future research should prioritize optimizing these self-refinement techniques and refining prompt strategies to accommodate more deployment scenarios.

Our findings suggest that, with the right strategies and tool integrations, LLMs can significantly enhance automated deployment pipelines. However, it's important to note that achieving this will require ongoing optimization of their interactions with automated tools. Nevertheless, advancing LLM capabilities will likely enhance automated deployment workflows, potentially reshaping traditional DevOps roles.

Acknowledgements. We thank Ralph Hänsel and Christian Töbermann for providing GPU resources via JupyterHub and Jonas Flodin, Max Sternitzke, and Patrick Willnow for managing JupyterHub and our Kubernetes infrastructure. Only your support and expertise made this study possible.

References

1. Achiam, O.J., et al.: GPT-4 technical report (2023). https://api.semanticscholar.org/CorpusID:257532815
2. Kubernetes security hardening guide (2021). https://media.defense.gov/2022/Aug/29/2003066362/-1/-1/0/CTR_KUBERNETES_HARDENING_GUIDANCE_1.2_20220829.PDF
3. Chang, Y., et al.: A survey on evaluation of large language models. arXiv preprint arXiv:2307.03109 (2023)
4. Chen, B., Zhang, Z., Langrené, N., Zhu, S.: Unleashing the potential of prompt engineering in large language models: a comprehensive review. arXiv preprint arXiv:2310.14735 (2023)
5. Dubey, A., et al.: The llama 3 herd of models. arXiv preprint arXiv:2407.21783 (2024)
6. Gao, L., et al.: Pal: program-aided language models. arXiv abs/2211.10435 (2022). https://api.semanticscholar.org/CorpusID:253708270
7. Hou, X., et al.: Large language models for software engineering: a systematic literature review. arXiv preprint arXiv:2308.10620 (2023)
8. Hulbert, D.: Using tree-of-thought prompting to boost chatgpt's reasoning (2023). https://doi.org/10.5281/ZENODO.10323452
9. Jiang, A.Q., et al.: Mistral 7b. arXiv abs/2310.06825 (2023). https://api.semanticscholar.org/CorpusID:263830494
10. Kaddour, J., Harris, J., Mozes, M., Bradley, H., Raileanu, R., McHardy, R.: Challenges and applications of large language models. arXiv preprint arXiv:2307.10169 (2023)
11. Kaplan, J., et al.: Scaling laws for neural language models. arXiv abs/2001.08361 (2020). https://api.semanticscholar.org/CorpusID:210861095
12. Kojima, T., Gu, S.S., Reid, M., Matsuo, Y., Iwasawa, Y.: Large language models are zero-shot reasoners. arXiv abs/2205.11916 (2022). https://api.semanticscholar.org/CorpusID:249017743
13. Komal, S., et al.: Adarma auto-detection and auto-remediation of microservice anomalies by leveraging large language models. In: Proceedings of the 33rd Annual International Conference on Computer Science and Software Engineering, CASCON 2023, pp. 200–205. IBM Corp., USA (2023)
14. Kratzke, N.: Cloud-native Computing: Software Engineering von Diensten und Applikationen für die Cloud. Carl Hanser Verlag GmbH Co KG (2023)
15. Kratzke, N., Drews, A.: Don't train, just prompt: towards a prompt engineering approach for a more generative container orchestration management. In: Proceedings of the 14th International Conference on Cloud Computing and Services Science - Volume 1: CLOSER, pp. 248–256. INSTICC, SciTePress (2024). https://doi.org/10.5220/0012710300003711

16. Lanciano, G., Stein, M., Hilt, V., Cucinotta, T., et al.: Analyzing declarative deployment code with large language models. CLOSER **2023**, 289–296 (2023)
17. Lewis, P., et al.: Retrieval-augmented generation for knowledge-intensive NLP tasks. In: Proceedings of the 34th International Conference on Neural Information Processing Systems, NIPS 2020. Curran Associates Inc., Red Hook (2020)
18. Lin, J., Tang, J., Tang, H., Yang, S., Dang, X., Han, S.: AWQ: activation-aware weight quantization for LLM compression and acceleration. arXiv abs/2306.00978 (2023). https://api. semanticscholar.org/CorpusID:258999941
19. Liu, J., et al.: Generated knowledge prompting for commonsense reasoning. In: Annual Meeting of the Association for Computational Linguistics (2021). https://api. semanticscholar.org/CorpusID:239016123
20. Liu, P., Yuan, W., Fu, J., Jiang, Z., Hayashi, H., Neubig, G.: Pre-train, prompt, and predict: a systematic survey of prompting methods in natural language processing. ACM J. **55**(9) (2023)
21. Long, J.: Large language model guided tree-of-thought. arXiv abs/2305.08291 (2023). https://api.semanticscholar.org/CorpusID:258686311
22. Madaan, A., et al.: Self-refine: iterative refinement with self-feedback. arXiv abs/2303.17651 (2023). https://api.semanticscholar.org/CorpusID:257900871
23. Naveed, H., et al.: A comprehensive overview of large language models. arXiv preprint arXiv:2307.06435 (2023)
24. Achiam, J., et al.: GPT-4 technical report. arXiv preprint arXiv:2303.08774 (2024)
25. Paranjape, B., Lundberg, S.M., Singh, S., Hajishirzi, H., Zettlemoyer, L., Ribeiro, M.T.: Art: automatic multi-step reasoning and tool-use for large language models. arXiv abs/2303.09014 (2023). https://api.semanticscholar.org/CorpusID:257557449
26. Petroni, F., et al.: Language models as knowledge bases? arXiv preprint arXiv:1909.01066 (2019)
27. Quint, P.C., Kratzke, N.: Towards a lightweight multi-cloud DSL for elastic and transferable cloud-native applications (2019)
28. Sultan, S., Ahmad, I., Dimitriou, T.: Container security: issues, challenges, and the road ahead. IEEE Access **7**, 52976–52996 (2019)
29. Topsakal, O., Akinci, T.C.: Creating large language model applications utilizing langchain: a primer on developing LLM apps fast. In: International Conference on Applied Engineering and Natural Sciences (2023). https://api.semanticscholar.org/CorpusID:260223847
30. Tosatto, A., Ruiu, P., Attanasio, A.: Container-based orchestration in cloud: state of the art and challenges. In: 2015 Ninth International Conference on Complex, Intelligent, and Software Intensive Systems, pp. 70–75. IEEE (2015)
31. Touvron, H., et al.: Llama: open and efficient foundation language models. arXiv abs/2302.13971 (2023). https://api.semanticscholar.org/CorpusID:257219404
32. Touvron, H., et al.: Llama 2: open foundation and fine-tuned chat models. arXiv abs/2307.09288 (2023). https://api.semanticscholar.org/CorpusID:259950998
33. Wang, X., et al.: Self-consistency improves chain of thought reasoning in language models. arXiv abs/2203.11171 (2022). https://api.semanticscholar.org/CorpusID:247595263
34. Wei, J., et al.: Finetuned language models are zero-shot learners. arXiv abs/2109.01652 (2021). https://api.semanticscholar.org/CorpusID:237416585
35. Wei, J., et al.: Chain of thought prompting elicits reasoning in large language models. arXiv abs/2201.11903 (2022). https://api.semanticscholar.org/CorpusID:246411621
36. Xu, Y., et al.: Cloudeval-yaml: a realistic and scalable benchmark for cloud configuration generation (2023). https://mlforsystems.org/assets/papers/neurips2023/paper33.pdf
37. Yao, S., et al.: Tree of thoughts: deliberate problem solving with large language models. arXiv abs/2305.10601 (2023). https://api.semanticscholar.org/CorpusID:258762525

38. Yao, S., et al.: React: synergizing reasoning and acting in language models. arXiv abs/2210.03629 (2022). https://api.semanticscholar.org/CorpusID:252762395
39. Ye, J., et al.: A comprehensive capability analysis of GPT-3 and GPT-3.5 series models. arXiv abs/2303.10420 (2023). https://api.semanticscholar.org/CorpusID:257632113
40. Zhao, X., et al.: Domain specialization as the key to make large language models disruptive: a comprehensive survey. arXiv preprint arXiv:2305.18703 (2023)

Efficient Online Application Placement Strategies in Mobile Edge Clouds

Chanh Nguyen[(✉)] [iD], Cristian Klein [iD], and Erik Elmroth [iD]

Department of Computing Science, Umeå University, 901 87 Umeå, Sweden
{chanh,cklein,elmroth}@cs.umu.se

Abstract. Mobile Edge Clouds (MECs) are emerging as a key complement to centralized cloud infrastructures by bringing computing and storage resources closer to the network edge, thereby reducing network bandwidth, latency, and jitter. A critical challenge in leveraging MECs effectively is the application placement problem, which seeks to minimize operational costs while ensuring end-user Quality of Service (QoS). This problem is further complicated by user mobility, as applications must migrate to maintain optimal QoS, yet frequent migrations can lead to unnecessary bandwidth consumption due to state transfer.

In this paper, we tackle the application placement problem for stateful applications in MEC environments. We model the dynamic workloads, applications, and infrastructure typical of MECs and define the associated costs: resource utilization, migration, and QoS degradation. Based on this model, we propose two online placement algorithms – *Gale-Shapley*-based and *Follow-me* – designed to minimize the total cost of operating applications. These algorithms are compared against an offline benchmark that has complete future knowledge.

Experimental results demonstrate that both proposed algorithms efficiently place applications in MECs, achieving operating costs within 8% of the global optimum approximated by the offline algorithm. Furthermore, the Gale-Shapley-based algorithm outperforms the Follow-me algorithm, reducing operating costs by up to 17% and improving load balancing across MECs to mitigate resource scarcity.

Keywords: Mobile edge clouds · Service orchestration · Optimization · Application placement

1 Introduction

The growth of mobile technology together with the roll-out of 5G networks enable the development of a new generation of applications with strict requirements for low jitter, low latency and high bandwidth. For instance, real-time gaming applications require delays of no more than a few milliseconds to avoid significant reductions in Quality of Service (QoS) [18,30]. To deal with such requirements, a Content Delivery Network (CDN) [7] is typically employed, which is an infrastructure consisting in placing caching servers at Internet Exchange Points (IXPs). However, CDNs are mostly useful to reduce latency when serving static content. In contrast, the new generation of

C. Pahl and M. van Steen (Eds.): CLOSER 2024, CCIS 2851, pp. 98–123, 2026.
https://doi.org/10.1007/978-3-032-17286-0_5

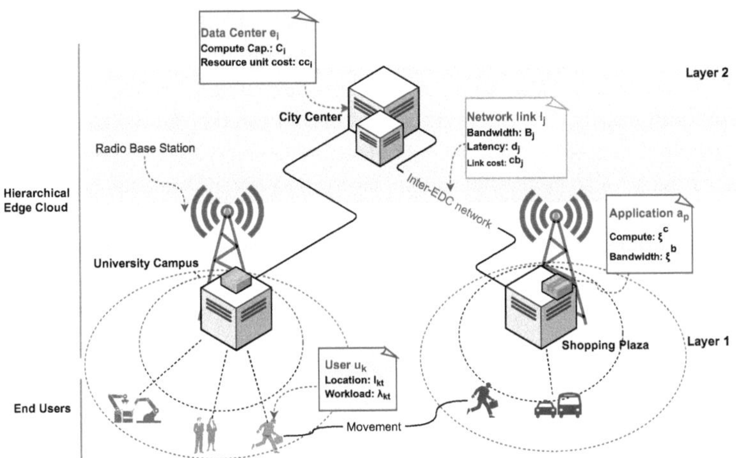

Fig. 1. A MEC platform with lower layer EDCs connecting to higher layer EDCs.

applications require fully programmable computing and storage capacity needs to be installed in closer vicinity of end-users.

To this end, recent years have seen a paradigm shift from current centralized cloud computing data-centers towards a distributed computing infrastructure called Mobile Edge Clouds (MECs). MECs are envisioned to distribute computing and storage capacity at the edge of the network, in so-called Edge Data Centers (EDCs) that are located in close proximity to end-users, for example in base stations. Recent works [12,23] have proposed hierarchical MECs with heterogeneous costs and capacities (see Fig. 1). EDCs are organized in layers, with EDCs in higher layers offering greater capacities and lower compute costs but also being more distant from the end-user, leading to higher latency and bandwidth costs.

Such MECs could be highly flexible, allowing applications to be placed in ways that meet their requirements while delivering the best of both worlds: cheap computation and proximity to end-users. In fact, many algorithms have been proposed for placing stateless applications on MECs, including dynamic placement algorithms for efficiently dealing with user mobility [11,25,28]. For example, user mobility can be predicted to deal with application start-up delay and ensure that capacity is allocated in the right EDCs just-in-time [16].

However, many envisioned MEC applications are stateful. For example, augmented reality applications must store generated meshes, world data, generated textures, etc. Employing stateless placement algorithms for stateful applications risks introducing unnecessary costs due to wastage of the bandwidth required to migrate user state from one EDC to another.

In this paper, we propose two online state-aware application placement algorithms for MECs, named *Follow-me* and *Gale-Shapley*-based algorithms. We start by thoroughly modeling the costs incurred by stateful applications on MECs, namely the resource cost (consisting of computing cost and application bandwidth cost), QoS degradation cost, and migration cost. The two proposed online placement algorithms aim to minimize the total operating cost, i.e. the sum of these three individual costs. In essence, the *Follow-me* placement strategy attempts to deploy applications in the EDC closest to the end-users, so as to minimize application bandwidth cost; applications are only migrated with the users' movement if the migration cost is smaller than the expected application bandwidth cost reduction. Conversely, the *Gale-Shapley*-based placement strategy strives to match applications to the EDCs that return the lowest resource cost and bandwidth consumption in the physical network links.

We evaluate these two algorithms using an MEC topology consisting of base stations geographically distributed across the San Francisco area. User mobility is modeled using real mobility traces of taxis in San Francisco. Finally, users' transition between applications are modeled based on a Markov model. We compare the total operating costs returned by *Follow-me* and *Gale-Shapley* to that of an offline precognition algorithm that has access to future user locations. While this offline algorithm is not usable in practice, it provides insight into how close our solution is to a theoretical optimum. Further, we present extensive experimental comparisons of the two online algorithms based on their performance and behavior on different application types (compute-intensive and bandwidth-intensive applications).

The contributions of this paper are three-fold:

- We comprehensively model the cost of stateful applications on MECs (see Sect. 3).
- We propose the two simple but efficient online placement strategies to place stateful applications among EDCs so as to minimize the total operating cost (see Sect. 4).
- We perform extensive experiments to evaluate the performance of the proposed placement strategies (see Sect. 6).

Our results show that the two proposed online placement algorithms can efficiently decide where to place applications among EDCs, reaching a total operation cost only 8% below the approximate global optimal placement provided by the benchmark offline algorithm. Of the two online algorithms, the Gale-Shapley-based algorithm achieves better optimal solutions than the Follow-me algorithm, reducing operating costs by up to 17% while helping MECs to effectively balance workloads to mitigate resource scarcity.

2   Related Work

The heterogeneity of resource capacity and cost of EDCs combined with end-user mobility makes application placement in MECs challenging. In this section, we provide a comprehensive review of the literature addressing the MEC application placement problem.

Wang et al. [28] proposed a *graph-based* mechanism to find optimal placements for multi-component applications in MECs. In their work, they abstracted both MECs and applications as un-directed tree graphs: Each tree application graph consists of nodes representing computational modules, and each edge represents communication between said nodes. The authors then proposed online approximation algorithms for placing the tree application graphs (with and without pre-specified junction nodes) onto the tree MEC graph so as to minimize the maximum resource utilization at both compute nodes and network links. Through rigorous theoretical analysis, the authors proved that the proposed online placement algorithms achieve an approximate optimal solution with a competitive ratio of $O(logN)$ and time complexity $O(V^3 N^2)$, where N is the number of servers in the MEC and V is the number of application components. Gao et al. [9] chose to regard the online service placement problem on MECs as two sub-tasks, i.e., choosing the access network; and then choosing places to deploy services. Differ from our work, the objective of the work is to find an optimal placement solution that improve the QoS by balancing the access, switching and communication delay. To this end, they divided the long-term optimization problem into a series of one-shot problems and used an *iterative-based* algorithm to obtain a near-optimal solution. This approach was shown to return a near-optimal solution with a feasible competitive ratio relative to the offline optimum.

Tong et al. [23] proposed a hierarchical MEC architecture and demonstrated its efficiency at handling peak loads. They additionally proposed a workload placement algorithm inspired by the Simulated Annealing process which the time complexity is a big concern depending on the size of the search space (i.e., number of EDCs and applications). In our work, we emulate the MEC platform following the same hierarchical architecture. We also implement an offline placement algorithm driven from the Simulated Annealing process as a baseline for performance evaluation.

Ouyang et al. [17] proposed an online approach for service placement on MECs where the main optimization objectives are the user's latency and the service migration cost. The placement mechanism overcomes the challenge of lacking future system information, and takes the user preferences into account to adaptively decide locations to place services. A theoretical analysis and a performance evaluation showed that the proposed algorithm can achieve better performance as compared to alternative algorithms. Wang et al. [27] targeted social virtual reality (VR) applications and presented an iterative approach called ITEM to help MEC optimally deploy such applications. Evaluation with large-scale real data traces show that the proposed algorithm outperforms the baseline approach by a factor of at least 1.3. Notably in this work, the authors proposed the *co-location cost* incurred due to resource contention among applications placed on the same EDC. The underlying idea is that there may be performance degradation due to application co-location and "noisy neighborhood" effects. Co-location costs were therefore used as soft constraints for the number of workloads hosted by an EDC. In our current work, we implement this idea by introducing dynamic unit costs for resources. In essence, we model the unit price of compute resources at a given EDC and of bandwidth at a given network link using linear functions that are inversely proportional to the workload intensity.

In recent years, the concept of the *cloud-edge continuum* has gained significant attention, facilitating seamless integration between centralized cloud data centers and edge data centers. This integration forms a continuous spectrum of computing capabilities [1, 14, 24], aligning with the geographical and hierarchical topology of MEC, which underpins this work. Service orchestration and application placement in such environments have been investigated [10, 21], with a focus on multiple objectives, including cost efficiency [20] and resource constraints [4], to optimize system performance.

In this work, our problem formulation differs from prior studies in several key aspects. First, we address dynamic workloads that vary across time slots, introducing a temporal dimension to the placement problem. Second, we explicitly account for data exchange costs, specifically the bandwidth cost along the network path between the connecting EDC (i.e., the one co-located with the tower nearest to the end-user) and the EDC responsible for serving the workload. Lastly, we consider resource unit costs as dynamic, reflecting fluctuations based on supply and demand principles.

3   Problem Definition

This section first outlines the models for each component considered in the application placement problem, including the MEC infrastructure, applications, user mobility, workload, and cost model. Based on these models, a formal statement of the problem is then formulated.

3.1   Mobile Edge Clouds

Geo-distributed EDCs organized in a hierarchical structure have been shown to provide efficient infrastructures for supporting anticipated MEC workloads [12,22,23,28,29]. We therefore focus on a MEC with EDCs organized into a hierarchical topology in this work (see Fig. 2).

A MEC is modeled as a set of N EDCs distributed geographically within a given area, represented by $\mathcal{E} = \{i | i = 1, 2, ..., N\}$. Each EDC is characterized by its geographic location loc_i and the layer to which it belongs. In layer 1, every EDC i is colocated with either a cellular base station or a WiFi access point, from which end-users send requests to an application hosted by the MEC. Each EDC contains a specific number of servers providing a pool of virtualized computing resources, with higher-layer EDCs offering greater computing capacities. The computing capacity of EDC i is denoted by C_i.

The EDCs are interconnected through a network modeled as follows. The set of all physical network links in the MEC is represented by $\mathcal{L} = \{j | j = 1, 2, ..., M\}$. Each link j connects an EDC i to its nearest ancestor and is defined by its network delay d_j and maximum bandwidth, referred to as bandwidth capacity, denoted by B_j. Any pair of EDCs can communicate via the shortest network path. Let $\mathcal{P}i, i' \subseteq \mathcal{L}$ represent the set of all physical network links on the shortest path between two EDCs i and i'. It is important to note that the total bandwidth consumed on a given physical network link j is the sum of the bandwidth consumed across all paths $\mathcal{P}i, i'$ that include j.

3.2   Application

Let $\mathcal{A} = \{p | p = 1, 2, .., P\}$ be the set of applications hosted in the MEC. An application p is characterized by the following parameters:

- **Compute** ξ_p^c describes the amount of computational resource units required by p to serve an end-user. The unit is CPU $\times$ seconds/user.
- **Bandwidth** ξ_p^b describes the amount of network bandwidth required by p to serve an end-user. The unit is KB/user.

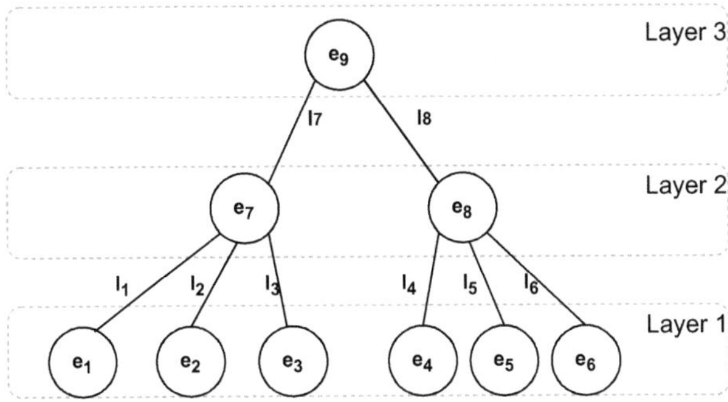

Fig. 2. The MEC model, illustrating the hierarchical organization of EDCs across multiple layers and the physical network connections linking the EDCs. Reference source [3].

- **State** ξ_p^s describes the amount of state stored by p for each served end-user. This is the amount of network bandwidth required to transfer the application from one EDC to another. The unit is KB/user.

The compute-bandwidth-usage ratio per application request (CPU-h/GB), denoted by A_{cl} [12], is used to determine whether a particular application is compute-intensive or bandwidth-intensive. The value of A_{cl} ranges from $[0.01, 10]$. To ensure the desired QoS, the system must allocate sufficient resources (both compute and bandwidth) to accommodate the total workload generated by users.

3.3   User and Workload

Consider a set of users, $\mathcal{U} = \{k \mid k = 1, 2, ..., K\}$, moving dynamically within the MEC coverage area. At each time slot t, user k wirelessly connects to the geographically nearest EDC, referred to as the *connecting* EDC. The access delay, defined as the delay introduced by the wireless network between user k and the connecting EDC i, is represented by $d_{k,t}$.

At each time slot t, user k connects to an application $p \in \mathcal{A}$, as specified by $\lambda_{k,t}$. After each time slot, user k may either continue using the same application or switch to a different one.

To serve a user, the placement algorithm allocates resources to the application in a *serving EDC*. The serving EDC may or may not be the same as the connecting EDC, depending on the algorithm's decision. Let $s_{k,t,i}$ denote the decision regarding whether the requested application p from user k is hosted on EDC i during time slot t:

$$s_{k,t,i} = \begin{cases} 1, & \text{if } p \text{ is hosted in EDC } i \text{ for user } k \\ 0, & \text{otherwise} \end{cases} \tag{1}$$

with

$$\sum_i s_{k,t,i} = 1 \tag{2}$$

Let $\text{tb}_{j,t}$ denote the total bandwidth allocated on link j during time slot t, comprising the bandwidth used for serving applications and that used for migrating applications. This is given by:

$$\text{tb}_{j,t} = \xi^b_{j,t} + \xi^s_{j,t} \tag{3}$$

where $\xi^b_{j,t}$ denotes the total bandwidth allocated on network link j for serving applications, and $\xi^s_{j,t}$ denotes the total bandwidth allocated on network link j for migrating applications, both during time slot t.

3.4   Cost

To serve end-users, the system responsible for placing applications in MECs must consider several costs:

- **The Resource Cost.** This cost encompasses the compute and bandwidth costs, which represent typical expenses such as hardware, service maintenance, and energy consumption. The unit price for compute resources at EDC i and bandwidth on network link j is modeled as inversely proportional to their current capacities. This approach is grounded in the law of supply and demand in microeconomics [13] and reflects the impact of economies of scale on both energy and maintenance costs. Let $g_*(.)$ denote the function that determines the resource unit price[1]:

$$g_*(x_t) = (b - a) \times x_t + a \tag{4}$$

Here,

$$x_t = \begin{cases} \sum_k \dfrac{s_{k,t-1,i} \times \xi^c_{\lambda_{k,t-1}}}{C_i}, & \text{for the compute resource} \\ \dfrac{\text{tb}_{j,t-1}}{B_j}, & \text{for the bandwidth resource} \end{cases} \tag{5}$$

and a, b are the minimum and maximum resource unit price, which are predefined differently for each i, j.

Then, the resource cost Cost_{res} is then calculated as below:

$$\text{Cost}_{res} = \sum_t \sum_i \sum_k s_{k,t,i} \times \left(g_i \times \xi^c_{\lambda_{k,t}} + \sum_{j \in \mathcal{P}_{\text{loc}_{k,t,i}}} g_j \times \xi^b_{\lambda_{k,t}} \right) \tag{6}$$

Here, $\mathcal{P}_{\text{loc}_{k,t,i}}$ is the network path as defined in Sect. 3.1.

The total bandwidth allocated on a particular physical network link j for serving applications is equal to the sum of the bandwidth consumed on paths $\mathcal{P}_{\text{loc}_{k,t,i}}$ go through j, which is decided by $s_{k,t,i}$:

$$\xi^b_{j,t} = \sum_k \sum_{j \in \mathcal{P}_{\text{loc}_{k,t,i}}} s_{k,t,i} \times \xi^b_{\lambda_{k,t}} \tag{7}$$

---

[1] It is important to note that the resource unit price function in Eq. 4 can be customized to fit stakeholder definitions and specific scenarios.

– **The Migration Cost.** This cost is incurred when a user's application p is migrated from EDC i at time slot $t - 1$ to another EDC i' at time slot t. It depends on the size of the application's state data (or service profile) for each user. Transferring this data between EDCs consumes bandwidth from the inter-EDC network connecting i and i'.

The migration flag, $\mathrm{MF}k, t, i, i'$, is set to 1 if and only if user k requests the same application in consecutive time slots (i.e., $\lambda_{k,t} = \lambda_{k,t-1}$), and the application is hosted on different EDCs in those time slots (i.e., $\langle s_{k,t} \cdot s_{k,t-1} \rangle = 0$):

$$
\mathrm{MF}_{k,t,i,i'} = \begin{cases} 1, & \lambda_{k,t} = \lambda_{k,t-1}, \\ & \text{and } s_{k,i',t} = 1 \\ & \text{and } s_{k,i,t-1} = 1 \\ 0, & \text{otherwise} \end{cases} \tag{8}
$$

Here, i represents the source EDC, and i' is the destination EDC for the migration. The total migration cost is then calculated as:

$$
\mathrm{Cost}_{mig} = \sum_t \sum_k \sum_i \sum_{i'} \left(\mathrm{MF}_{k,t,i,i'} \times \sum_{j \in \mathcal{P}_{i,i'}} g_j \times \xi^s_{\lambda_{k,t}} \right) \tag{9}
$$

The total bandwidth allocated on a network link j for application migrations is the sum of the bandwidth allocated for migrating applications along the paths $\mathcal{P}_{i,i'}$ that pass through j:

$$
\xi^s_{j,t} = \sum_k \sum_i \sum_{i'} \mathrm{MF}_{k,t,i,i'} \times \sum_{j \in \mathcal{P}_{i,i'}} \xi^s_{\lambda_{k,t}} \tag{10}
$$

– **The Service Quality Degradation Cost.** This cost results from delays caused by three factors: (i) the start-up time required to provision new virtual resources for user-requested applications, (ii) the wireless network delay between user k and the connected EDC i, and (iii) the transmission delay across network link j, including delays related to the migration of application state data.

Given $\xi^c_{\lambda_{k,t-1}}$ and $\xi^c_{\lambda_{k,t}}$, the increase in resource allocation for EDC i between time slots t and $t - 1$ is calculated as follows:

$$
\delta_{t,i} = \max \left\{ \sum_k \left(s_{k,t,i} \times \xi^c_{\lambda_{k,t}} - s_{k,t-1,i} \times \xi^c_{\lambda_{k,t-1}} \right), 0 \right\} \tag{11}
$$

Let st represent the average start-up time for a new virtual resource. It is assumed that new virtual resources are invoked in parallel at each EDC i during time slot t. The start-up time for the newly added virtual resources, denoted as $d_{st,t}$, is then given by the following expression:

$$
d_{st,t} = \begin{cases} st, & \text{for } \delta_{t,i} > 0 \\ 0, & \text{for } \delta_{t,i} = 0 \end{cases} \tag{12}
$$

To model the relationship between network latency and injection bandwidth for each physical link j, the relative latency is treated as a function of the offered traffic in a simple network. As previously demonstrated [5, 15], network latency in an interconnection network increases to infinity as throughput approaches saturation. In such scenarios, this relationship is well represented by an exponential distribution.

In our model, the total bandwidth allocated on each link j at time t is capped by the link's maximum bandwidth, thus disregarding certain waiting times (e.g., queuing latency) that may occur in real networks. The network delay on link j is modeled using an exponential distribution:

$$\text{delay}_{j,t} = \frac{e^{\left(\frac{\text{tb}_{j,t}}{B_j}\right)}}{1 - \frac{\text{tb}_{j,t}}{B_j}} + d_j \tag{13}$$

Let cc_{qos} be the unit price of the service quality downgrade due to delay. The service quality degradation cost, Cost_{qos}, can then be calculated as follows:

$$\text{Cost}_{qos} = \text{cc}_{qos} \times \sum_t \left(d_{st,t} + \left(\sum_k d_{k,t} + \sum_{l_j} \text{delay}_{l_j,t} \right) \right) \tag{14}$$

3.5 Cost Optimization Formulation

After describing the different costs involved in placing applications on MECs to serve end-users while maintaining QoS, the total cost is expressed as the sum of all these costs: $\text{Cost}res + \text{Cost}mig + \text{Cost}_{qos}$. The application placement optimization problem can thus be formalized as:

$$\text{minimize:} \quad \mathbb{P} = \text{Cost}_{res} + \text{Cost}_{mig} + \text{Cost}_{qos} \tag{15}$$

$$\text{subject to:} \quad \sum_k \xi^c_{\lambda_{k,t}} \times s_{k,i,t} \leq C_i, \forall i, t, \tag{16}$$

$$\text{tb}_{j,t} \leq B_j, \forall j, t \tag{17}$$

Here, constraints 16 and 17 ensure that the system's capacity limit is not exceeded (i.e. the load on each EDC does not exceed its compute capacity; and the traffic through each network link does not exceed its maximum bandwidth).

In each time slot $t \in \mathcal{T}$, the system must determine $s_{k,t,i}$, specifying which EDC will host the requested application p for user k. These decisions affect the total compute resource allocation at each EDC i and the total bandwidth usage on each link j. The goal is to minimize the aggregated operating cost over the time window $\mathcal{T}$.

3.6 An Illustrative Example

To more clearly explain the application placement problem and the challenges of finding an optimal solution, we present a simple example of how the optimal placement could be decided.

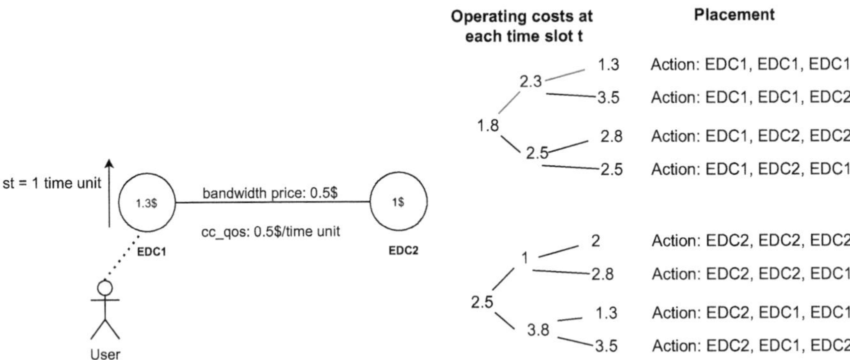

(a) An MEC with two EDCs and their resource unit prices.

(b) Placement decisions and corresponding costs.

Fig. 3. A simple illustration of the application placement challenge in MECs.

Consider a MEC with two EDCs both in layer 1 (i.e., each EDC is collocated with a base station to which users connect directly). The costs of compute units in each EDC, network links, and the QoS violations cost are presented in Fig. 3a. Please note that in this example, the prices are chosen to be static for the sake of clarity, i.e., the minimum and maximum prices are equal. However, our problem statement generalizes to dynamic prices.

Assume a single user with the following mobility: At t_0 the user is close to EDC 1 and makes requests with a rate $\lambda_{t_0} = 1$. At t_1, the user moves close to EDC 2 and makes requests with a rate $\lambda_{t_1} = 1$. At t_2, the user moves back close to EDC 1 and makes requests with a rate $\lambda_{t_2} = 1$.

Assume that all applications requested by the user demand 1 compute resource unit and 1 bandwidth unit, and that the start-up time delay is 1 time unit.

The problem is to find the optimal application placement that minimizes total cost over the time window $\mathcal{T} = \{t_0, t_1, t_2\}$. Figure 3b presents all potential placement decisions and the resulting total cost. It is apparent that serving the requests from EDC 1 for all time slots $t \in \mathcal{T}$ is the decision that minimizes total cost, giving a total cost is $1.8 + 2.3 + 1.3 = 5.4$. This placement choice – which includes QoS degradation cost and extra bandwidth cost when the user moves close to EDC 2 – is better than moving the allocation to EDC 2 with the user.

This example is only meant to illustrate the placement trade-offs that can be made when the location of user is known *a priori* for the whole time window. However, practical algorithms must operate online and have no knowledge of future changes. In our example, we can observe that until time slot t_1, the optimal solution is to place workload on EDC2 for both time slots t_0 and t_1; the total operating cost being $2.5+1 = 3.5$. This shows how an online algorithm can easily get trapped in a local optimum leading to an inferior global optimum.

4 Online Application Placement Algorithm

This section introduces a mathematical transformation to simplify the original placement problem described in Sect. 3. The placement problem is proven to be NP-hard, meaning that an exact solution cannot be achieved in polynomial time. To address this challenge, two online placement algorithms are proposed: the *Follow-me* strategy and a *Gale-Shapley*-based placement approach.

4.1 Mathematical Transformation and Proof that the Problem is NP-Hard

In time slot t, placement decisions from previous time slots are fixed, but the placement in time slot $t - 1$ affects the decision at time t. Thus, the original total operation cost $\mathbb{P}$ from Eq. (15) can be re-written as follows (with $\mathcal{T} = [1, T]$):

$$\mathbb{P}_{t \in [1,T]} = \mathbb{P}_{t \in [1,T-1]} + \mathbb{P}_{t=T} \tag{18}$$

Finding an optimal operating cost $\mathbb{P}_{t \in [1,T]}$ thus becomes a recursive process of finding an optimal operating cost $\mathbb{P}_{t=T}$ based on the current system's state, assuming the application placements in previous time slots $t \leq T - 1$ are optimal. In each time slot $t \in \mathcal{T}$, the total compute resource allocated at each EDC i, $\sum_k \xi^c_{k,t-1} \times s_{k,t-1,i}$ and the total bandwidth resource allocated at each network link j, $\mathrm{tb}_{j,t-1}$ are known. These values together with the users' application requests and their location during t are the inputs for the placement problem, $\mathbb{P}_{t=T}$. The original placement problem thus becomes an assignment problem: to which EDC should each user's requested applications be assigned so as to minimize the total operating cost at every time slot t.

This problem can be shown to be *NP-hard* as follows:

Let $\pi_{k,i}$ represent the operating cost, which is the sum of the three individual costs outlined in the previous section, incurred when serving the workload λ_k for user k on EDC i. $\mathbb{P}_{t=T}$ can be rewritten as:

$$\mathbb{P}_{t=T} = \sum_i \sum_k \pi_{k,i} \times s_{k,i} \tag{19}$$

Let $\mathbb{Z}_{t=T} = -\mathbb{P}_{t=T}$. Then, minimizing $\mathbb{P}_{t=T}$ becomes equivalent to solving the problem:

$$\text{maximize:} \quad \mathbb{Z}_{t=T} \tag{20}$$

$$\text{subject to:} \quad \sum_k \xi^c_{\lambda_k} \times s_{k,i} \leq C_i, \forall i, \tag{21}$$

$$\mathrm{tb}_j \leq B_j, \forall j \tag{22}$$

$$\sum_i s_{k,i} = 1, \forall i, \tag{23}$$

$$s_{k,i} \in \{0, 1\} \tag{24}$$

This is the generalized assignment problem, which is a proven NP-hard problem [6], Our problem is thus NP-hard. $\square$

It is impossible to find an optimal solution for the original application placement problem in polynomial time unless $P = NP$. We must therefore design efficient algorithms that provide near-optimal solutions for minimizing $\mathbb{P}_{t=T}$ in polynomial time. To this end, we introduce two efficient heuristic algorithms, i.e., *Follow-me*, and *Gale-Shapley*-based algorithm.

4.2 Follow-Me Strategy

Intuitively, applications with high bandwidth requirements (i.e., bandwidth-intensive applications) increase the total operating cost to a greater degree if placed on EDCs far from the connected EDC. Therefore, one should place such applications as close as possible to the connected end-users. To this end, the *Follow-me* strategy (as presented in Algorithm 1) first sorts all the requested applications in decreasing order of their bandwidth requirements $\xi^b_{\lambda_{k,t}}$, and state size $\xi^s_{\lambda_{k,t}}$ (line 3). It then loops through the set of workloads W to place the requested applications at the EDCs closest to their end-users (line 5–13). Specifically, for each $\lambda_{k,t}$, the algorithm searches for ancestor EDCs from layers above that to which the user is currently connected (line 7). It then picks the EDC that delivers the lowest total operating cost from the set of $ancestorDCs_{\lambda_{k,t}}$ with suitable compute resources to host the requested application (line 8).

If the hierarchical infrastructure of the MEC has l layers and it hosts m applications, then the run-time complexity of the Follow-me strategy is $O(l \times m)$.

4.3 Gale-Shapley Based Strategy

The *Gale-Shapley* algorithm [8] finds attainable optimal solutions to the *stable matching problem*. The algorithm has been used in mathematics and economics due to its polynomial time complexity. In general, our problem of assigning requested applications to EDCs in each time slot t to minimize $\mathbb{P}_{t=T}$ is analogous to the *college admissions* discussed by Gale and Shapley [8]: The set of n EDCs $\mathcal{E}$ can be compared to the set of n colleges, in which each EDC $i \in \mathcal{E}$ has a "quota" C_i. Similarly, the set of m requested applications to assigned to the n EDCs can be compared to the m applicants to be assigned to the n colleges. We therefore considered the *Gale-Shapley*-based placement strategy presented in Algorithm 2. The algorithm takes the same inputs as the *Follow-me* placement strategy, and perform in every time slot t. To perform Gale-Shapley assignment, our algorithm first formulates the application preference matrix $\mathbb{M}_{\text{app}}(n \times m)$ in which each column p ranks EDCs in decreasing order of the operating cost incurred when placing application p on them(line 3). Similarly, the algorithm formulates an EDC preference matrix $\mathbb{M}_{\text{edc}}(m \times n)$, in which each column i ranks the requested applications in decreasing order of the bandwidth consumed when placed on EDC i (line 4). This preference ensures that each application is hosted on an EDC that minimizes network congestion. Finally, it call the *Gale-Shapley* method to conduct the assignment using the two matrices above as inputs (line 5).

With n EDCs and m applications, the run-time complexity of the *Gale-Shapley*-based strategy is $O(n \times m)$.

Algorithm 1. Follow-me Placement Strategy.

$\triangleright$ Executed in every time slot

1: **Input:** *Previous application placement* (from $t - 1$),
    Resource availability for all EDCs (up to t),
    Bandwidth availability for all network links (up to t),
    End-users' locations u_k *and workloads at time* t, $W = \{\lambda_{k,t}\}$.
2: **Update:** Compute unit price for each EDC i, and bandwidth unit price for each network link j.
3: **Sort:** Workloads W in descending order of bandwidth requirements $\xi^b_{\lambda_{k,t}}$ and state size $\xi^s_{\lambda_{k,t}}$.
4: **Initialize:** $n \leftarrow 0$,
    total cost $\leftarrow 0$,
    $s_{k,i} \leftarrow 0$ (initial application placement state for each workload).
5: **while** W is not empty **do**
6:      Take workload $W[n] = \lambda_{k,t}$.
7:      Find ancestorDCs$_{\lambda_{k,t}}$ = all closest ancestor EDCs for user u_k.
8:      **for** each $e_i \in$ ancestorDCs$_{\lambda_{k,t}}$ **do**
9:          **if** EDC i has sufficient resources and network path has enough bandwidth **then**
10:              Set $s_{k,i} \leftarrow 1$ and minimize Cost$_{total}$.
11:          **end if**
12:      **end for**
13:      Remove $W[n]$ from W.
14:      Update compute resource availability of EDCs and bandwidth availability of network links.
15:      Calculate cost for $\lambda_{k,t}$: cost$_k$.
16:      *total cost* $\leftarrow$ *total cost* + cost$_k$.
17: **end while**
18: **Return:** $\{s_{k,i}\}$ and *total cost*.

Algorithm 2. Gale-Shapley Based Placement Strategy.

$\triangleright$ Performed for every time slot

1: **Input:** *Previous application placement* (from $t - 1$),
    EDCs' available resources (up to t),
    Network links' available bandwidth (up to t),
    End-users' locations u_k *and workload at time* t, $W = \{\lambda_{k,t}\}$.
2: **Update:** Compute unit price for each EDC i, and bandwidth unit price for each network link j.
3: **Formulate** $\mathbb{M}_{\text{app}}$ ($n \times m$) – the application preference matrix. Each column p ranks EDCs in the order of lowest operating cost if application p is placed on it.
4: **Formulate** $\mathbb{M}_{\text{edc}}$ ($m \times n$) – the EDC preference matrix. Each column i ranks applications in the order of least bandwidth consumption.
5: **Perform Matching:** Run Gale-Shapley algorithm using $\mathbb{M}_{\text{edc}}$ and $\mathbb{M}_{\text{app}}$.
6: **Return:** Application placement $\{s_{k,i}\}$ and total cost.

---

5   Experimental Setting and Methodology

This section presents our simulation-based evaluation. First, we describe an MEC infrastructure with EDCs distributed in a metropolitan area connected in tree topology. Then, we describe the parameters of simulated applications and end-users workload. Finally, we describe the implementation and setup of our proposed placement algorithm, as well as the baseline placement algorithm.

5.1   Infrastructure: An MEC Platform

A hierarchical MEC platform is simulated with EDCs distributed over a metropolitan area, following the MEC model outlined in [12]. The capacities and compute unit prices (minimum and maximum) of EDCs across different layers, along with the capacities and costs of network links between successive layers, are summarized in Table 1. The physical network links between layer 1 and layer 2 are modeled as OC-3 (optical carrier level 3), while those between layer 2 and layer 3 are modeled as OC-12.

Layer 1 EDCs are geographically distributed and collocated with base stations, enabling direct connections for end-users. The geographical coordinates of these EDCs are derived from a dataset of real-world cellular tower locations in San Francisco, US[2]. From this dataset, six tower locations were selected as deployment sites for layer 1 EDCs, as illustrated in Fig. 4. Although datacenter deployment is not the primary focus of this work, these locations were chosen to maximize coverage in areas with high user density, based on the experimental mobility trace dataset, as discussed in Sect. 5.3.

Fig. 4. Distribution of 6 EDCs collocated with cellular base stations in layer 1. Reference source [3].

---

[2] http://www.city-data.com/towers/cell-San-Francisco-California.html.

Table 1. Experiment Configuration. Reference source [3].

MEC topology		
Layer	Capacity (#VMs)	Cost ($/CPU-h)
1	150	(0.115, 0.206)
2	1500	(0.091, 0.127)
3	15000	(0.075, 0.086)
Network Link		
Link	Capacity (Mbps)	Cost ($/GB)
OC3	155	(0.3078, 0.46)
OC12	622	(0.98, 1.47)
Application		
A_{cl} (CPU-h/GB)	(0.01, 10)	

5.2 Application

We simulate multiple applications, each with a distinct resource usage profile. For this, we use the *compute-to-bandwidth usage ratio* per user (CPU-h/GB), denoted as A_{cl} [12], to generate 10 unique applications. The A_{cl} values range from 0.01 to 10, reflecting different levels of CPU and bandwidth demands. Additionally, each application is defined by an average state size, which influences the bandwidth needed for state transfers during migration. In stateful application migration, a general correlation exists between the size of the migrating operator and the incoming data rate, where higher loads result in larger saved states [2]. For simplicity, the state size is modeled as a linear function of the application's average bandwidth usage:

$$\text{state\_size} = \nu \times \text{bandwidth\_usage} \tag{25}$$

Here, ν is a uniform random deviate in the range $(0.5, 1)$.

5.3 User Mobility and Workload

To simulate user mobility, real-world mobility traces from San Francisco-based Yellow cab vehicles [19] are utilized, as the dataset reflects the movements of end-users within the same geographic region as the simulated MEC. The dataset captures the mobility patterns of 536 taxi cabs in the San Francisco Bay area over a 25-day period starting on May 17, 2008. The original dataset contains four attributes: longitude, latitude, datetime, and the number of passengers. The trace data were preprocessed to remove invalid records, with a maximum velocity threshold of $V_{\max} = 115$ km/h, established in accordance with relevant urban traffic regulations.

User locations are assumed to remain fixed within each time slot t, but may vary between time slots. Each time slot is set to 1 min in duration. During time slot t, a user connects to an application hosted on the MEC. The session length is modeled as the smallest integer greater than or equal to an exponentially distributed random variable with a given rate parameter:

$$\text{rate} = \frac{1}{\text{average\_session\_length}} \tag{26}$$

The parameter *average_session_length* denotes the average duration of sessions for users utilizing a specific application. This parameter is assigned values based on the average session durations of the five most popular mobile social networking applications in the US as of September 2019[3]. At the beginning of each subsequent time slot t, the simulation assesses whether the current session has concluded. If the session has ended, the user uniformly selects another application. Consequently, the simulation records the following data for each user in each time slot: the layer 1 EDC to which the user connects, the application accessed, and the user's influence on the application in terms of CPU usage, bandwidth consumption, and state size.

5.4   Off-Line Placement Strategy - Precognition Strategy

To evaluate the performance of the proposed algorithms, we benchmark it against an approximately optimal off-line placement strategy, referred to as *Precognition*. This strategy assumes full knowledge of future events over the entire time horizon $\mathcal{T}$. Specifically, it has access to complete information regarding end-user locations, their application requests, and the available capacities of each EDC and network link at every time slot within $\mathcal{T}$. Although such future knowledge is unattainable in real-world scenarios, this comparison provides insight into how closely our algorithm approximates an optimal solution based on perfect foresight.

To this end, we employ *Simulated Annealing*(SA) [26], a well-known meta-heuristic method, to approximate the global optimum. With full access to the aforementioned information over the time window $\mathcal{T}$, we reformulate the placement problem as a shortest path problem. We construct a graph $\mathcal{G} = (\mathcal{V}, \mathcal{E})$ to represent all potential placement decisions within $\mathcal{T}$, where the weight assigned to each edge (connecting vertices in successive time slots) reflects the operational cost incurred at each time slot $t \in \mathcal{T}$. The shortest path from the initial vertex (at $t = -1$) to the terminal vertex (at $t = T + 1$) corresponds to the minimum total operational cost across the entire time horizon $\mathcal{T}$. The pseudo-code of the clairvoyant strategy is presented in Algorithm 3.

The input to the algorithm consists of data from the MEC system, including the compute resource capacities of the EDCs, the bandwidth capacities of the network links, and complete workload information over the time window $\mathcal{T}$. The Simulated Annealing algorithm requires the specification of two key parameters: the *Temperature* (T), which must be initialized to a sufficiently high value, and the *Cooling Factor* $(c \in (0, 1))$, which governs the rate of temperature decrease and indirectly controls the time budget

---

[3] https://www.statista.com/statistics/579411/top-us-social-networking-apps-ranked-by-session-length/.

Algorithm 3. Precognition Placement Strategy.

1: **Input:** Temperature T, Cooling factor c,
        Best initial placement solution s_0 and its cost $cost_0$,
        Datacenters' resource capacity,
        Network links' bandwidth capacity,
        Users' locations and their workload over the time window T.
2: **Initialize:** $s_{best} \leftarrow s_0$,
        $cost_{best} \leftarrow cost_0$,
        $s_{current} \leftarrow s_0$,
        $cost_{current} \leftarrow cost_0$,
        $temp_{current} \leftarrow T$.
3: **while** $temp_{current} > 1$ **do**
4:      Create a new solution s_{new} by selecting a neighbor of $s_{current}$ randomly.
5:      Calculate the cost $cost_{new}$ of the solution s_{new}.
6:      **if** $\text{Random}() < e^{\frac{cost_{current} - cost_{new}}{temp_{current}}}$ **then**
7:          $s_{current} \leftarrow s_{new}$
8:          $cost_{current} \leftarrow cost_{new}$
9:      **end if**
10:     **if** $cost_{current} < cost_{best}$ **then**
11:        $s_{best} \leftarrow s_{current}$
12:        $cost_{best} \leftarrow cost_{current}$
13:     **end if**
14:     Update temperature: $temp_{current} \leftarrow temp_{current} \times c$
15: **end while**
16: **Return:** s_{best} and $cost_{best}$

---

allocated for exploring potential solutions. Initially, the algorithm uses the best solution obtained from the two proposed algorithms as the starting point (line 2). This initialization step ensures that the SA algorithm begins from a high-quality solution, reducing the likelihood of starting from a suboptimal configuration.

At each iteration of the loop (line 3 - 9), the algorithm generates a neighboring solution by perturbing the current solution – specifically, by altering the placement decision at a given time slot t. The acceptance of this new solution is probabilistic (line 6), determined by comparing its cost to the current solution in relation to the current temperature. If the new solution offers a lower cost than the best-known solution, it is accepted as the new best solution (line 7). This iterative process continues, gradually refining the solution while balancing exploration and exploitation through temperature reduction.

With N EDCs, K users, and a time window of length T, the total number of possible solutions in the search space is $(N^K)^T$. Consequently, as these parameters increase, it becomes computationally infeasible for the precognition algorithm to find the optimal solution within a fixed time frame. To address this, we conduct the experiments using smaller values for these parameters. The approximate minimum operating cost produced by the precognition strategy is then used as a benchmark to assess how closely the Gale-Shapley-based and Follow-me algorithms approach the global optimum.

5.5   Evaluation Metrics

We evaluate the performance of our approach based on the following metrics:

- **Total Operation Cost.** This metric, formally defined in Sect. 3, representes the total cost of operations. The goal for each algorithm is to minimize this quantity.
- **Resource Usage.** The utilization of compute resources at EDCs and bandwidth on network links is analyzed to evaluate how effectively each algorithm manages resource allocation and mitigates capacity constraints.
- **Mean Execution Time.** This metric measures the average time taken by each algorithm to make placement decisions at each time slot over the entire time window T, providing a benchmark for computational efficiency.

All experiments were conducted on a machine equipped with an Intel i7-4790 CPU and 32 GB of RAM, utilizing a single-threaded implementation.

6   Result and Discussion

In this section, we evaluate the proposed placement strategies using the experimental setup presented in the preceding section.

Table 2. Total operating cost difference between the two proposed strategies (Follow-me and Gale-Shapley) and the Precognition strategy.

# Users	T	Follow-me		Gale-Shapley	
		CompInApp	BandInApp	CompInApp	BandInApp
3	1	1.5×10^{-16}	1.5×10^{-16}	0	0
	3	0.06	0.06	0.05	0.05
	5	0.08	0.08	0.07	0.07
	10	0.06	0.08	0.05	0.08
	20	0.02	0.04	0.05	0.02
	30	0.02	0.03	0.05	0.01
5	1	0	0	0	0
	3	0.04	0.03	0.03	0.02
	5	0.04	0.05	0.02	0.03
	10	0.01	0.04	0.05	0.07
	20	0.01	3.5×10^{-3}	0.02	1.5×10^{-3}
	30	0	0	0.01	0.01
10	1	0	0	0	0
	3	0.04	0.03	0.04	0.03
	5	0.03	0.03	0.03	0.03
	10	8.5×10^{-3}	6.4×10^{-3}	4.8×10^{-3}	4.4×10^{-3}
	20	0	0	0.03	0.03
	30	0	0	0.03	0.02

6.1 How Do the Proposed Online Strategies Compare to the Precognition Strategy in Terms of Total Operating Cost?

The objective of answering this question is to quantitatively determine how the performance of the two proposed online placement strategies compares to that of the off-line placement strategy. As mentioned in the previous section, if the search space is large, the Precognition placement strategy cannot achieve an approximate optimal solution in a feasible time. Therefore, to address this question, we perform experiments with a reduced number of users and a shortened time window. This is done by randomly selecting an appropriate number of users (and the corresponding workloads, shortened to the given time window length) from the original trace. For the Precognition strategy, we set the *Temperature* parameter to $10e+11$, and the *CoolingFactor* parameter to 0.995, to ensure it obtains a solution within a reasonable amount of time. We collect the results returned by the three algorithms and calculate the difference in total operating cost using the following equation:

$$\text{difference} = \frac{\text{cost}_{\text{(proposed)}} - \text{cost}_{\text{(Precognition)}}}{\text{cost}_{\text{(Precognition)}}}$$

In Table 2, we show the differences between the total operating costs achieved with the two proposed strategies and that for the Precognition strategy for various numbers of users (i.e., 3, 5, and 10 users) and time window lengths (i.e., 1, 3, 5, 10, 20, and 30 time slots). As observed, **The total operating costs achieved with the two online placement strategies are pretty close to the approximate optimal values returned by Precognition; the maximum difference in total operating costs is around 8%.**

The results presented in Table 2 are not sufficient to conclusively state which of the two online algorithms performs better. This is due to the use of a reduced set of users and a short time window, which makes the difference between the resulting total costs non-significant. To better compare these two online algorithms, we perform experiments with more users (number of users is set to 536) and a larger time window (time window length is set to 144 time slots). Each placement strategy is evaluated with two workloads: one featuring compute-intensive applications, and one featuring bandwidth-intensive applications.

Figure 5 and Fig. 6 present the individual costs and the total operating costs achieved with the two online placement strategies in the experiments with bandwidth-intensive applications and compute-intensive applications, respectively. The intrinsic idea of the *Follow-me* strategy is to place applications in close proximity to users, so the requested applications are mainly allocated capacity on layer 1 EDCs, which causes resource costs to exceed those for the *Gale-Shapley* strategy. The resource cost difference between these two strategies is more significant for compute-intensive applications, as shown in Fig. 5a and Fig. 6a. Furthermore, the *Follow-me* strategy may migrate the requested applications with the users movement, resulting in higher migration costs, as shown in Fig. 5b and Fig. 6b. Consequently, **the Gale-Shapley strategy reduces the total cost by 6% and 17% as compared with the Follow-me strategy for experiments with bandwidth-intensive applications, and compute-intensive applications respectively.**

6.2 What Are the Execution Times of the Two Online Algorithms?

We now evaluate the scalability of our proposed algorithms, and their suitability for real MECs where real-time decision-making is required. As presented in Sect. 4, the *Follow-me* strategy's execution time depends on the number of users m and the number of layers l of the MEC infrastructure, i.e., its time complexity is $O(l \times m)$. Conversely, the *Gale-Shapley*-based strategy's execution time depends on the number of EDCs n and the number of users m, i.e., its time complexity is $O(n \times m)$. To confirm that both algorithms' execution times are linear with respect to the number of users in a fixed infrastructure, we measure the mean execution time per time slot for both strategies with varying number of users. In essence, we use the same emulated MECs as in previous experiments and increase the number of users per experiment.

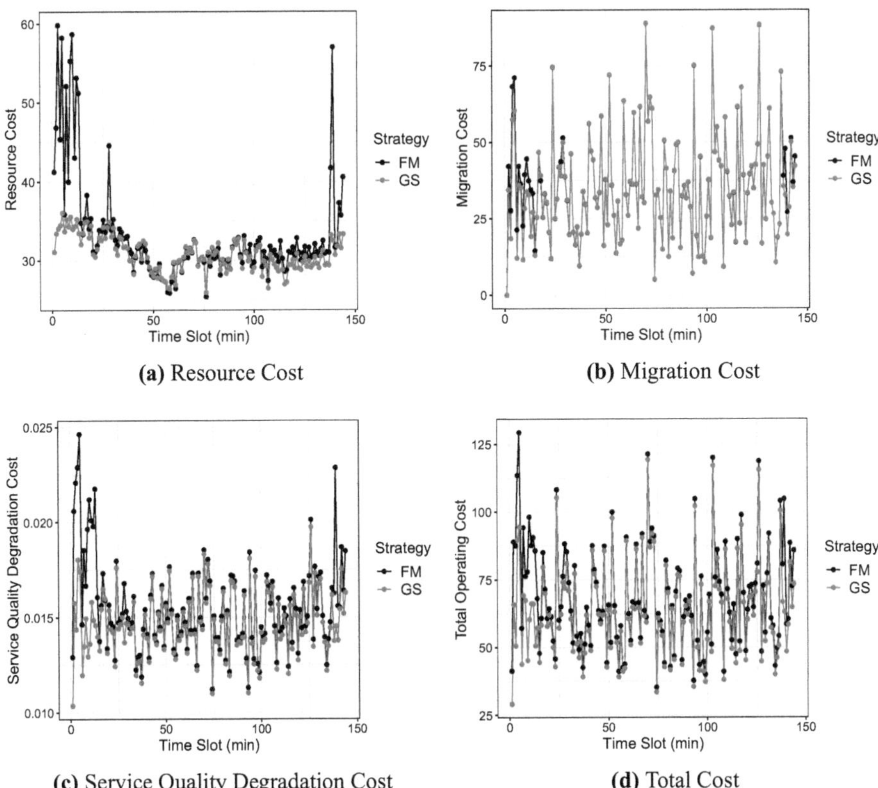

(a) Resource Cost

(b) Migration Cost

(c) Service Quality Degradation Cost

(d) Total Cost

Fig. 5. Individual costs and total operating costs achieved with the two online strategies for bandwidth intensive applications. FM: Follow-me strategy; GS: Gale-Shapley strategy.

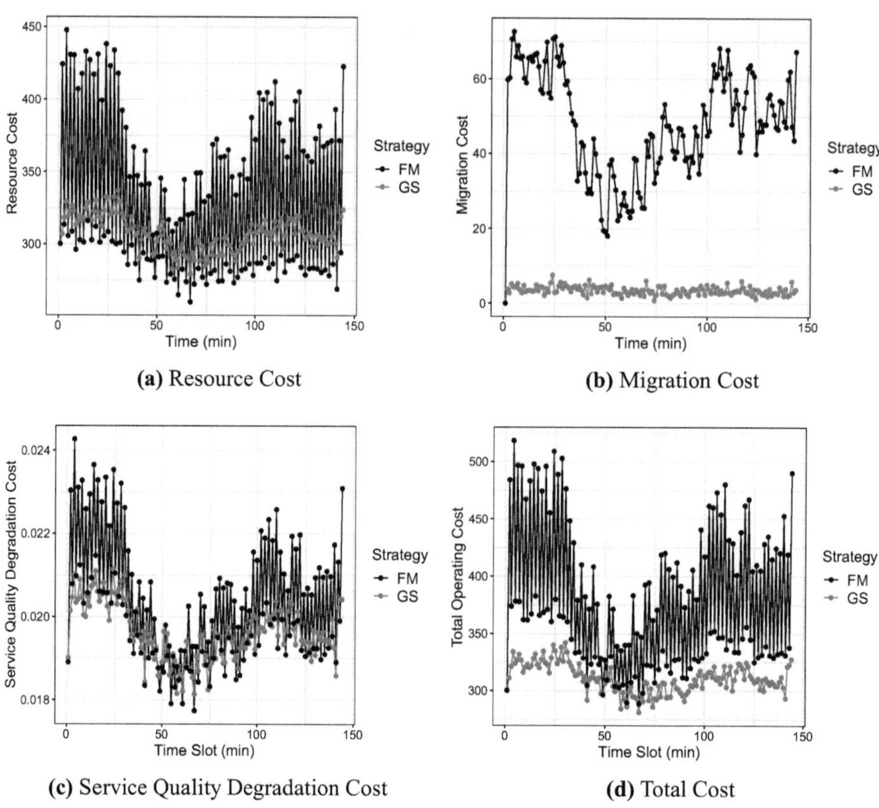

(a) Resource Cost

(b) Migration Cost

(c) Service Quality Degradation Cost

(d) Total Cost

Fig. 6. Individual costs and total operating costs achieved with the two online strategies for compute intensive applications. FM: Follow-me strategy; GS: Gale-Shapley strategy.

Figure 7 shows the mean execution time per time slot of the two algorithms as the number of users is raised from 500 to 5500 users. As observed, the execution time per time slot increases linearly with the number of users. Additionally, the execution time of the *Gale-Shapley* algorithm is initially much lower but then increases rapidly and roughly reaches the execution time of *Follow-me*. However, the execution times per time slot for both strategies (approximately below 100 ms for the experiment with 5500 users) are reasonably small compared to the length of the time slots (1 min). When adding more EDCs to the MEC, the execution time of the algorithms could be reduced further through parallelization. **Because the two proposed algorithms have such small execution times and achieve near-global-optimum placement, they are both suitable for deployment in real MEC systems.** They can help the system rapidly decide where to allocate application capacity among various EDCs to minimize the total operating cost.

6.3 Where Are Applications Placed by the Two Online Algorithms?

We analyse the placement produced by the two online strategies to better understand their behavior. By design, we expect the *Follow-me* strategy to place application in the closest EDC to the end-users. In order to prevent resource scarcity in EDCs and congestion in network links, the *Follow-me* strategy also utilizes resources from ancestor EDCs of the connected EDC to place applications. In contrast, the *Gale-Shapley* placement strategy aims to place applications in a way that returns the lowest resource cost, which in turn minimizes bandwidth consumption.

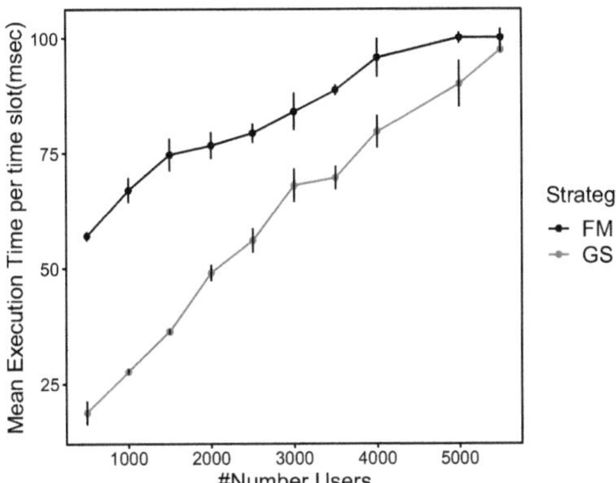

Fig. 7. Mean execution time per time slot for the two proposed online strategies with the number of users is set to values between 500 and 5500. FM: Follow-me strategy; GS: Gale-Shapley strategy.

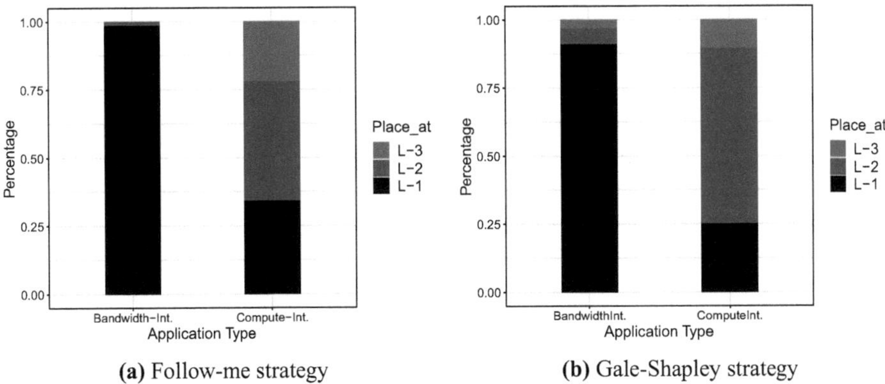

(a) Follow-me strategy   **(b)** Gale-Shapley strategy

Fig. 8. Behavior of the two online placement strategies for bandwidth-intensive and compute-intensive applications. L-1, L-2, L-3 denote layers 1, 2, and 3 in the simulated MEC, respectively.

Figure 8 shows where these applications are placed over the whole experiment. For the bandwidth-intensive applications, in order to reduce network bandwidth as much as possible, which helps reduce overall operating costs, the *Follow-me* strategy preferentially places applications at the EDC to which their user is directly connected. As a result, 99.85% of bandwidth-intensive applications are placed on the EDC to which their end-users is connected, and only 0.15% of such applications are placed on the layer 2 ancestor of the connecting EDCs. Similarly, the Gale-Shapley strategy places 91% of bandwidth-intensive applications on the connecting EDCs of the users, while approximately 6% are placed on layer 2 EDCs, and 3% on layer 3 EDCs.

For compute-intensive applications, both the *Follow-me* strategy and the *Gale-Shapley* strategy use larger amounts of resources from EDCs in higher layers, which have lower resources unit prices. More specifically, the *Follow-me* strategy places 21.9% of the applications in layer 3 EDCs, 43.9% in lever-2 EDCs, and leaving 34.2% of the applications are placed in the connected EDCs. In contrast, the *Gale-Shapley* strategy places 25.1% of the compute-intensive applications on the connected EDCs, 64% in layer 2 EDCs, and 10.4% in layer 3 EDCs. The observed results show that the *Gale-Shapley* strategy allows MECs to achieve better resource usage balance than the *Follow-me* strategy.

We further analyze the percentage of resource usage in each layer during a period of peak workload intensity with many simultaneous users. The *Follow-me* strategy fails to balance resource usage as effectively as the *Gale-Shapley* strategy: using the *Follow-me* strategy, EDCs in layer 1 reach 96.5% resource utilization, whereas those in layer 2 and layer 3 have average resource utilization values of only 40% and 0.04%, respectively. Conversely, the *Gale-Shapley* strategy balances the workload more efficiently with high-layer EDCs, hence the average resource utilization values for EDCs in layer 1, layer 2 and layer 3 are 54%, 17% and 11%, respectively.

We also measured the bandwidth usage (expressed as a percentage of the total capacity) in each link j of the simulated MEC in during experiments (Fig. 9). In general, the placement decisions taken by *Follow-me* increase the system's bandwidth consumption (i.e., data traffic must traverse more links) compared to those taken by *Gale-Shapley*. For experiments with compute-intensive applications (Fig. 9a), due to more applications being placed in layer 3, the *Follow-me* strategy makes a larger average bandwidth usage (i.e., 17%) on the links connecting layer 2 and layer 3 as compared to the *Gale-Shapley* strategy (i.e., 1.9%). Furthermore, the average bandwidth usage on the links connecting layer 1 and layer 2 when using the *Follow-me* strategy is also greater than when using the *Gale-Shapley* strategy (24% versus 18%).

In the experiments with bandwidth-intensive applications (Fig. 9b), the *Follow-me* strategy only uses network links connecting layer 1 and layer 2 to transfer applications data; the observed average bandwidth usage on these links is 2.2%. Conversely, the *Gale-Shapley* strategy distributes applications bandwidth to the network links in the higher layer; as a result, the observed average bandwidth usage on the links between layer 1 and layer 2 is 0.9%, while that for links between layer 2 and layer 3 is 0.11%.

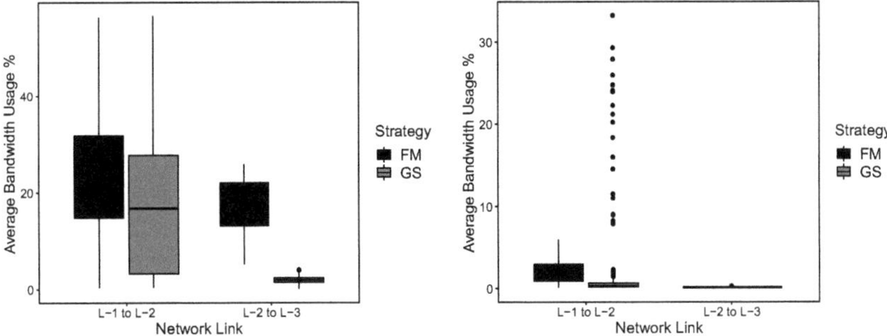

(a) Experiment with compute-intensive applications

(b) Experiment with bandwidth-intensive applications

Fig. 9. Bandwidth usage in the network links of the MEC.

Our result confirms the finding in [12], which shows the benefits of having the intermediate layer of EDCs in terms of operating cost saving, avoiding compute capacity scarcity and network congestion in MECs.

7   Conclusion and Future Work

In this paper, we address the problem of placing stateful applications in MECs. First, we thoroughly model the workloads, applications, and infrastructures to be expected in MECs. We then formulate the various costs associated with operating the application, namely resource cost, migration cost, and service quality degradation cost. Finally, we propose two efficient online placement algorithms, *Follow-me* and *Gale-Shapley*-based algorithm. Our experimental results show that both of these algorithms can help MECs rapidly decide where to place allocate capacity for applications, achieving total operating costs that are no more than 8% higher than the approximate global optimal returned by an offline precognition algorithm. The *Gale-Shapley*-based algorithm achieves better results than the *Follow-me* algorithm, with up to 17% total operating cost reduction while helping MECs to effectively balance workloads to mitigate resource scarcity.

Several promising directions remain for future research. First, the proposed placement algorithms in this study treat all applications uniformly. In practice, however, some mission-critical applications may have strict locality requirements and must be hosted on resources within EDCs located near end-users. To address this, we aim to extend the current application model by incorporating application priorities and adapting the placement algorithms accordingly. Second, we plan to explore distributed placement algorithms that can be executed across all EDCs. A key objective will be to ensure that the execution time of these distributed algorithms is independent of the number of EDCs, enhancing their scalability.

References

1. Balouek-Thomert, D., Renart, E.G., Zamani, A.R., Simonet, A., Parashar, M.: Towards a computing continuum: enabling edge-to-cloud integration for data-driven workflows. Int. J. High Perform. Comput. Appl. **33**(6), 1159–1174 (2019). https://doi.org/10.1177/1094342019877

2. Cardellini, V., Nardelli, M., Luzi, D.: Elastic stateful stream processing in storm. In: 2016 International Conference on High Performance Computing & Simulation (HPCS), pp. 583–590. IEEE (2016). https://doi.org/10.1109/HPCSim.2016.7568388

3. Chanh, N., Cristian, K., Erik, E.: State-aware application placement in mobile edge clouds. In: 14th International Conference on Cloud Computing and Services Science (CLOSER 2024), pp. 117–128 (2024). https://doi.org/10.5220/0012326300003711

4. Cohen, I., Chiasserini, C.F., Giaccone, P., Scalosub, G.: Dynamic service provisioning in the edge-cloud continuum with bounded resources. IEEE/ACM Trans. Networking **31**(6), 3096–3111 (2023). https://doi.org/10.1109/TNET.2023.3271674

5. Dally, W.J., Towles, B.P.: Principles and practices of interconnection networks. Elsevier Science (2004)

6. Fisher, M.L., Jaikumar, R., Van Wassenhove, L.N.: A multiplier adjustment method for the generalized assignment problem. Manage. Sci. **32**(9), 1095–1103 (1986). https://doi.org/10.1287/mnsc.32.9.1095

7. Gagliardi, J.D., Munger, T.S.: Content delivery network, US Patent 7,962,580 (2011)

8. Gale, D., Shapley, L.S.: College admissions and the stability of marriage. Am. Math. Mon. **69**(1), 9–15 (1962). https://doi.org/10.2307/2312726

9. Gao, B., Zhou, Z., Liu, F., Xu, F.: Winning at the starting line: joint network selection and service placement for mobile edge computing. In: IEEE INFOCOM 2019-IEEE Conference on Computer Communications, pp. 1459–1467. IEEE (2019). https://doi.org/10.1109/INFOCOM.2019.8737543

10. He, X., Xu, H., Xu, X., Chen, Y., Wang, Z.: An efficient algorithm for microservice placement in cloud-edge collaborative computing environment. IEEE Trans. Serv. Comput. (2024). https://doi.org/10.1109/TSC.2024.3399650

11. Ksentini, A., Taleb, T., Chen, M.: A Markov decision process-based service migration procedure for follow me cloud. In: 2014 IEEE International Conference on Communications (ICC), pp. 1350–1354. IEEE (2014). https://doi.org/10.1109/ICC.2014.6883509

12. Mehta, A., Tärneberg, W., Klein, C., Tordsson, J., Kihl, M., Elmroth, E.: How beneficial are intermediate layer data centers in mobile edge networks? In: 2016 IEEE 1st International Workshops on Foundations and Applications of Self* Systems (FAS* W), pp. 222–229. IEEE (2016). https://doi.org/10.1109/FAS-W.2016.55

13. Moore, H.L.: A moving equilibrium of demand and supply. Q. J. Econ. **39**(3), 357–371 (1925). https://doi.org/10.2307/1882433

14. Moreschini, S., Pecorelli, F., Li, X., Naz, S., Hästbacka, D., Taibi, D.: Cloud continuum: the definition. IEEE Access **10**, 131876–131886 (2022). https://doi.org/10.1109/ACCESS.2022.3229185

15. Moudi, M., Othman, M.: On the relation between network throughput and delay curves. Automatika **61**(3), 415–424 (2020). https://doi.org/10.1080/00051144.2020.1774731

16. Nguyen, C., Klein, C., Elmroth, E.: Multivariate LSTM-based location-aware workload prediction for edge data centers. In: 2019 19th IEEE/ACM International Symposium on Cluster, Cloud and Grid Computing (CCGRID), pp. 341–350. IEEE (2019). https://doi.org/10.1109/CCGRID.2019.00048

17. Ouyang, T., Li, R., Chen, X., Zhou, Z., Tang, X.: Adaptive user-managed service placement for mobile edge computing: an online learning approach. In: IEEE INFOCOM 2019-IEEE Conference on Computer Communications, pp. 1468–1476. IEEE (2019). https://doi.org/10.1109/INFOCOM.2019.8737560

18. Pantel, L., Wolf, L.C.: On the impact of delay on real-time multiplayer games. In: Proceedings of the 12th International Workshop on Network and Operating Systems Support for Digital Audio and Video, pp. 23–29. Association for Computing Machinery (2002). https://doi.org/10.1145/507670.507674

19. Piorkowski, M., Sarafijanovoc-Djukic, N., Grossglauser, M.: CRAWDAD dataset epfl/mobility (v. 2009-02-24) (2009). https://crawdad.org/epfl/mobility/20090224. https://doi.org/10.15783/C7J010

20. Rac, S., Brorsson, M.: Cost-aware service placement and scheduling in the edge-cloud continuum. ACM Trans. Archit. Code Optim. **21**(2), 1–24 (2024). https://doi.org/10.1145/3640823

21. Sarkohaki, F., Sharifi, M.: Service placement in fog–cloud computing environments: a comprehensive literature review. J. Supercomput. 1–33 (2024). https://doi.org/10.1007/s11227-024-06151-4

22. Tärneberg, W., et al.: Dynamic application placement in the mobile cloud network. Futur. Gener. Comput. Syst. **70**, 163–177 (2017). https://doi.org/10.1016/j.future.2016.06.021

23. Tong, L., Li, Y., Gao, W.: A hierarchical edge cloud architecture for mobile computing. In: IEEE INFOCOM 2016-The 35th Annual IEEE International Conference on Computer Communications, pp. 1–9. IEEE (2016). https://doi.org/10.1109/INFOCOM.2016.7524340

24. Ullah, A., et al.: Orchestration in the cloud-to-things compute continuum: taxonomy, survey and future directions. J. Cloud Comput. **12**(1), 135 (2023). https://doi.org/10.1186/s13677-023-00516-5

25. Urgaonkar, R., Wang, S., He, T., Zafer, M., Chan, K., Leung, K.K.: Dynamic service migration and workload scheduling in edge-clouds. Perform. Eval. **91**, 205–228 (2015). https://doi.org/10.1016/j.peva.2015.06.013

26. Van Laarhoven, P.J., Aarts, E.H.: Simulated annealing. In: Simulated Annealing: Theory and Applications, pp. 7–15. Springer (1987). https://doi.org/10.1007/978-94-015-7744-1_2

27. Wang, L., Jiao, L., He, T., Li, J., Mühlhäuser, M.: Service entity placement for social virtual reality applications in edge computing. In: IEEE INFOCOM 2018-IEEE Conference on Computer Communications, pp. 468–476. IEEE (2018). https://doi.org/10.1109/INFOCOM.2018.8486411

28. Wang, S., Zafer, M., Leung, K.K.: Online placement of multi-component applications in edge computing environments. IEEE Access **5**, 2514–2533 (2017). https://doi.org/10.1109/ACCESS.2017.2665971

29. Yang, B., Chai, W.K., Xu, Z., Katsaros, K.V., Pavlou, G.: Cost-efficient NFV-enabled mobile edge-cloud for low latency mobile applications. IEEE Trans. Netw. Serv. Manage. **15**(1), 475–488 (2018). https://doi.org/10.1109/TNSM.2018.2790081

30. Zervas, N.: White paper: understanding and reducing latency in video compression systems (2013). https://www.cast-inc.com/blog/white-paper-reducing-video-latency/. Accessed 30 Sept 2020

Edge AI Collaborative Learning: Bayesian Approaches to Uncertainty Estimation

Gleb Radchenko[1(✉)] [iD] and Victoria Andrea Fill[2] [iD]

[1] Silicon Austria Labs, Sandgasse 34, 8010 Graz, Austria
gleb.radchenko@silicon-austria.com
[2] FH Joanneum, Alte Poststraße 149, 8020 Graz, Austria
victoria.fill@edu.fh-joanneum.at

Abstract. Recent advancements in edge computing have significantly enhanced the AI capabilities of Internet of Things (IoT) devices. However, these advancements introduce new challenges in knowledge exchange and resource management, particularly addressing the spatiotemporal data locality in edge computing environments. This study examines algorithms and methods for deploying distributed machine learning within autonomous, network-capable, AI-enabled edge devices. We focus on determining confidence levels in learning outcomes considering the spatial variability of data encountered by independent agents. Using collaborative mapping as a case study, we explore the application of the Distributed Neural Network Optimization (DiNNO) algorithm extended with Bayesian neural networks (BNNs) for uncertainty estimation. We implement a 3D environment simulation using the Webots platform to simulate collaborative mapping tasks, decouple the DiNNO algorithm into independent processes for asynchronous network communication in distributed learning, and integrate distributed uncertainty estimation using BNNs. Our experiments demonstrate that BNNs can effectively support uncertainty estimation in a distributed learning context, with precise tuning of learning hyperparameters crucial for effective uncertainty assessment. Notably, applying Kullback–Leibler divergence for parameter regularization resulted in a 12–30% reduction in validation loss during distributed BNN training compared to other regularization strategies.

Keywords: Edge computing · Edge learning · Distributed machine learning · Fog computing · Machine learning · IoT

1 Introduction

Recent advancements in edge computing have significantly increased the computational capabilities of Internet of Things (IoT) devices, enabling more complex data processing at the network edge [17,25,35]. This evolution in edge device capabilities introduces new challenges and opportunities in distributed data processing and analysis.

Integrating advanced processing capabilities into edge devices aims to optimize local data handling and enhance device autonomy. This approach is particularly relevant when low-latency processing, data privacy, and network efficiency are critical. However, implementing machine learning (ML) algorithms on edge devices introduces several challenges:

C. Pahl and M. van Steen (Eds.): CLOSER 2024, CCIS 2851, pp. 124–145, 2026.
https://doi.org/10.1007/978-3-032-17286-0_6

- **Distributed Learning.** How can we effectively implement distributed learning on edge devices, transitioning from traditional inference-only models to active participation in the learning process while ensuring data privacy and efficient knowledge sharing? [18]
- **Resource Management and Communication Efficiency.** How do we optimally manage limited resources (e.g., power, processing capabilities, network bandwidth) on edge devices while maintaining efficient communication for data and model updates in dynamic network conditions? [24, 27]
- **Spatio-Temporal Locality and Non-IID Data.** What strategies most effectively incorporate localized and non-IID data to improve accuracy in distributed ML models? Evaluating the uncertainty at the level of both the individual agent and the aggregated model is essential. [12, 38]

1.1 Contribution

This study focuses on algorithms and methods for deploying distributed ML within autonomous, network-capable, sensor-equipped, AI-enabled edge devices. Specifically, it addresses determining confidence levels in learning outcomes, considering the spatial variability of data sets encountered by independent agents. To address this issue, we investigate the potential of the Distributed Neural Network Optimization (DiNNO) algorithm [39], aiming to extend it for organizing distributed data processing and uncertainty estimation using Bayesian neural networks (BNN) [12].

Our research examines the interactions of AI-enabled edge devices within a collaborative mapping task. To meet our objectives, we need to address the following tasks:

1. Decoupling the DiNNO algorithm implementation into independent processes, enabling asynchronous network communication for distributed learning.
2. Integrating distributed uncertainty estimation into the resulting neural network models by applying BNNs and evaluating the applicability of BNNs in the context of distributed learning.
3. Implementing the proposed approaches within a case study: simulation of robots, augmented with LiDAR sensors for environmental mapping, navigating a 3D environment using the Webots platform.
4. Evaluating the effectiveness of distributed uncertainty estimation using BNNs in a distributed learning context, including tuning of learning hyperparameters and applying Kullback–Leibler divergence for NN parameter regularization.

This paper is an extended version of the work entitled "Uncertainty Estimation in Multi-Agent Distributed Learning for AI-Enabled Edge Devices" [26], which was presented at the 14th International Conference on Cloud Computing and Services Science (CLOSER). This extended version expands upon the previous work by providing an expanded analysis of distributed ML algorithms and evaluating the feasibility of an online learning approach within the collaborative mapping case.

1.2 Outline

The remainder of this paper is structured as follows. In Sect. 2, we provide an overview of the related work in distributed edge-based ML methods and Bayesian Neural Networks. Section 3 presents the collaborative mapping case study. Sections 4 and 5 elaborate on the distributed edge learning approach and uncertainty estimation method. In Sect. 6, we describe the implementation and evaluation of the proposed methods. Finally, Sect. 7 presents conclusions and suggestions for future work.

2 Related Work

2.1 Edge Learning Methods

Edge computing has recently enabled local devices to perform AI tasks that were once limited to centralized systems. Initially, these devices only supported edge-based inference, using pre-trained models to process local data [16,30]. However, with the development of Edge Learning (EL), these devices can now both train and update models locally [22]. By enabling data processing directly where it is generated, EL improves adaptability and personalization. Moreover, because the data remains on edge devices and is not transferred to centralized cloud servers, EL reduces bandwidth usage and mitigates privacy risks [32,33,40]. This advancement not only enhances the capabilities of edge devices but also marks a significant step forward in the field of distributed ML [11].

Distributed ML algorithms can be categorized based on their communication mechanisms, which primarily involve the exchange of model parameters, model outputs, or hidden activations. These exchanges are typically facilitated through peer-to-peer or client-server architectures [24]. Among the various approaches to organizing distributed and edge learning, the most widely used methods include Federated Learning, Federated Distillation, Split Learning, and a range of decentralized learning techniques based on the Alternating Direction Method of Multipliers and its derivatives.

Federated Learning (FL). (see Fig. 1a) orchestrates the periodic transmission of local training parameters from edge nodes to the Federated Learning Server. The server sends the global model P to all edge nodes. Each edge node then trains the model on its local data $[X_i, Y_i]$ collected from sensors, updating its local parameters p_i. These local parameters are returned to the server and aggregated ($\text{AGGREGATE}(p_{1..n})$) to update the global model P. This updated global model is then distributed back to the edge nodes, and the process repeats iteratively.

FL has emerged as a promising strategy for EL, offering a viable solution to various challenges in edge computing environments, including the potential to preserve data privacy by avoiding the need for raw data exchange. Originally proposed to enable distributed learning using mobile devices [20], FL can enhance communication efficiency by allowing for adjustable transmission intervals, which helps to optimize resource usage and reduce bandwidth demands [18]. The authors of [1] further emphasize that FL addresses issues such as unwanted bandwidth loss, data privacy concerns, and legal

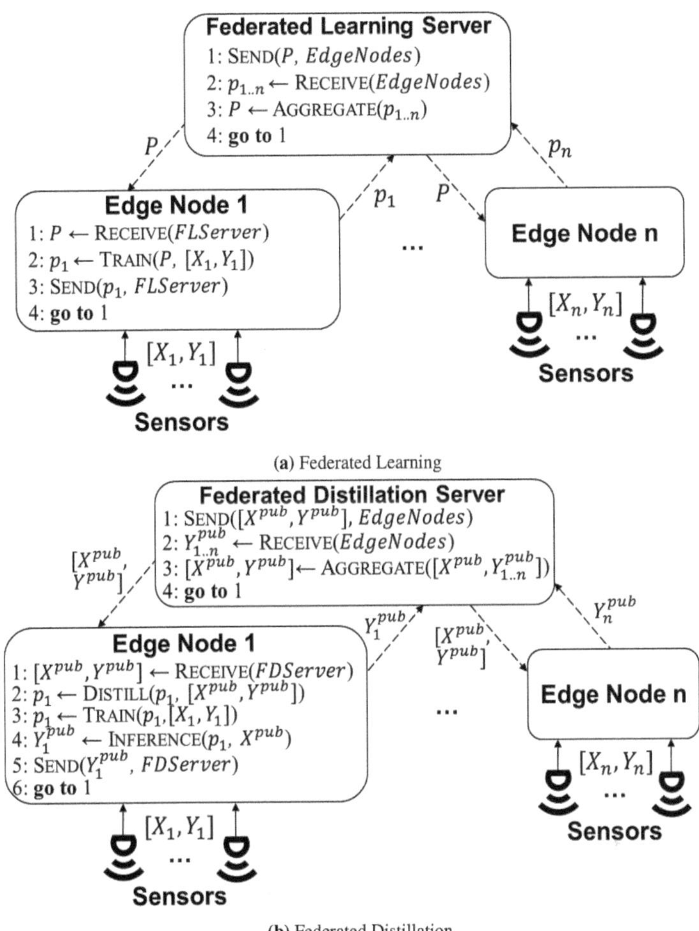

(a) Federated Learning

(b) Federated Distillation

Fig. 1. Graphical representation of (a) Federated Learning and (b) Federated Distillation process.

compliance. They highlight that FL facilitates the co-training of models across distributed clients—from mobile phones to automobiles and hospitals—via a centralized server while ensuring that the data remains localized. The authors of [23] propose an extension of the FL model called FedFog designed to enable FL over a wireless fog-cloud system. The authors address key challenges such as non-identically distributed data and user heterogeneity. The FedFog algorithm performs local aggregation of gradient parameters at fog servers and a global training update in the cloud.

On the other hand, recent research has highlighted several limitations of FL, particularly in terms of privacy and robustness. For instance, FL is vulnerable to malicious servers and actors, which can compromise the privacy of sensitive information [21]. Furthermore, the work of Lyu et al. [19] discusses how these vulnerabilities might undermine the privacy guarantees typically associated with FL.

Federated Distillation (FD). (see Fig. 1b) takes a distinct approach to communicating knowledge obtained during local training. Unlike traditional FL, which involves transmitting model parameters, FD leverages model distillation. In this technique, knowledge is transferred from one model (the "teacher") to another (the "student") by training the student on the teacher's outputs (soft-label predictions) rather than the raw data. A widely known application of knowledge distillation is model compression, through which the knowledge of a large pre-trained model may be transferred to a smaller one [2].

Instead of sharing the parameterization of locally trained models, the knowledge in FD is communicated through soft-label predictions on a public distillation dataset [28]. FD orchestrates an iterative knowledge-sharing process between a central server and multiple edge nodes. At the start of each round, the server sends aggregated soft labels Y^{pub} on a public dataset X^{pub} to the participating edge nodes. Each edge node then performs the following steps:

1. **Distillation.** The node updates its local model using the soft labels received, incorporating global knowledge.
2. **Local Training.** The node further refines the distilled model on its private local data $[X_i, Y_i]$, improving the local model's performance.
3. **Prediction.** The node generates new soft labels Y_i^{pub} by running the refined model on the public dataset X^{pub}.
4. **Communication.** These newly generated soft labels Y_i^{pub} are returned to the server.

The server aggregates the soft labels received from all participating nodes (AGGREGATE$[X^{pub}, Y_{1..n}^{pub}]$) to update the global public dataset. This iterative process improves collective knowledge while ensuring that raw local data remains private.

The soft-label exchange in FD significantly reduces the data that needs to be transferred during training compared to the exchange of full model parameters in FL. According to the authors of [36], FD can reduce communication costs by up to 94.89% compared to the classical FedAvg [20] FL method. Another advantage of FD is its flexibility in accommodating different model architectures on edge nodes. Since model parameters are not exchanged between the edge nodes and the FD server, the models on the server and the edge nodes can vary significantly in structure. Additionally, FD effectively addresses challenges in collaborative learning under non-independent and identically distributed (non-IID) data conditions. The Selective-FD algorithm proposed in [29] demonstrates high accuracy even in severe non-IID environments, enabling a communication-efficient and heterogeneity-adaptive EL.

Split Learning (SL). (see Fig. 2a) partitions a multi-layer neural network (NN) into segments, enabling the training of large-scale deep NNs that exceed the memory capacities of a single edge device [34]. This approach divides the NN into two segments: a lower NN segment p_i, which resides on the edge devices containing the raw data, and an upper NN segment P_{server}, hosted on a parameter server [9]. The NN cut layer serves as the boundary between these segments.

During the forward pass, the edge devices compute the activations at the NN cut layer and transmit these activations a_i, along with the true labels Y_i, to the parameter server. The parameter server then uses these activations as inputs to the upper NN

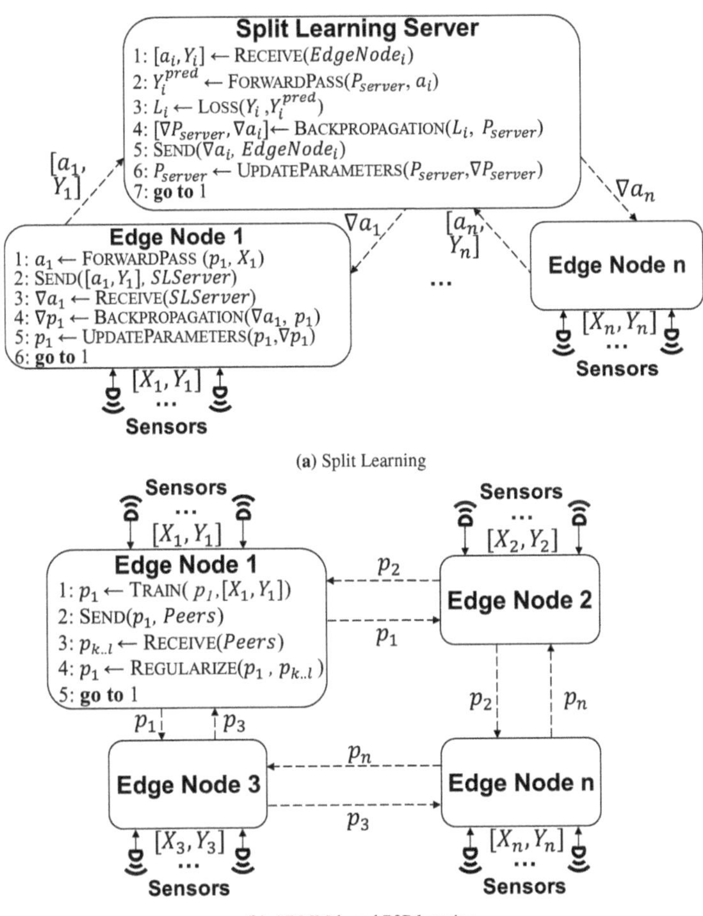

(a) Split Learning

(b) ADMM-based P2P learning

Fig. 2. Graphical representation of (a) Split Learning and (b) a decentralized learning process using the Alternating Direction Method of Multipliers.

segment to continue the forward pass and compute the final predictions Y_i^{pred}. Subsequently, the server calculates the loss L_i by comparing the predictions with the true labels and initiates the backward pass.

The gradients ∇a_i, computed at the NN cut layer during backpropagation, are returned to the edge devices. The edge devices then use these gradients to update the weights of the lower NN segments, completing the training loop. This iterative process continues until the model converges.

While this description covers the most basic form of Split Learning, it's important to note that several SL implementations differ in how the NN is partitioned and distributed between the edge and server nodes [10,37]. These variants address different challenges and trade-offs, particularly regarding communication efficiency, which remains an active area of research [14].

Alternating Direction Method of Multipliers (ADMM): is a general-purpose decentralized convex optimization algorithm, particularly well suited to problems in applied statistics and machine learning. It takes the form of a decomposition-coordination procedure, in which the solutions to small local subproblems are coordinated to find a solution to a large global problem [5]. Distributed machine learning algorithms derived from ADMM, such as Distributed Neural Network Optimization (DiNNO) [39] and Group Alternating Direction Method of Multipliers (GADMM) [8], enable decentralized learning without the need for a coordinating server by allowing direct communication between the edge nodes in a peer-to-peer (P2P) manner (see Fig. 2b). The strong convergence properties of ADMM ensure that all learning P2P agents eventually reach a consensus on the machine-learning model parameters.

In these methods, each edge node independently trains its local model parameters p_i on its private data $[X_i, Y_i]$ collected from sensors. The trained parameters p_i are then shared with neighboring edge nodes. Each node receives the parameters $p_{k..l}$ from its peers, which are then used to regularize its model by incorporating the knowledge from the neighboring nodes. This process is repeated as nodes exchange and regularize their model parameters.

One of the critical issues with such P2P learning methods is the communication overhead, which is proportional to the number of model parameters and learning agents. This overhead can limit the effectiveness of ADMM-derived methods in supporting deep NNs [8]. However, despite this limitation, ADMM-derived methods offer a decentralized alternative to FL, particularly when a central server is unavailable or impractical.

2.2   Uncertainty Estimation and Bayesian Neural Networks

Bayesian Neural Networks. In a conventional NN architecture, a linear neuron is characterized by a weight (w), a bias (b), and an activation function (f_{act}). Given an input x, a single linear neuron performs the following operation:

$$y = f_{act}(w \cdot x + b) \tag{1}$$

where y is the output of the neuron.

However, as we explore more complex and uncertain environments, the deterministic nature of classical NNs becomes a limitation. The ability of NNs to generalize to data that lies outside the training distribution remains an area of ongoing research. The potential lack of generalization, coupled with the inherent instability of NNs, can lead to the appearance of false structures in their predictions. These false structures, often referred to as hallucinations, may occur when the reconstruction method incorrectly estimates parts of the initial data set that either did not contribute to the observed measurement data or cannot be recovered in a stable manner [4]. A promising approach to addressing these challenges is using Bayesian neural networks, which incorporate uncertainty estimates directly into their predictions.

Bayesian Neural Networks (BNNs) adopt a Bayesian framework to train neural networks with stochastic behavior [12]. Instead of relying on fixed, deterministic values for weights and biases, BNNs employ probability distributions, typically denoted as $P(w)$

for weights and $P(b)$ for biases. These distributions are often approximated by Gaussian distributions, with the mean and standard deviation determined from the training data. As a result, a Bayesian neuron does not produce a single output but rather a range of possible values. The operation of a Bayesian Linear neuron can thus be described as:

$$P(y|x) = f_{act}(P(w) \times x + P(b)) \tag{2}$$

In the context of BNNs, the Gaussian distributions for both weights and biases are characterized by a mean (μ) and a standard deviation (σ). Specifically, the weight distribution $P(w)$ is modeled as a Gaussian with a mean w_μ and a standard deviation w_σ, where:

$$w_\sigma = \log(1 + e^{w_\rho}) \tag{3}$$

The parameter w_ρ ensures that the standard deviation remains positive. Similarly, the bias distribution $P(b)$ is represented by a Gaussian with a mean b_μ and a standard deviation b_σ, defined as:

$$b_\sigma = \log(1 + e^{b_\rho}) \tag{4}$$

In the forward pass of a Bayesian neuron, weights and biases are drawn from their respective probability distributions for each neuron. These sampled values are then utilized to calculate the neuron's output. Throughout the training process, the parameters w_μ, w_ρ, b_μ, and b_ρ are adjusted to enhance the overall performance of the network.

Unlike traditional neural networks, where repeated forward passes yield the same output, BNNs generate different outputs with each forward pass due to the stochastic nature of the sampled weights and biases. After multiple passes, the mean and standard deviation of the outputs can be calculated, effectively capturing the uncertainty in the predictions. This ability to quantify uncertainty provides BNNs with the advantage of offering detailed insights into how confident the model is about each prediction.

Kullback-Leibler Divergence. Kullback-Leibler Divergence (KL Divergence) [6, 15] allows us to measure the difference between the Gaussian distributions representing the parameters in a BNN. KL Divergence quantifies the dissimilarity between two probability distributions and is calculated as:

$$D_{KL}(g||h) = \int g(x) \log\left(\frac{g(x)}{h(x)}\right) dx \tag{5}$$

where $g(x)$ and $h(x)$ are two probability density functions over the same domain.

As explained in [3], when the distributions $N_0(\mu_0, \sigma_0)$ and $N_1(\mu_1, \sigma_1)$ are both normal, Eq. (5) may be reduced to:

$$D_{KL}(N_0||N_1) = \frac{1}{2}\left[\log\left(\frac{\sigma_1^2}{\sigma_0^2}\right) + \frac{\sigma_0^2 + (\mu_0 - \mu_1)^2}{\sigma_1^2} - 1\right] \tag{6}$$

In the context of BNNs, KL Divergence is applied to quantify the deviation of the network's parameter distributions from a predefined prior distribution. The total loss in a BNN is typically expressed as:

$$total_{loss} = base_{loss} + kl_{weight} \times kl_{loss} \tag{7}$$

where $base_{loss}$ corresponds to the standard loss function, such as Binary Cross-Entropy or Mean Squared Error; the term kl_{weight} represents a hyperparameter that controls the influence of uncertainty on the model's predictions; and kl_{loss} represents the sum of the KL Divergence between the distributions of the BNN parameters $N_0(\mu_0, \sigma_0)$ and a specified normal distribution $N_1(\mu_1, \sigma_1)$.

3   Collaborative Mapping Case Study

For our case study on edge AI collaborative learning, we focused on addressing a collaborative environment mapping problem using a network of robotic edge devices. These autonomous robots, each starting from different locations, work together to construct a comprehensive map of their surroundings by utilizing onboard sensors and sharing knowledge with each other.

Each robot is designed to update its local ML model with new data acquired from its sensors while also communicating with other robots via a network interface. The architecture of these AI-enabled edge devices is provided in Fig. 3. Each edge device is equipped with specialized computational cores tailored to handle specific tasks:

- Real-time core: Handles immediate sensor data processing and controls the actuators, ensuring timely responses to environmental changes.
- General-purpose core: Manages overall device operations and coordinates between different components.
- AI core: Supports the edge training cycle by processing the data, updating the model, and facilitating knowledge exchange with other devices in the network.

These components work together to ensure that each robot can process data locally and interact with its peers to contribute to a global understanding of the environment.

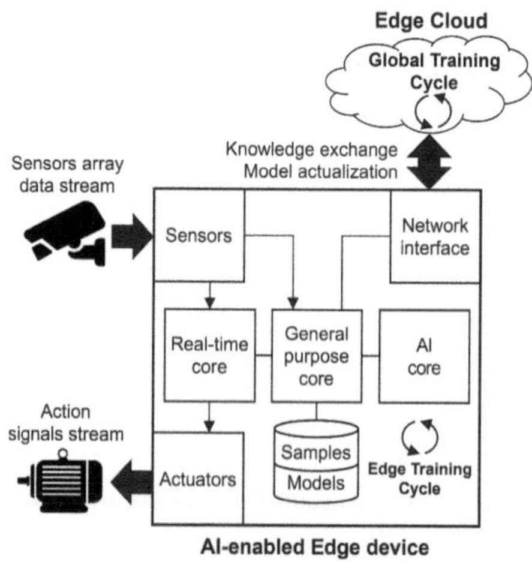

Fig. 3. Components of AI-Enabled edge device [26].

To address the distributed machine learning challenge in our study, we employed the Distributed Neural Network Optimization (DiNNO) algorithm [39]. DiNNO facilitates decentralized learning by allowing each robot to optimize its NN model locally and iteratively share the learned parameters with its neighbors. Unlike centralized methods that require aggregating all data at a central node, DiNNO operates over a mesh network where robots communicate directly, ensuring robustness against node failures and preserving data privacy.

DiNNO builds on the ADMM algorithm, allowing it to efficiently converge to a consensus on the NN parameters across all robots. The algorithm's ability to work with time-varying communication graphs and streaming data is particularly suited to the dynamic and distributed nature of multi-robot systems. Each robot refines its NN model using local sensory inputs. Then, it exchanges updated parameters with its neighbors, implementing a collective learning process that eventually aligns the models across the entire network.

In our experiment, we utilized the CubiCasa5K dataset [13] to generate floor plans for the environment mapping task. Figure 4 illustrates the paths taken by the robots during the mapping process. The solid colored lines represent the trajectories of various robots as they navigate the environment, with the red solid line highlighting a particular robot's path as it explores a designated area. The dotted line surrounding the robot indicates the range of its LiDAR sensor, which acts as a source for the training data.

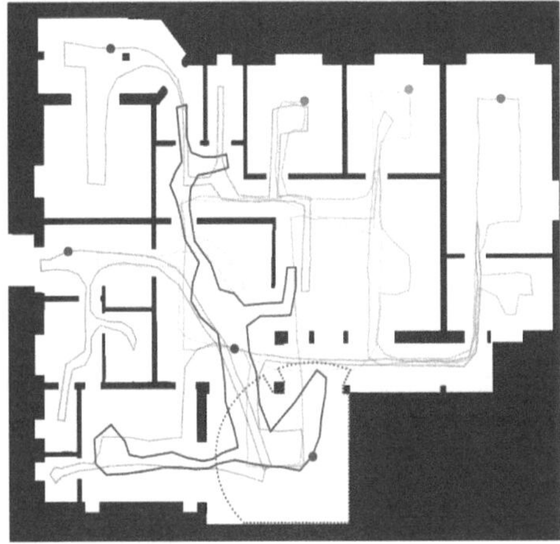

Fig. 4. Visualization of the environment map including starting points, exploration pathways, and LiDAR range for the robotic agents as described by [39]. Adapted from [26].

4   Peers State Exchange Algorithm

The original implementation of the DiNNO algorithm was constrained by several limitations that significantly impacted its applicability to edge AI collaborative learning.

The original framework featured a sequential approach to the learning process and a centralized experimental architecture, which could benefit from a more distributed design to simulate data exchange better. In this setup, agents were part of a monolithic data structure processed within a single, tightly coupled computational process. This design led to "quasi-agents" that directly accessed each other's memory during the learning process, which, while efficient, did not fully embrace the potential of distributed learning.

To overcome these limitations, we restructured the DiNNO algorithm implementation to make it suitable for edge computing environments. Each agent now operates autonomously, independently processing local LiDAR data and optimizing NN parameters. A key improvement in this updated approach is the introduction of an epoch-based decentralized consensus algorithm, which helps agents exchange NN parameters with each other in a peer-to-peer way (see Algorithm 1).

The peers state exchange algorithm starts with the following inputs: the maximum number of synchronization epochs ($MaxRound$), network socket ($Socket$), unique peer identifier (Id), and the initial state of the NN parameters ($State$). The algorithm uses two data structures to keep track of the communications process: $PeerComplete[]$, which monitors whether each peer has finished a round, and $PeerState[]$, which stores the current NN parameters for each peer.

The algorithm revolves around the P2P exchange of two message types: $State$ and $RoundComplete$. The $RoundComplete$ message signals the completion of a round by a peer, while the $State$ message contains the peer's NN parameters state for the current round. Including the $RoundComplete$ message along with a round finalization logic addresses the challenges posed by network latency—such as out-of-order messages, delayed status updates, and potential desynchronization between peers. To mitigate the latency issues, the algorithm ensures that a $RoundComplete$ message is dispatched by a peer only after successfully receiving all $State$ messages from the other peers. This ensures that no peer progresses to the subsequent round until all peers have synchronized on the current round, preventing the risk of desynchronization caused by delayed or missing messages.

When a peer receives a $State$ message from a future round, the algorithm triggers the FINISHROUND function, prompting the peer to align with the correct round. This mechanism manages out-of-order deliveries, ensuring consistency and synchronization across all agents.

This version of the algorithm assumes that all messages will eventually reach their intended recipients, excluding the consideration of scenarios involving agent malfunctions, computational halts, or permanent network failures that could result in irreversible message loss or total communication breakdown.

Algorithm 1. Peers State Exchange [26].

Require: $MaxRound, Socket, Id, State$
 1: **Initialize:** $Round, PeerComplete[], PeerState[]$
 2: $Message \leftarrow (State, 0)$
 3: SEND($Socket, Message, Id$)
 4: **while** $Round < MaxRound$ **do**
 5:     $(Message, PeerId) \leftarrow$ RECEIVE($Socket$)
 6:     **if** $Message$ is $RoundComplete$ **then**
 7:         $PeerComplete[PeerId] \leftarrow$ TRUE
 8:     **else**
 9:         **if** $Round < Message.Round$ **then**
10:             FINISHROUND
11:         **end if**
12:         $PeerState[PeerId] \leftarrow Message.State$
13:     **end if**
14:     **if** $\forall s \in PeerState, s \neq \emptyset$ **then**
15:         $State \leftarrow$ NodeUpdate($State, PeerState$)
16:         $\forall s \in PeerState, s \leftarrow \emptyset$
17:         $PeerComplete[Id] \leftarrow$ TRUE
18:         $PeerState[Id] \leftarrow State$
19:         $Message \leftarrow RoundComplete$
20:         SEND($Socket, Message, Id$)
21:     **end if**
22:     **if** $\forall p \in PeerComplete, p =$ TRUE **then**
23:         FINISHROUND
24:     **end if**
25: **end while**
26: **function** FINISHROUND
27:     $\forall p \in PeerComplete, p \leftarrow$ FALSE
28:     $Round \leftarrow Round + 1$
29:     $Message.State \leftarrow State$
30:     $Message.Round \leftarrow Round$
31:     SEND($Socket, Message, Id$)
32: **end function**

---

5   Distributed Uncertainty Estimation

To address uncertainty estimation in the distributed mapping problem, we developed a BNN incorporating Bayesian Linear Layers in the neural network (see Fig. 5).

The architecture of the BNN is detailed as follows:

- **Input Layer (2).** The input consists of coordinates x, y, representing a global position on the map.
- **SIREN Layer (256).** A layer with a sinusoidal activation function, designed for Neural Implicit Mapping, as described by [31].
- **4 x Bayesian Linear Layers (256).** Four Bayesian Linear Layers, each with 256 nodes and activated by the ReLU function. These layers are probabilistic and support uncertainty estimation.

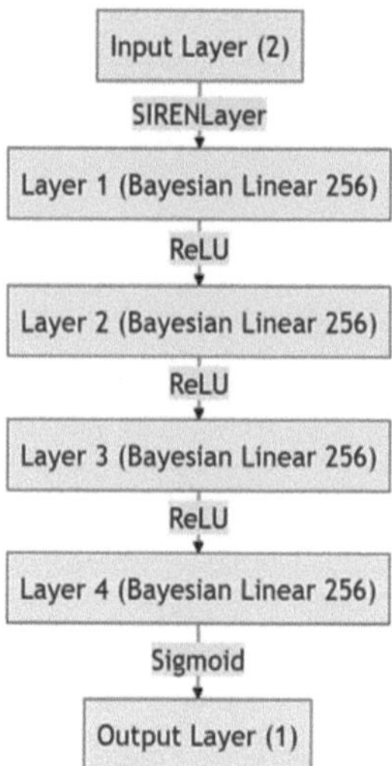

Fig. 5. Visualization of the proposed collaborative mapping BNN architecture.

- **Output Layer (1).** A linear layer with one node, activated by the Sigmoid function. An output of 0 indicates empty space, while an output of 1 indicates occupied space (e.g., a wall).

Unlike deterministic networks that produce only a single output, BNNs are distinguished by their ability to estimate prediction uncertainty. By conducting multiple forward passes to compute the mean and standard deviation of the outputs, BNNs provide valuable insights into the model's confidence for each mesh grid point. To correctly regularize the BNN parameters during the distributed learning phase, we developed Algorithm 2, which takes into account the specific roles of the median (μ) and standard deviation (ρ) parameters of BNN neurons. For regularizing the BNN ρ-parameters across models of individual actors, we employ KL Divergence, as detailed in Eq. (6).

Algorithm 2. Optimization of BNN Parameters [26].

Require: $Model, Optimizer_\mu, Optimizer_\rho, W_\mu, W_\rho, Iter, \theta_{\mathrm{reg}\mu}, \theta_{\mathrm{reg}\rho}, Duals_\mu, Duals_\rho$
1: **for** $i \leftarrow 1$ to $Iter$ **do**
2:     Reset gradients of $Optimizer_\mu$ and $Optimizer_\rho$
3:     $PredLoss \leftarrow \textsc{ComputeLoss}(Model)$
4:     $\theta_\mu, \theta_\rho \leftarrow \textsc{ExtractParameters}(Model)$
5:     $Reg_\mu \leftarrow \textsc{L2Regularization}(\theta_\mu, \theta_{\mathrm{reg}\mu})$
6:     $Reg_\rho \leftarrow D_{KL}(\theta_\rho, \theta_{\mathrm{reg}\rho})$
7:     $Loss_\mu \leftarrow PredLoss + \langle \theta_\mu, Duals_\mu \rangle + W_\mu \times Reg_\mu$
8:     $Loss_\rho \leftarrow \langle \theta_\rho, Duals_\rho \rangle + W_\rho \times Reg_\rho$
9:     $\textsc{UpdateParameters}(Optimizer_\mu, Loss_\mu)$
10:    $\textsc{UpdateParameters}(Optimizer_\rho, Loss_\rho)$
11: **end for**

---

6   Implementation and Evaluation of the Edge AI Collaborative Learning

To simulate a realistic environment for robotic exploration, we utilized floor plan data from the CubiCasa5K dataset to generate three-dimensional interior models in STL format. These models were subsequently imported into the Webots simulation platform, where TurtleBot robots were programmed to navigate through the space (see Fig. 6). In our simulation, the TurtleBots were equipped with essential sensors, including LiDAR, which introduced realistic sensor noise and measurement uncertainties.

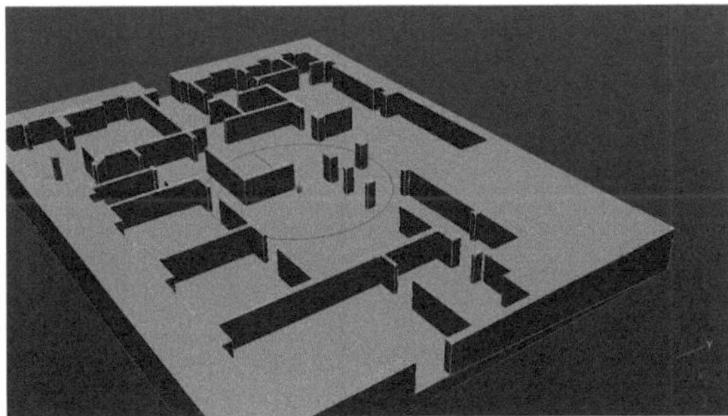

Fig. 6. Visualization of the 3D model of the environment generated from the floor plan showcasing a LiDAR-equipped TurtleBot navigating the space in a Webots simulation [26].

The environment was designed to represent real-world conditions, allowing for the testing of mapping algorithms. The experiment involved launching seven independent TurtleBot agents that gradually collected information from LiDAR sensors while exploring a virtual interior space. TurtleBot movement was controlled by a Python-based script that guided the robots through the environment. This controller managed robot orientation and movement using a compass and GPS data. The study assumed that all robots had access to global positioning information.

Agents' movement paths were predefined to create simulation programs for their interior navigation. LiDAR sensor data collection was simulated as a Webots data stream during navigation. The LiDAR sensor scanned the surroundings and updated an occupancy grid map, where each cell was classified as unknown, free, or occupied. LiDAR data was transformed to fit the Neural Implicit Mapping framework, converting raw scans into a point set with values ranging from 0 to 1. In this mapping, a value of 1 indicated the presence of a wall, while 0 represented empty space.

Within the experiment's framework, each agent ran as a separate Python process. Agent communication was implemented via direct TCP connections between processes on the same virtual local network. The ZeroMQ library was used for asynchronous data exchange. Containerization of agent processes was achieved using Singularity containers provided with GPU access. In the experiments outlined, all processes were initiated on GPU enabled computing nodes managed by the SLURM workload manager.

6.1 Uncertainty Evaluation: Individual Agent Case

To evaluate the effectiveness of the BNN architecture proposed in Sect. 5 for estimating uncertainty in NN outcomes, we designed an experiment to demonstrate how the BNN captures and represents uncertainty in its predictions, particularly in areas where the agent has no prior data. The robotic agent was trained exclusively on local data during the experiment without exchanging information with other agents. The visualization of the training results is presented in Fig. 7.

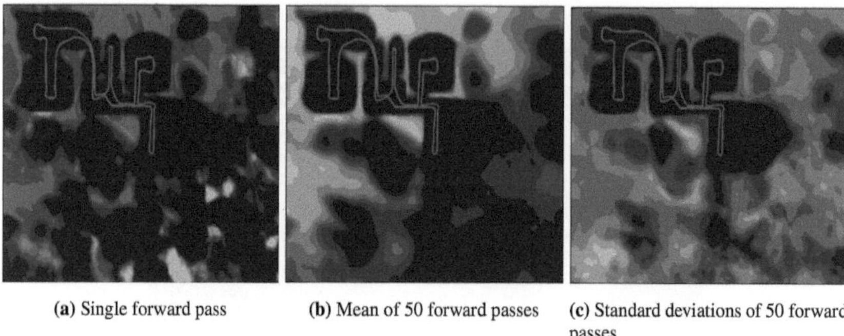

(a) Single forward pass   (b) Mean of 50 forward passes   (c) Standard deviations of 50 forward passes

Fig. 7. Visualization of the individual agent BNN training results. The red line represents the path of the single agent through the environment. (Color figure online)

To generate outputs from the BNN, 50 queries were made for each pair of input coordinates (x, y). Subsequently, a visualization was created to illustrate the mean values and standard deviations of the NN responses. The red line on the graph indicates the actual path taken by the agent, while the surrounding colors represent the network's prediction of the environment's state based on the agent's current understanding.

Subplot 7a depicts the results of a single forward pass through the BNN. This visualization displays a significant amount of noise in regions the agent has not explored, indicating high uncertainty in those areas. Subplot 7b shows the mean of 50 forward passes, resulting in a much smoother and more accurate representation of the investigated environment, highlighting the BNN's capability to refine its predictions by reducing uncertainty through repeated passes. Finally, subplot 7c illustrates the standard deviation across the 50 forward passes, effectively visualizing the uncertainty associated with the network's predictions. Higher standard deviations indicate regions where the network is less certain about its predictions, often corresponding to areas with less data or where the agent has less experience.

Following this initial test, we conducted a series of experiments to evaluate the impact of the kl_{weight} parameter from Eq. (7) on the training results. The visualization of the experiments results is presented in Fig. 8.

A low value of the kl_{weight} parameter was observed to lead to a low variance in the NN's results, which does not allow for distinguishing the hallucinations of the NN from areas with sufficient data to form a general understanding of the environment. onversely,

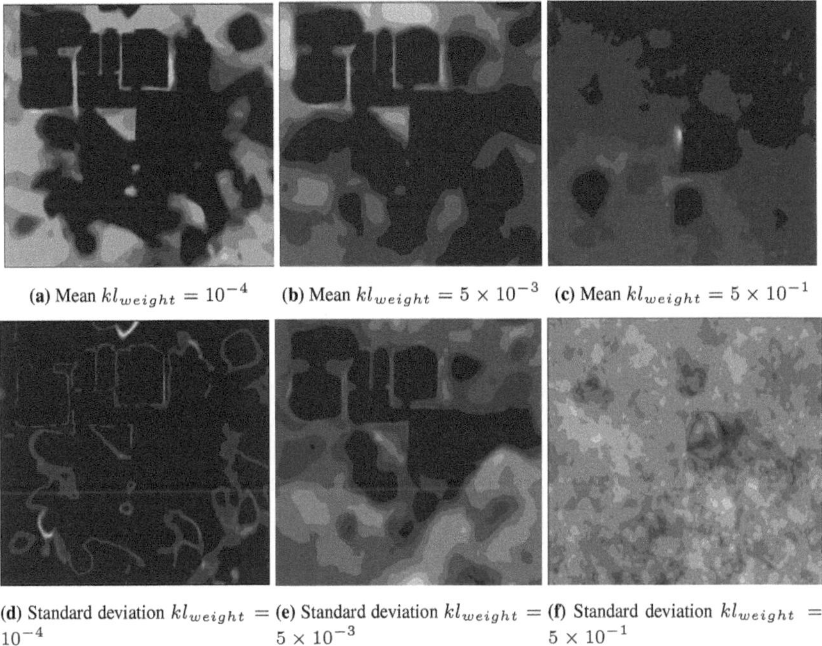

(a) Mean $kl_{weight} = 10^{-4}$ (b) Mean $kl_{weight} = 5 \times 10^{-3}$ (c) Mean $kl_{weight} = 5 \times 10^{-1}$

(d) Standard deviation $kl_{weight} = 10^{-4}$ (e) Standard deviation $kl_{weight} = 5 \times 10^{-3}$ (f) Standard deviation $kl_{weight} = 5 \times 10^{-1}$

Fig. 8. Comparative visualization of the influence of the kl_{weight} parameter on the single-agent uncertainty estimation. Adapted from [26].

a high kl_{weight} parameter value results in excessive noise and high uncertainty in the NN's results. Therefore, to ensure that the BNN provides an effective assessment of uncertainty, fine-tuning the kl_{weight} parameter during the training process is required.

6.2 Online Learning Process Evaluation

Previously, we explored the results derived from analyzing data sets collected and processed collectively after the agents completed their traversal. This approach is necessary due to the substantial processing power and energy resources required for NN training, which may not be readily available to autonomous edge devices operating in a mobile investigation mode.

To evaluate the applicability of online training—combining agent exploration with the learning process—we implemented a simulation that used real-time data gathering alongside a batch training approach. This simulation was built using the ZeroMQ library to implement the communication between components. A streamer broker was initiated as a subprocess from the Webots controller, while the NN training process was launched as a parallel subprocess, acting as the data receiver. The data-sending function was embedded directly within the Webots controller. As the robot traversed its path, it periodically sent LiDAR data to the broker after scanning a set number of positions. The NN training process then added this data to the training pool, allowing for a gradual compilation of training data as the path was navigated.

The experiment aimed to assess the effectiveness of the training process based on partial data collection. To structure this process, we introduced the "Communication Rounds" (CR) concept, which segmented the path into discrete parts, each representing a phase of data collection and subsequent training. The agent gathered LiDAR data for each CR segment and transmitted this information to the training algorithm for partial data training at the segment's end.

We specifically investigated two scenarios in our experiments:

- **Cumulative Data Retention (CDR).** In this scenario, the algorithm retained all previously received data, using it alongside new data for subsequent training sessions. This method was intended to continuously enrich the training dataset, potentially enhancing the NN's accuracy and adaptability.
- **Data Refresh (DR).** In contrast, this approach trained the NN solely on the newly acquired dataset for each CR, discarding all previous datasets. The only remnants of prior data were the pre-trained weights of the NN, which could influence the training outcome based on past learning but did not directly reuse old data.

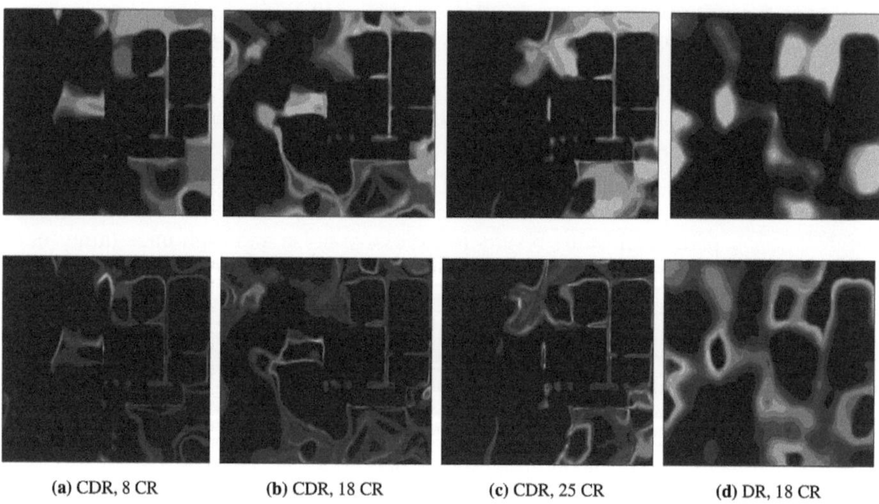

(a) CDR, 8 CR   (b) CDR, 18 CR   (c) CDR, 25 CR   (d) DR, 18 CR

Fig. 9. Visualization of the Mean (top row) and Standard Deviation (bottom row) of the online training process results under different configurations of Cumulative Data Retention (CDR) and Data Refresh (DR) scenarios.

The results of these experiments are visualized in Fig. 9. Each column in the figure corresponds to different configurations of the online training process, with varying numbers of communication rounds and the implementation of either Cumulative Data Retention (CDR) or Data Refresh (DR) strategies. As the number of communication rounds increases, the quality of the environment mapping improves, reflecting more accurate mean predictions and reduced standard deviations. In the CDR scenario, the

NN demonstrates better stability and consistency in its predictions across all communication rounds, indicating that the accumulation of data significantly benefits the learning process. On the other hand, in the DR scenario, while initial rounds show promising results, later rounds exhibit increased noise and uncertainty, suggesting that the DR strategy may lead to a significant loss of valuable information, affecting the overall performance of the NN.

6.3   Uncertainty Evaluation: Multi-agent Case

In Sect. 6.1, we demonstrated that BNNs can effectively estimate uncertainty in the context of a single learning agent. In this section, we extend that analysis to explore whether the same capabilities of BNNs are in decentralized multi-agent training environments. To investigate this, we evaluated different regularization strategies to understand their impact on the quality of decentralized BNN training, with a particular focus on assessing validation loss under the following approaches:

1. Applying a uniform L2 regularization across all neural network parameters without differentiating between parameter types;
2. Applying separate L2 regularization for standard neural network parameters and Bayesian parameters;
3. Using distinct regularization techniques for standard and Bayesian parameters, with L2 regularization for the standard parameters and Kullback-Leibler divergence for the Bayesian parameters (see Algorithm 2).

The findings from these evaluations are illustrated in Fig. 10. Notably, the use of KL divergence for regularizing Bayesian parameters, as detailed in Algorithm 2) led to a 12–30% reduction in validation loss compared to the other approaches. This strategy also enhanced the stability of the training process.

The results of the decentralized BNN training using this method are visualized in Fig. 11.

The figure depicts the results of 50 forward passes of a generalized model that the seven individual agents converged to during the training process utilizing Algorithms 1 and 2. During the training, all agents reached a consensus on a unified model. Subfigure 11a shows the mean predictions across the environment, representing a general map that encapsulates the knowledge gathered by all seven agents. Subfigure 11b illustrates the standard deviation of these predictions, which can be interpreted as the level of uncertainty associated with the model's output. Higher standard deviations indicate regions where the model is less certain about its predictions.

As an uncertainty baseline, Subfigure 11c shows the density of LiDAR data points used for model training. In this subfigure, darker areas represent regions with a higher concentration of data points, offering a reference for comparing the uncertainty visualized in Subfigure 11b against the actual data distribution. To estimate the density of the LiDAR data points, we employed the Kernel Density Estimation method [7] with a Gaussian kernel.

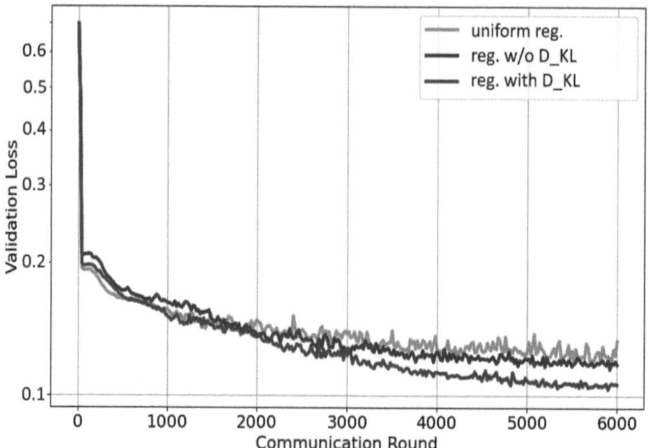

Fig. 10. Comparison of validation loss during distributed BNN training 1) with uniform L2 regularization (**uniform reg.**); 2) separate L2 regularization (**reg. w/o D_KL**); 3) Kullback-Leibler divergence for regularization of BNN ρ-parameters (**reg. with D_KL**) [26].

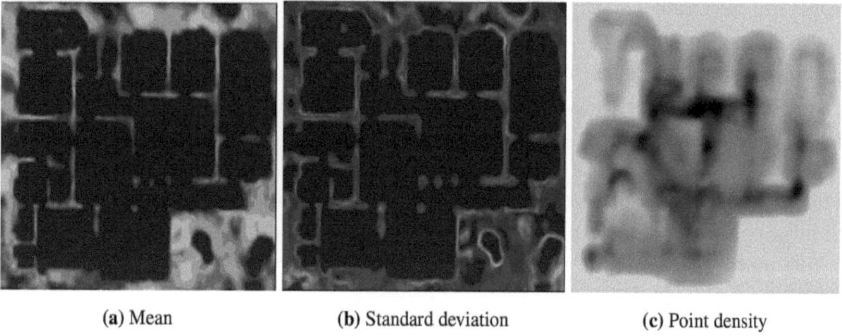

(a) Mean   (b) Standard deviation   (c) Point density

Fig. 11. Visualization of the decentralized BNN training results according to Algorithm 2: (a) mean; (b) standard deviation; (c) point density of the original data set. Adapted from [26].

7 Conclusions

This paper addressed the problem of uncertainty estimation in edge collaborative learning. Through a targeted case study on collaborative mapping, we developed and evaluated a decentralized learning framework based on the Webots simulation platform and Distributed Neural Network Optimization algorithm. Our main contributions include the design of an epoch-based decentralized consensus algorithm to support the peer-to-peer exchange of neural network parameters among distributed agents and integrating BNNs to incorporate uncertainty estimation into this decentralized learning context.

We reviewed EL methods and their applicability to AI-enabled edge devices alongside our practical implementations. This review covered several approaches, including Federated Learning, Federated Distillation, Split Learning, and decentralized techniques based on the Alternating Direction Method of Multipliers. We examined the benefits and drawbacks of these methods and discussed how they could be adapted and applied to enhance edge learning environments. Additionally, we explored how BNNs could be used for uncertainty estimation, emphasizing the potential of stochastic modeling to improve the generalization capabilities of neural networks in complex and uncertain scenarios.

Our findings show that BNNs are effective in estimating uncertainty within distributed learning environments, but they also highlight the importance of precise hyperparameter tuning to achieve reliable uncertainty assessments. Among the regularization strategies evaluated, using Kullback–Leibler divergence for Bayesian parameter regularization was particularly beneficial, resulting in a 12–30% reduction in validation loss compared to other strategies. This approach also contributed to greater stability during training, demonstrating the practical value of integrating BNNs into distributed learning frameworks.

Future work should focus on optimizing these distributed learning techniques for implementation on embedded AI hardware, where computational resources are limited. This will require refining neural network architectures and EL methods to fit the specific constraints of edge devices. Furthermore, there is a need to explore advanced task management and offloading strategies within the multi-layered fog and hybrid edge-fog-cloud infrastructures to enhance computational efficiency and resource utilization in dynamic and resource-constrained environments.

Acknowledgments. The research reported in this paper has been partly funded by the European Union's Horizon 2020 research and innovation program within the framework of Chips Joint Undertaking (Grant No. 101112268). This work has been supported by Silicon Austria Labs (SAL) owned by the Republic of Austria, the Styrian Business Promotion Agency (SFG), the federal state of Carinthia, the Upper Austrian Research (UAR), and the Austrian Association for the Electric and Electronics Industry (FEEI).

References

1. Abreha, H.G., Hayajneh, M., Serhani, M.A.: Federated learning in edge computing: a systematic survey (2022). https://doi.org/10.3390/s22020450
2. Ahn, J.H., Simeone, O., Kang, J.: Wireless federated distillation for distributed edge learning with heterogeneous data, vol. 2019-September (2019). https://doi.org/10.1109/PIMRC.2019.8904164
3. Belov, D.I., Armstrong, R.D.: Distributions of the Kullback-Leibler divergence with applications. Br. J. Math. Stat. Psychol. **64**, 291–309 (2011). https://doi.org/10.1348/000711010X522227
4. Bhadra, S., Kelkar, V.A., Brooks, F.J., Anastasio, M.A.: On hallucinations in tomographic image reconstruction. IEEE Trans. Med. Imaging **40**, 3249–3260 (2021). https://doi.org/10.1109/TMI.2021.3077857
5. Boyd, S.: Distributed Optimization and Statistical Learning via the Alternating Direction Method of Multipliers, vol. 3 (2010). https://doi.org/10.1561/2200000016
6. Claici, S., Yurochkin, M., Ghosh, S., Solomon, J.: Model fusion with Kullback-Leibler divergence, vol. PartF168147-3 (2020)
7. D., S.: Kernel Density Estimators, pp. 137–216 (2015). https://doi.org/10.1002/9781118575574.ch6. https://onlinelibrary.wiley.com/doi/10.1002/9781118575574.ch6

8. Elgabli, A., Park, J., Bedi, A.S., Bennis, M., Aggarwal, V.: Gadmm: fast and communication efficient framework for distributed machine learning. J. Mach. Learn. Res. **21** (2020)
9. Gupta, O., Raskar, R.: Distributed learning of deep neural network over multiple agents. J. Netw. Comput. Appl. **116**, 1–8 (2018). https://doi.org/10.1016/j.jnca.2018.05.003
10. Ha, Y.J., et al.: Spatio-temporal split learning for privacy-preserving medical platforms: case studies with covid-19 CT, X-ray, and cholesterol data. IEEE Access **9**, 121046–121059 (2021). https://doi.org/10.1109/ACCESS.2021.3108455
11. Jiang, Z., Yu, G., Cai, Y., Jiang, Y.: Decentralized edge learning via unreliable device-to-device communications. IEEE Trans. Wirel. Commun. **21**, 9041–9055 (2022). https://doi.org/10.1109/TWC.2022.3172147
12. Jospin, L.V., Laga, H., Boussaid, F., Buntine, W., Bennamoun, M.: Hands-on Bayesian neural networks–a tutorial for deep learning users. IEEE Comput. Intell. Mag. **17**, 29–48 (2022). https://doi.org/10.1109/MCI.2022.3155327
13. Kalervo, A., Ylioinas, J., Häikiö, M., Karhu, A., Kannala, J.: CubiCasa5K: a dataset and an improved multi-task model for floorplan image analysis. In: Felsberg, M., Forssén, P.-E., Sintorn, I.-M., Unger, J. (eds.) SCIA 2019. LNCS, vol. 11482, pp. 28–40. Springer, Cham (2019). https://doi.org/10.1007/978-3-030-20205-7_3
14. Koda, Y., et al.: Communication-efficient multimodal split learning for mmwave received power prediction. IEEE Commun. Lett. **24** (2020). https://doi.org/10.1109/LCOMM.2020.2978824
15. Kullback, S., Leibler, R.A.: On information and sufficiency. Ann. Math. Stat. **22**, 79–86 (1951). https://doi.org/10.1214/aoms/1177729694
16. Li, E., Zeng, L., Zhou, Z., Chen, X.: Edge AI: on-demand accelerating deep neural network inference via edge computing. IEEE Trans. Wirel. Commun. **19**, 447–457 (2020). https://doi.org/10.1109/TWC.2019.2946140
17. Liang, Q., Hanafy, W.A., Ali-Eldin, A., Shenoy, P.: Model-driven cluster resource management for AI workloads in edge clouds. ACM Trans. Auton. Adaptive Syst. **18**, 1–26 (2023). https://doi.org/10.1145/3582080
18. Lim, W.Y.B., et al.: Federated learning in mobile edge networks: a comprehensive survey. IEEE Commun. Surv. Tutor. **22**, 2031–2063 (2020). https://doi.org/10.1109/COMST.2020.2986024
19. Lyu, L., et al.: Privacy and robustness in federated learning: attacks and defenses. IEEE Trans. Neural Netw. Learn. Syst. **35**, 8726–8746 (2024). https://doi.org/10.1109/TNNLS.2022.3216981
20. McMahan, H.B., Moore, E., Ramage, D., Hampson, S., Arcas, B.A.: Communication-efficient learning of deep networks from decentralized data. In: Proceedings of the 20th International Conference on Artificial Intelligence and Statistics, AISTATS 2017 (2017)
21. Melis, L., Song, C., Cristofaro, E.D., Shmatikov, V.: Exploiting unintended feature leakage in collaborative learning. In: 2019 IEEE Symposium on Security and Privacy (SP), pp. 691–706. IEEE (2019). https://doi.org/10.1109/SP.2019.00029
22. Merenda, M., Porcaro, C., Iero, D.: Edge machine learning for AI-enabled IoT devices: a review. Sensors **20**, 2533 (2020). https://doi.org/10.3390/s20092533
23. Nguyen, V.D., Chatzinotas, S., Ottersten, B., Duong, T.Q.: Fedfog: Network-aware optimization of federated learning over wireless fog-cloud systems. IEEE Trans. Wirel. Commun. **21** (2022). https://doi.org/10.1109/TWC.2022.3167263
24. Park, J., et al.: Communication-efficient and distributed learning over wireless networks: principles and applications. Proc. IEEE **109**, 796–819 (2021). https://doi.org/10.1109/JPROC.2021.3055679
25. Parmar, V., Sarwar, S.S., Li, Z., Lee, H.H.S., Salvo, B.D., Suri, M.: Exploring memory-oriented design optimization of edge AI hardware for extended reality applications. IEEE Micro **43**, 40–49 (2023). https://doi.org/10.1109/MM.2023.3321249

26. Radchenko, G., Fill, V.: Uncertainty estimation in multi-agent distributed learning for AI-enabled edge devices. In: Proceedings of the 14th International Conference on Cloud Computing and Services Science, pp. 311–318. SCITEPRESS - Science and Technology Publications (2024). https://doi.org/10.5220/0012728500003711

27. Samie, F., Tsoutsouras, V., Bauer, L., Xydis, S., Soudris, D., Henkel, J.: Computation offloading and resource allocation for low-power IoT edge devices, pp. 7–12. IEEE (2016). https://doi.org/10.1109/WF-IoT.2016.7845499

28. Sattler, F., Marban, A., Rischke, R., Samek, W.: CFD: communication-efficient federated distillation via soft-label quantization and delta coding. IEEE Trans. Netw. Sci. Eng. **9**, 2025–2038 (2022). https://doi.org/10.1109/TNSE.2021.3081748

29. Shao, J., Wu, F., Zhang, J.: Selective knowledge sharing for privacy-preserving federated distillation without a good teacher. Nat. Commun. **15**, 349 (2024). https://doi.org/10.1038/s41467-023-44383-9

30. Shao, J., Zhang, J.: Communication-computation trade-off in resource-constrained edge inference. IEEE Commun. Mag. **58**, 20–26 (2020). https://doi.org/10.1109/MCOM.001.2000373

31. Sitzmann, V., Martel, J.N., Bergman, A.W., Lindell, D.B., Wetzstein, G.: Implicit neural representations with periodic activation functions. In: Advances in Neural Information Processing Systems, vol. 2020-December (2020)

32. Sudharsan, B., Breslin, J.G., Ali, M.I.: Edge2train: a framework to train machine learning models (SVMs) on resource-constrained IoT edge devices. In: Proceedings of the 10th International Conference on the Internet of Things, pp. 1–8. ACM (2020). https://doi.org/10.1145/3410992.3411014

33. Tak, A., Cherkaoui, S.: Federated edge learning: design issues and challenges. IEEE Netw. **35**, 252–258 (2021). https://doi.org/10.1109/MNET.011.2000478

34. Vepakomma, P., Gupta, O., Swedish, T., Raskar, R.: Split learning for health: distributed deep learning without sharing raw patient data. arXiv preprint arXiv:1812.00564 (2018)

35. Wang, B., Dong, K., Zakaria, N.A.B., Upadhyay, M., Wong, W.F., Peh, L.S.: Network-on-chip-centric accelerator architectures for edge AI computing, pp. 243–244. IEEE (2022). https://doi.org/10.1109/ISOCC56007.2022.10031356

36. Wu, C., Wu, F., Lyu, L., Huang, Y., Xie, X.: Communication-efficient federated learning via knowledge distillation. Nat. Commun. **13**, 2032 (2022). https://doi.org/10.1038/s41467-022-29763-x

37. Wu, W., et al.: Split learning over wireless networks: parallel design and resource management. IEEE J. Sel. Areas Commun. **41**, 1051–1066 (2023). https://doi.org/10.1109/JSAC.2023.3242704

38. Yang, K., et al.: Spatio-temporal domain awareness for multi-agent collaborative perception. In: 2023 IEEE/CVF International Conference on Computer Vision (ICCV), pp. 23326–23335. IEEE (2023). https://doi.org/10.1109/ICCV51070.2023.02137

39. Yu, J., Vincent, J.A., Schwager, M.: Dinno: distributed neural network optimization for multi-robot collaborative learning. IEEE Robot. Autom. Lett. **7**, 1896–1903 (2022). https://doi.org/10.1109/LRA.2022.3142402

40. Zhang, J., et al.: Edge learning: the enabling technology for distributed big data analytics in the edge. ACM Comput. Surv. **54**, 1–36 (2022). https://doi.org/10.1145/3464419

Threat Analysis and Security Assessment of an HPC System

Raffaele Elia[1]([✉])(iD), Daniele Granata[2](iD), and Massimiliano Rak[1](iD)

[1] Department of Engineering, University of Campania Luigi Vanvitelli,
Via Roma 9, Aversa, CE, Italy
`{raffaele.elia,massimiliano.rak}@unicampania.it`
[2] DiSEGIM, University of Naples Parthenope, 80143 Naples, Italy
`daniele.granata@uniparthenope.it`

Abstract. High Performance Computing (HPC) defines a computing paradigm characterized by extraordinarily powerful computing capacity. An HPC infrastructure is also equipped with high-bandwidth network connections, and extensive storage. The mentioned resources make their employment in academic and industrial environments clear, as well as the manipulation of huge amounts of sensitive and critical data. Since HPC infrastructures involve a broad quantity of desirable resources, including confidential data, and are employed for research and industry tasks, they become an attractive target for malicious entities. Furthermore, the heterogeneous resources involved in the HPC systems and their consideration as "trusted" systems worsen the situation. Applying traditional security measures to individual nodes of the infrastructure is an inadequate strategy because it does not consider the system as a whole. To enhance security, use a "defense-in-depth" strategy by implementing multiple layers of controls across the system, ensuring that if one or two layers fail, others remain in place to thwart potential attacks. While not ensuring absolute security, it makes successful attacks highly challenging. Clearly, this approach does not provide absolute security but only offers the means to make a successful attack so difficult to execute that it becomes unsustainable for an attacker. These considerations push the necessity to identify the threats that an HPC infrastructure may be affected to and how the security of these systems may be assessed to understand: the security level of the analyzed infrastructure; the applied security controls, if they are implemented; and the possible ones that may be applied to improve the security level. By following this direction, with this work, we propose: (i) a threat analysis for an HPC system through a fine-grained threat modeling technique; and (ii) a possible approach to perform a security assessment of an HPC system. Additionally, we propose a possible approach to selecting suitable security controls to improve the security level of an HPC infrastructure. Lastly, we present some results for V:HPCCRI: the supercomputer of the University of Campania Luigi Vanvitelli.

Keywords: HPC · Threat modelling · High performance computing · Security assessment

C. Pahl and M. van Steen (Eds.): CLOSER 2024, CCIS 2851, pp. 146–175, 2026.
https://doi.org/10.1007/978-3-032-17286-0_7

1   Introduction

High-Performance Computing (HPC) denotes a computing paradigm characterized by extraordinarily powerful computing capacity. HPC has evolved to achieve petaflops [7] levels after its initial introduction in the 1960s by Seymour Cray at the University of Manchester [17]. Besides the exceptionally powerful computing capacity, an HPC infrastructure is equipped with high-bandwidth network connections, and extensive storage [11]. The mentioned resources that characterise an HPC system make it clear their employment in academic and industrial environments as well as the manipulation of huge amounts of sensitive and critical data. Since HPC infrastructures involve a broad quantity of desirable resources, including confidential data, and are employed for research and industry tasks, they become an attractive target for malicious entities.

Furthermore, the heterogeneous resources involved in the HPC systems and their consideration as "trusted" systems. On one hand, using different technologies extends the attack vectors, making it more difficult to ensure the security of the systems. On the other hand, since they have historically originated in academic and research environments, they are often regarded as "trusted" systems: users have significant rights, and sophisticated protective measures are rarely in place for those with access to the system. Applying traditional security measures to individual nodes of the infrastructure is an inadequate strategy because it does not consider the system as a whole. There is no single solution to guarantee the complete security of an HPC centre, and, of course, there never will be. The key idea to achieve an adequate level of security is the use of an approach known as "defence-in-depth": multiple layers of security controls are placed throughout the system, so that, if one or two layers fail, others still exist and may stop the attack [19].

Clearly, this approach does not provide absolute security but only offers the means to make a successful attack so difficult to execute that it becomes unsustainable for an attacker. These considerations push the necessity to identify the threats that an HPC infrastructure may be affected to and how the security of these systems may be assessed to understand: the security level of the analyzed infrastructure; the applied security controls, if they are implemented; and the possible ones that may be applied to improve the security level.

By following this direction, with this work, we aim to extend our conference paper [3] by proposing: (i) a threat analysis for an HPC system, based on our modeling technique (MACM) [5] and a well-detailed HPC threat catalogue we built; and (ii) a possible approach to perform a security assessment of an HPC system, using the Framework Nazionale per la Cybersecurity e la Data Protection [9], based on the HPC contextualization we defined. Additionally, we propose a possible approach to selecting suitable security controls to improve the security level of an HPC infrastructure. Lastly, we present some results for V:HPCCRI: the supercomputer of the University of Campania Luigi Vanvitelli.

The structure of this work is organized to guide the reader through a comprehensive examination of security in High-Performance Computing (HPC) systems. In Sect. 2, we begin by providing an overview of the significant contributions to the fields of security assessment and threat modeling for HPC systems. Moving forward, Sect. 3 elaborates on the specific methodology we employed for evaluating the security of these systems.

Next, Sect. 4 introduces HPC systems and details the approach we used to model them for our study. Following this, Sect. 5 uses a Systematic Literature Review (SLR) method to identify potential threats and develop a threat catalogue in the context of HPC. In Sect. 7, we propose a method for assessing the security of HPC systems and determining effective countermeasures.

The methodology is then applied to a practical case study of our supercomputer, which is presented in Sect. 8. Finally, Sect. 9 summarizes our conclusions and future works.

2   Related Work

As anticipated above, our aim is both to build a threat catalogue containing the fine-grained threats [4] affecting HPC components that can be used to support our threat modelling technique and to assess the security of the system by considering the related countermeasures. To achieve this, we began by investigating the threat analysis and security assessment techniques presented in the literature to highlight the originality of our approach.

2.1   Threat Analysis for HPC Systems

NIST Special Publication 800-223 [6] offers a detailed description of the HPC key components and the threats that can affect these assets by underlining their security. The HPC architecture, its main components, and their analysis will be described in detail in Sect. 4. It is important to note that the document divides an HPC architecture into Zones and evaluates the threats each zone may face. The selection phase plays a crucial role in the identification of threats. It simplifies and enhances the process of recognizing potential malicious behaviours. However, it is important to note that this approach operates at a high level when modeling threats. This means that it takes a broad perspective and may not align with our specific approach or methodology for addressing threats. In essence, while the selection phase facilitates the identification process, its high-level nature might diverge from our more detailed and nuanced approach to modeling and managing threats. A detailed analysis of the HPC architecture is reported in Sect. 4. Hou et al.'s recent research [7] took into account the advanced security requirements unique to High-Performance Computing (HPC) systems, highlighting the differences from general-purpose computers and assessing related security threats. The study particularly stresses the importance of a robust access control policy to mitigate confidentiality-related threats in HPC environments. This emphasis underscores the critical role of stringent access control mechanisms and user management in safeguarding HPC systems, significantly enhancing our understanding of security challenges in this field.

Several notable scientific authors advocate for a systematic and comprehensive threat analysis tailored to the specific characteristics of HPC clusters. For instance, Mogilevsky et al. [11] recommend using a structured Confidentiality, Integrity, and Availability (CIA) model as the foundation for their proposed threat model. Despite this, the literature often lacks detailed methodologies for extracting threats and security issues from HPC systems, as many studies do not specify how threats are identified and extracted from the model. To address this gap, we employed a well-established technique to systematically expand our threat catalogue within the HPC context. This catalogue is designed to identify detailed threats impacting various components of a supercomputer.

2.2 Security Assessment Approaches

Several scientific works delve into security assessment and monitoring of HPC infrastructures, each employing distinct techniques for this purpose. Malin et al. [10] have made a noteworthy contribution by proposing an adaptation of continuous monitoring within the HPC context. Their work investigates potential alterations in compliance and articulates technical objectives for implementing continuous monitoring. While recognizing the potential for enhancing HPC security, the paper highlights a limitation in existing Commercial Off-The-Shelf (COTS) tools and NIST-approved benchmarks, which are primarily tailored for desktop environments. The authors advocate for a proactive approach to managing HPC systems within US government organizations. The authors propose collaboration among HPC sites to develop suitable approaches, tools, and techniques that align with compliance requirements and bolster cybersecurity. This proactive stance is crucial, considering the unique challenges posed by HPC environments, which are distinct from conventional desktop setups. To support this problem, Arcutek organization [2] has developed a security service called *HEAP* (HPC Evaluation And Plan) that aims at configuring security solutions for connections, computing, handling files, etc. Even though the project is currently open, it represents a step forward into practically evaluating the security of supercomputers.

3 Methodology

As already mentioned, this work aims to collect a detailed catalogue of HPC threats from literature to support our fine-grained threat model generation technique as well as assess the security of the system by using the Framework Nazionale per la Cybersecurity e la Data Protection. To achieve our goal, we propose a methodology, shown in Fig. 1.

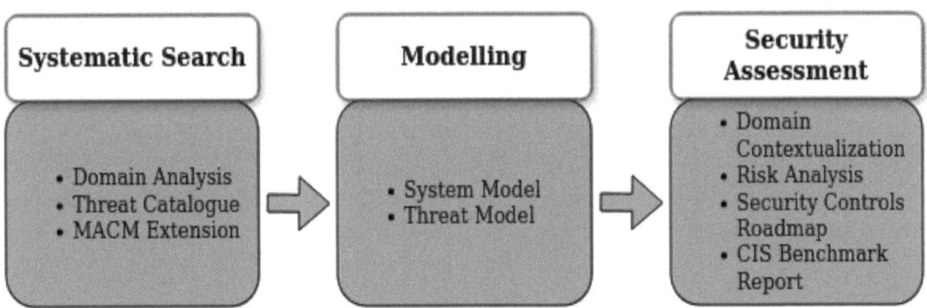

Fig. 1. Methodology Steps.

The methodology consists of three phases: Systematic Search, Modelling, and Security Assessment. Here is a general explanation of each phase, which will be detailed further in the following sections.

The initial phase, Systematic Search, already described in detail in our previous works [3,4]), focuses on collecting and analyzing relevant information related to the system components and the security issues that may affect each component from the scientific literature. This phase involves creating a Domain Analysis Report, which provides a detailed examination of the application domain, identifying the assets (i.e. resources that need to be protected). Additionally, a Threat Catalogue is compiled to list potential threats pertinent to the analyzed domains associated with the components characterizing the specific domain (in this paper, HPC). The phase also includes the extension of our modelling technique, ensuring a more precise and targeted evaluation.

The next phase, Modelling, is dedicated to developing detailed models of the system and the associated threats for our case study. It is different from the threat catalogue phase since, in this case, the threats are generated from our algorithm [15]), while in the previous step, threats have been collected from the literature.

This includes creating a System Model that represents the system's functioning, encompassing components and their interactions using the MACM model [5]. Alongside this, a Threat Model is developed to identify and describe specific threats to the system, based on the threat catalogue produced above.

The final phase, Security Assessment, focuses on evaluating the system's security and planning countermeasures. This involves Domain Contextualization, which integrates the collected information and developed models to provide a comprehensive view of the system's security using the contextualization provided by Framework Nazionale per la Cybersecurity e la Data Protection [9]. A Risk Analysis is conducted to assess the likelihood and impact of identified threats (in our case we adopted the OWASP risk rating methodology), helping to prioritize mitigation actions. Subsequently, a Countermeasures Roadmap is created, outlining the steps to implement to mitigate identified risks and enhance the system's security. Additionally, a CIS Benchmark Report is produced, based on the Center for Internet Security (CIS) benchmarks that highlight vulnerabilities that indicate which controls are missing. It is worth noting that the CIS framework is one of the available cybersecurity frameworks in the literature, but the methodology can be adapted to each chosen framework.

4 HPC Domain Analysis

First of all, we conducted a domain analysis related to high performance computing systems: specifically, we considered the reference architecture proposed by NIST [6]. It allows us to have a comprehensive architectural overview and identify the assets that may be involved in the analysis. Lastly, the section described our modelling technique and its extension necessary to model an HPC system, emphasizing which new asset types we added and why.

4.1 HPC Reference Architecture

An HPC system is constituted by a huge number of nodes organized in four different function zones: (i) access zone, a set of one or more nodes connected to external networks aiming at providing authentication and authorization services; (ii) computing zone, an ensemble of nodes with the purpose to run parallel jobs at scale; (iii) data storage zone, a set of one or multiple high-speed file systems aiming at providing data storage services for user data; and (iv) management zone, a group of nodes with the goal to offer services aiming at manage the entire infrastructure [6]. Each zone is connected to the others by means of one or more networks (Fig. 2).

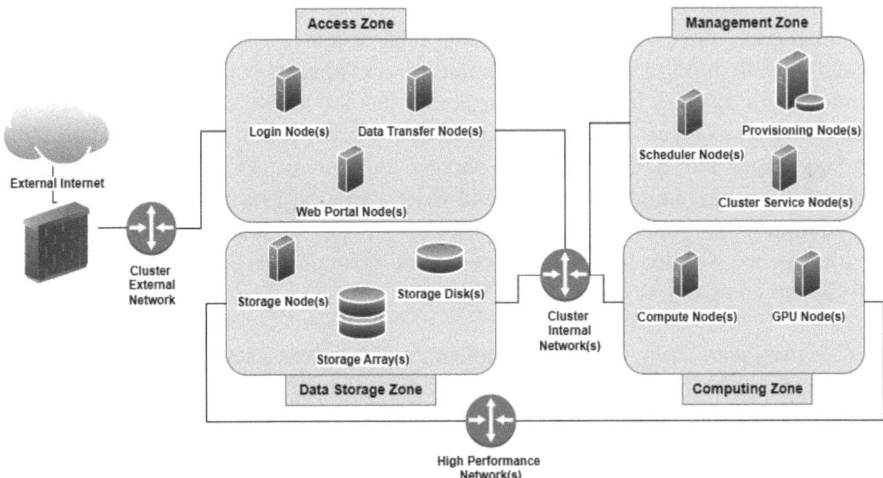

Fig. 2. HPC Reference Architecture.

HPC Access Zone. The Access Zone is crucial for allowing users and administrators to access and operate the HPC infrastructure. Accordingly, it consists of one or more nodes, connected to external networks, that offer authentication and authorization services. Generally, at least one of these nodes provides shells that users can use to launch interactive or batch jobs. Furthermore, this zone may contain one or more data transfer nodes that allow to: (i) transfer data into and out of the HPC system; and (ii) offer storage-mounting services like Network File System (NFS), Server Message Block (SMB), and others. Numerous HPC infrastructures currently offer web portals through dedicated web portal nodes, allowing for a range of web-based interfaces to access HPC system services.

HPC Computing Zone. An HPC infrastructure comprises a set of independent computing systems (i.e., compute nodes) which are interconnected via high-speed network and that involve CPU cores, memory, disk space and networking interface cards. Compared to a typical laptop or desktop computer, HPC systems boast significantly more CPU cores and memory. They include different types of nodes designed for specific tasks, and some nodes are equipped with hardware accelerators, such as GPUs, to enhance application performance. The quantity of compute nodes can vary from just a few nodes to hundreds and even thousands of nodes. This zone communicates with the Management and Access Zone through a non-high-performance communication networks (e.g., Ethernet). Anyway, the Computing Zone'purpose pushes the necessity to employ an high-performance communication networks (i.e., networks characterized by high bandwidth and ultra-low latency) to connect Computing Zone with Data Storage Zone. The most common interconnect networking encompasses InfiniBand, Omni-Path, and Slingshot.

HPC Data Storage Zone. The Data Storage Zone aims to offer data storage services for user data using one or multiple high-speed parallel file systems. In detail, it stores the initial data, intermediate outcomes, and final results of applications, making them accessible both during the application's runtime and after its completion. Typically, the mentioned file systems have storage capacities that are measured in petabytes and can even extend to exabytes. Generally, the storage systems within the Data Storage Zone can be grouped into three classes: (i) parallel file systems (PFS), designed to handle applications needing high-speed read and write operations, supporting both sequential and random access patterns at speeds up to terabytes per second; (ii) node-local storage, for low-latency workloads; and (iii) archival file systems, that defend against data loss and support campaign storage.

HPC Management Zone. The Management Zone involves a set of nodes and network switches that facilitate a range of functions aimed at efficiently, effectively, and stably managing the infrastructure. To accomplish their purposes, nodes within the other zones of the infrastructure, require specific protocols and services that are provided by this zone. As an example, we can mention: the Network Time Protocol (NTP), essential for synchronization, log management, and version-controlled repositories; authentication, and authorization services provided by an LDAP server; as well as Domain Name Services (DNS) and Dynamic Host Configuration Protocol (DHCP). The reported services can be executed either on designated hardware platforms or as virtual machines. Furthermore, the management zone comprises the storage systems to store configuration data and node images, it also stores logs of the entire HPC system and comprises servers that aim to analyze the logs and alert administrators if specific events occur. It is worth noting that, since HPC systems are characterized by a distributed nature, this zone comprises nodes that host job schedulers in order to coordinate the requests of resources for specific workloads. The most used job scheduler are SLURM and Portable Batch System (PBS).

4.2   Asset Identification

Asset Identification aims at enumerating all assets (i.e., valuable resources that must be protected) by leveraging reference architecture. This is a crucial step because it allowed us to individuate new assets, specific to the HPC domain in order to assess their security. Specifically, the analysis of reference architecture enabled the identification of hardware and software assets, as well as network assets resulting in 23 assets.

Since Access Zone is connected to an external network, each node within the zone, and each service it hosts, requires protection: in fact, if one or multiple nodes (or some service they host) are compromised, a malicious user may gain access to the infrastructure, transferring malicious data into the system or running unauthorized jobs. Therefore, we individuated: the login node, data transfer node, and web portal node.

From Computing Zone we identified two physical assets: the compute node and GPU node, necessary to distinguish nodes equipped with GPU hardware accelerator from those without. They represent two valuable resources because through their compromise an attacker might execute its illegal jobs or discover information related to the legitimate user jobs. Additionally, we selected the container platform as a software service asset because an attacker might escape from a container to the underlying host, with the intent to either move to other containers from the host or perform actions directly on the host itself.

Also, the protection of the nodes within the Data Storage Zone is mandatory: in fact, on one hand this zone stores and manages data and final results of users' applications; on the other hand, by default, it is characterized by the lack of backup services. Therefore, by compromising this zone an attacker could get access to application data and deletes and corrupts data or injects false data. Accordingly, we identified data storage node, storage disk, and storage array as physical assets; and distributed file system (e.g., HDFS, Lustre, etc.) as software service assets.

The Management Zone's nodes host essential services for managing and proper functioning of the HPC infrastructure so, all physical hardware and each service they host require to be safeguarded. Indeed, compromising a scheduler node, a malicious user might give their own jobs higher priority or modify the legitimate users' job priorities; instead, impairing cluster services nodes, an attacker might obtain access to log data of the entire infrastructure and, possibly, tampers them or make unavailable essential services; additionally, the compromise of provisioning nodes might entail, for example, the leak or tamper of stored images; lastly, through time tampering, synchronization issues could occur. Accordingly, we selected: the scheduler node, cluster services node, and provisioning node as physical assets, as well as services like LDAP, NTP, DHCP, job scheduler, and so on. In this regard, as described in the following sections, it is important to point out that our approach to protocol modeling considers the services they support, rather than solely focusing on communication aspects.

Lastly, we identified cluster external and internal networks and high performance networks as network asset since their compromise might lead to unauthorized access to sensitive data or materialization of various threats such as message replay, topology disclosure, and so on.

5   Systematic Search

As anticipated in the introduction, this work aims to analyze and assess the security of an HPC system. Specifically, it seeks to understand: (i) the threats faced by HPC system assets; (ii) how to determine its security level through the application of available methodologies for conducting a security assessment, if they exist; and (iii) the security controls that should be applied to enhance the security level of the analyzed infrastructure. To address these objectives, we performed a Systematic Literature Review (SLR) to identify security threats and HPC-specific security assessment techniques.

5.1   SLR Protocol and Extraction

To achieve our purpose, we conducted an SLR in compliance with [8]. The authors propose a three-step process: Planning, Conducting, and Reporting. The Planning's purpose is to develop a protocol for querying various sources for articles and to include and exclude specific papers to address particular research questions. In the Conduction phase, the rules defined within the protocol are applied to select a set of suitable papers to try to answer the research questions. The Reporting phase involves documenting the review's outcomes and sharing the results with interested parties.

Planning. The definition of a protocol initiates with the specification of the research questions. To address the mentioned challenges, we choose three research questions.

- *RQ1:* What are the threats that apply to an HPC system?
- *RQ2:* Which methodologies are used to produce a threat model of the HPC system?
- *RQ3:* What are the existing security assessment methodologies for an HPC system?

The answers to the questions are determined through data extracted from the selected suitable papers. To gather these papers, we used a keyword-based approach, which consists of first selecting appropriate keywords and then defining search queries. Specifically, we formulated two queries using the chosen keywords: one to address RQ1 and RQ2, and another for RQ3. They are reported below.

```
Q1: ((hpc OR ''high performance computing'') AND ("system" OR
    "data
center" OR "architecture" OR "infrastructure")) AND (threat AND
(analysis OR model OR modeling))

Q2: ((hpc OR "high performance computing") AND ("system" OR
    "data
center" OR "architecture" OR "infrastructure")) AND (("security
evaluation" OR "security control" OR "security assessment"))
```

The two shown queries were applied in Scopus, the most commonly used literature search engine because it includes papers, articles, and book chapters from other platforms like Springer, Google Scholar, and IEEE Explore. Additionally, we defined specific criteria - inclusion and exclusion criteria - to select suitable papers. It is reported in Table 1.

Table 1. Inclusion and Exclusion Criteria [3].

Inclusion Criteria	Exclusion Criteria
Proposes threat analysis/model for HPC system	It is not written in English
Describes threats for HPC system	Does not cover HPC security
Describes security assessment methodologies for HPC system	Does not concern threat analysis for HPC system
-	Does not concern HPC security threats

Conduction. The Conduction phase is by three steps: (i) study identification, which allows to gathering of the studies through the application of the two mentioned queries to the Scopus using its language; (ii) selection, which involves the application of inclusion and exclusion criteria to studies' abstract to reduce the large number of documents; (iii) extraction, which aims to extract data from selected papers through a detailed study and analysis.

The study identification allowed us to obtain 131 papers. It is worth noting that the results include further documents, such as paper related to HPC security technologies, that we decided to include in the next steps to have a comprehensive overview of the HPC domain. After that, by applying the inclusion and exclusion criteria to all studies' abstract, only 24 papers were selected for data extraction; whereas 107 were discarded in compliance to the exclusion criteria. Out of the 24 extracted papers, only 11 met the inclusion criteria, while 13 met the exclusion criteria. Therefore, 11 papers were selected to address the research questions.

Reporting Summary. The outcomes of the systematic literature review can be divided according to the three research questions.

Starting from the reason why an HPC system may represent a valuable target for a malicious user, parts of the results illustrate and describe some threats for an high-performance computer infrastructure, also describing the feasible attacks that an attacker may implement through the materialization of the mentioned threats. Additionally, some results specify what CIA requirement is compromised if a threat is materialized. Furthermore, much of the evidence provided us with a comprehensive overview of high-performance computing systems, with a focus on their architecture, differences from general-purpose systems, and the programming models employed. Additionally, we have gained detailed insights into security recommendations, requirements, challenges, mechanisms, technologies, and enhancement methods [7, 13, 14, 19].

As already discussed in Sect. 2, the outcomes show that not-specific methodologies have been employed to determine threats of an HPC system. For example, some authors enumerated part of the threats affecting a supercomputer by considering the security requirements they compromise. Consequently, threats were selected based on their impact on confidentiality, integrity and availability of services [11]. Other listed part of the threats according to the zone or the specific asset they compromise [6]. These results are significant for us since our approach systematically derives threats from a well-structured model.

Lastly, as we discussed earlier in the Sect. 2, the systematic literature review provided us two results about the existing methodologies used to evaluate the security of a target system. One focuses on continuous monitoring [10], while the other pertains to HEAP [2]. In particular, the study has highlighted that neither of them constitutes a specific security assessment methodology for an HPC system. The first one is employed in the context of general-purpose computers, while the second one is a security service. However, both can be used to evaluate the security of an HPC infrastructure. This answer justifies the choice to use the Framework Nazionale per la Cybersecurity e la Data Protection to perform the security assessment of the considered case study.

5.2 HPC Threat Catalogue

Through the study of the selected papers, we have been able to extract threats that may affect the assets obtained from the reference architecture. In particular, we organized these threats in an Excel sheet, thereby building an HPC Threat Catalogue, which is a structured representation of the threats to which HPC assets may be exposed.

In detail, we built the HPC Threat Catalogue through a two-step process: (i) threat collection; and (ii) data enhancement. With the first step, we gathered threats specific to each selected asset; in the second one, each pair (asset, threat) was enhanced with the following data model fields: description, STRIDE, Compromised, PreCondition, PostCondition.

Description field reports a brief description for each threat. *STRIDE* field denotes the STRIDE classification. The Compromised field takes into account threat that, affecting a component, are transmitted to neighbouring components (i.e., indirect threats). It can be *self* if it compromises the component itself; otherwise it follows the following format: *role(relationship)*. The *role* field can be either *source* or *target*, indicating whether the threat compromises the incoming or outgoing connections from the component. Meanwhile, the *relationship* field serves as a filter for the type of relation through which the threat can propagate. The *Precondition* and *PostCondition* are define through the triple *[LossOfConfidentiality, LossOfIntegrity, LossOfAvailability]*. While the first one refers to how much CIA requirements have to be impaired to materialize the threat; the second one refers to how much the threat materialization impact on the CIA requirements. The three fields within the triple *[LossOfConfidentiality, LossOfIntegrity, LossOfAvailability]* may assume three possible values: (i) n (i.e., no compromise); (ii) p (i.e., partial compromise); and (iii) f (i.e., full compromise).

As a result, a part of the threat catalogue is reported in the Table 2. Readers who are interested in the overall HPC Threat Catalogue, may get it by contacting the authors.

6 Modeling

This phase involves the modelling process that consists of the production of a model aimed at representing the system under analysis as well as evaluating the security of this system. Accordingly, in this section, we present our graph-based model, which we widely use to present the system and the related threat model.

6.1 MACM Extension

Once the asset typology was identified, we extended our modelling technique, the Multi-purpose Application Composition Model (MACM) [5], to support HPC components. Our model uses a formalism designed to provide a straightforward method for summarizing an application's architecture by focusing on its main assets. It is the modelling technique used for the case study under consideration. MACM is a graph-based model with nodes and edges: each node describes a system asset, and each edge represents the relationship between two distinct assets. Each node has a primary label identifying the component's class and an optional secondary label for additional details.

Table 2. Part of HPC Threat Catalogue [3].

Asset Type	Threat	Description	STRIDE	Comprom.	Post Con	Source
HW.PC. Login Node	Authentication Abuse	An attacker is able to access the node abusing the authentication system	S	self, target(hosts)	[p, p, n]	[6]
HW.PC. Cluster Services Node	Log Tampering	An attacker modifies and manipulates system logs or records	T	self, source(hosts)	[n, p, n]	[11]
Data Storage Disk	Lack of data backup services	Without data backup, higher risk of critical data loss from hardware failures, corruption, deletion, or cyberattacks	D	self	[n, n, p]	[6]
Service. Job Scheduler	Scheduler tampering	An attacker gives their own job higher priority and/or modifies the legitimate users' job priorities	T, D	self, source(uses)	[n, p, p]	[11]
Network. Wired. HPC	Subnet Manager Tampering	An attacker compromises the Subnet Manager (SM) with the aim to manipulates and alters configuration and management information associated to InfiniBand network elements	T	self	[n, n, n]	

Furthermore, each node is characterized by a set of properties that provide detailed information about specific attributes. The most important parameter in our model is the asset type, defining the component's typology. This mandatory label describes the functional behaviour of each component and can be associated with security issues. Labels influence the type of relationship in which a node can participate, and the permissible asset types for a node are determined by these labels. Each node must have an obligatory property referred to as asset type, which describes the asset's functional behaviour.

As a result of this phase, the new asset types related to HPC components are shown in Table 3.

6.2 Threat Model Generation

To generate the threat model, as outlined in our previous work [16], we start by identifying all threats that impact the system represented by the MACM. This involves creating a list of pairs, each consisting of a *(CompromisedAsset, MaliciousBehaviour)*. This approach leverages the data model described above, associating threats with each asset based on some parameters, including (i) asset-type parameter; (ii) protocol and role in communication; and (iii) compromised field.

First, we enumerate threats associated with the type of asset. For instance, a *Service.Web* asset type faces different threats than a *Service.DNS* asset type. Protocols involved in communication are considered based on the direction of the edges in the MACM's directed graph, which helps in assigning roles to the assets. For example, if a client (CSC) communicates with a web application using the HTTP protocol, the MACM model will attribute HTTP characteristics to the *uses* relationship, identifying the CSC as the HTTP client and the application as the server. Assets classified as client or server undergo role filtering, using the *Role* field to determine if a threat applies to the client, the server, or both.

The *Compromised* field accounts for indirect threats affecting a specific component and potentially spreading to adjacent components. This can be labelled as *self* if the component itself is compromised or follows a template like *Role (relationship)*. The *Role* field indicates whether the threat impacts in-going or out-going edges, labelled as *source* or *target*. The relationship defines the type of connection through which the threat may propagate. For example, *[self, source(uses)]* means the threat compromises the asset and all nodes that utilize that asset, while *source(connects)* applies the threat to all networks connecting to the asset.

It should be noted that our approach derives all threats from the MACM model semi-automatically.

7 Security Assessment

The last step of our methodology defines the way we evaluate the security level of an HPC infrastructure and determine the countermeasures that should be applied to improve it.

Since, to the best of our knowledge, no fit methodologies aim to perform an HPC security assessment, we opted for the *Framework Nazionale per la Cybersecurity e la Data Protection* [9]. CIS-Sapienza and CINI Cybersecurity National Lab created it and it is inspired by Cybersecurity Framework (CSF) [12] developed by NIST. Both frameworks use a risk-based approach; however, while the Framework Nazionale per la Cybersecurity e la Data Protection has been designed to address the specific needs of the Italian context; CSF, initially intended for use by US organizations, has subsequently been adopted globally by many other organizations and countries. This section also presents our risk analysis approach since, in order to have a comprehensive analysis of the security levels of the system, it is necessary to evaluate the risks (in terms of the probability that the threats may happen). Also, Risk rating helps the security administrator prioritize the countermeasures selection phase.

Table 3. Part of MACM Node Labels and Assets [3].

Primary Label	Secondary Label	Asset Type(s)	Description	Technology	HPCZone
HW	Server	HW.PC	A physical hosting hardware		
HW	Server	HW.PC.Login Node	Node that provides login services		HPC Access Zone
HW	Server	HW.PC.Data Storage Disk	Disk storage		HPC Storage Zone
HW	Server	HW.PC. Scheduler Node	Node that manages the HPC system		HPC Management Zone
HW	Server	HW.PC. ClusterServicesNode	Node that hosts services such as a DHCP server, a DNS server, and others		HPC ManagementZone
HW	Server	HW.PC. Provisioning Node	Node that hosts node images		HPC Management Zone
HW	Server	HW.PC. Compute Node	Compute node		HPC Computing Zone
Network	LAN	Network. Wired. HPC	Local Access Network used in HPC system that guarantee high bandwidth and low latency.	InfiniBand, Omni-Path, Slingshot	
Network	LAN	Network. Wired. Ethernet	Local Access Network used in HPC system that aims to connect nodes		
service	SaaS	Service.DNS	Domain Name System Protocol		
service	SaaS	Service.LDAP	Lightweight Directory Access Protocol		
service	SaaS	Service.Job Scheduler	Job Scheduler, the assets vary based on the technologies involved	PBS, SLURM, Torque	HPC Access Zone, HPC Management Zone, HPC Computing Zone
service	SaaS	Service. System Monitoring	Monitoring System	xClarity	HPC Management Zone

7.1 HPC Contextualization

The choice of a proper contextualization (i.e. a set of functions, categories, and subcategories with their respective definitions of priority and maturity level) is essential for using the Framework Nazionale per la Cybersecurity e la Data Protection correctly: in particular, a consistent contextualization within the considered domain represents the initial step upon which an organization can start to build a path aimed at improving its cybersecurity. To the best of our knowledge, despite various contextualizations being available, no one fit within high-performance computing context. Consequently, we developed a specific HPC contextualization.

Proper contextualization involves the selection of suitable subcategories and the assignment of the correct priority level to them. In compliance with [9], when a contextualization is determined is necessary to: (i) make explicit the concept of "implementation complexity" to distinguish between medium priority level and low; (ii) establish what must be implemented (regardless of complexity); and (iii) make explicit the reason why specific subcategories does not reduce cyber risk. These considerations push to the necessity to have a well-defined criteria to select subcategories and assign them the priority level. Accordingly, we defined a qualitative criteria that considers only subcategories that match with the conducted study so, each of them for which an implementation has not been found in the state of the art will be discarded. Selected subcategories will have a high priority level if they are related to data protection or regulations. Instead, to distinguish between medium and low priority levels, we defined three questions and relative answers, assigning a score – ranging from one to five – for each answer. So, the priority level is determined based on the MEDIUM of the scores related to the provided answers. Specifically, the priority level will be medium if the value is less than three; while it will be low if the value is greater than or equal to three. Table 4 shows the three questions and related answers; the score associated with each response is provided in parentheses.

Table 4. Qualitative Criteria: Questions and Answers.

Questions	Answer
How many distinct entities are involved?	Few entities (1), Enough entities (3), Many entities (5)
How expensive is the implementation in economic terms?	Few (1), Enough (3), Many (5)
How time-consuming is the implementation?	Few (1), Enough (3), Many (5)

Furthermore, each subcategory in the current profile must have a maturity level. We defined four possible maturity levels: (i) *insufficient*; (ii) *basic*; (iii) *normal*; and (iv) *advanced*. In detail, for a specific subcategory, the maturity level will be *basic* if only all essential practices and security controls provided for a specific subcategory or provided by a security process are implemented; it will be *normal* if only all essential and standard practices and security controls provided for a specific subcategory or provided by a security process are implemented; while it will be *advanced* if all practices and security controls provided for a specific subcategory or provided by a security process are implemented. Instead, if at least one basic security control will result in not being implemented, the maturity level for the considered subcategory will be *insufficient*.

Table 5 reports an abstract of HPC contextualization. It includes five fields in compliance with [9]. It is worth noting that the priority level for each subcategory is labelled differently based on the value resulting from the application of the described qualitative criteria; while in the Maturity Level field are listed all eligible maturity levels. Readers who are interested to overall contextualization may obtain it by reaching out to the authors.

7.2 Risk Analysis

Threat Modeling identifies the threats to the system under analysis, but addressing all threats might not align with time-to-market constraints and budget considerations. The Risk Analysis provides a rough estimate of the risk (i.e., the probability of a threat occurring) to prioritize the implementation of security controls. To do this, we adopted the OWASP Risk Rating Methodology [18], which assesses risk based on two indicators: *Likelihood* and *Impact*.

Likelihood indicates the probability of a threat being executed by a threat agent. OWASP quantifies this through two sets of factors: Threat Agent Factors and Vulnerability Factors. Threat Agent Factors include *skill level*, *motive*, *opportunity*, and *size* of the threat agent group. Vulnerability Factors consider the ease of exploiting a specific threat, including *ease of discovery*, *ease of exploit*, *awareness*, and *intrusion detection*.

Impact is measured through technical and business factors. Technical impact assesses how a threat affects the asset's security requirements, such as *Loss of Confidentiality*, *Loss of Integrity*, *Loss of Availability*, and *Loss of Accountability*. Business factors evaluate the significance to the company, including *financial damage*, *reputation damage*, *non-compliance*, and *privacy violation*.

OWASP provides criteria to assign a value between 1 and 10 to each factor. Likelihood and Impact are categorized as *Low*, *Medium*, or *High* if their average values fall within the ranges of 1–3, 4–6, or 7–10, respectively. The overall risk level of a threat is then determined by a table that cross-references Likelihood and Impact levels.

Using our approach, we can pre-determine the Threat Agents and, using our threat catalogue we can evaluate 12 out of 16 factors without user input. Default values are suggested for the business impact factors, which are closely tied to the application's context and market considerations.

In our paper, we detail the risk rating methodology to offer a thorough overview of the security assessment approach used for the HPC system. Additionally, we emphasize the link between risk calculation for threats and the identification of countermeasures that are essential for evaluating security. For a detailed explanation of the risk calculation methodology, please refer to [5].

Table 5. Abstract of HPC Contextualization.

Function	Category	Subcategory	Priority Level	Maturity Level
Identify (ID)	Asset Management (ID.AM)	`ID.AM-1`: The systems and physical devices in use within the organization are inventoried or listed.	MEDIUM	Insufficient; Basic, Normal, Advanced
	Asset Management (ID.AM)	`ID.AM-7`: Roles and responsibilities related to the processing and protection of personal data are defined and communicated to all personnel and relevant third parties (e.g., suppliers, clients, partners).	HIGH	Insufficient; Basic, Normal, Advanced
	Risk Assessment (ID.RA)	`ID.RA-1`: The vulnerabilities of the organization's resources (e.g., systems, premises, devices) are identified and documented.	LOW	Insufficient; Basic, Normal, Advanced
Protect (PR)	Awareness and Training (PR.AT)	`PR.AT-1`: All users are informed and trained.	LOW	Insufficient; Basic, Normal, Advanced
	Data Security (PR.DS)	`PR.DS-4`: The systems have adequate resources available to ensure availability.	MEDIUM	Insufficient; Basic, Normal, Advanced
	Maintenance (PR.MA)	`PR.MA-1`: Maintenance and repair of resources and systems are performed and recorded using controlled and authorized tools.	LOW	Insufficient; Basic, Normal, Advanced

7.3   Definition of Security Controls Roadmap

The application of Framework Nazionale per la Cybersecurity e la Data Protection allows to get an overview relative to the security level - expressed in term of *Overall Maturity Level (OML)* - of the analyzed profile through the *Profile Evaluation*. Additionally, its application provides a list of security controls that have not been implemented.

The implementation of all security controls is surely crucial; anyway, it's not necessarily required to implement all countermeasures. Accordingly, we defined a semi-automatic approach to individuate the *Security Controls Roadmap (SCR)*, which represents the set of security controls that must be applied to improve the security of the assets with the aim of mitigate the threats.

Our approach is based on the mapping between the primary label and CIS asset type: as previously mentioned, the primary label defines the class belonging to a considered MACM node; instead, CIS asset type defines the typology of the asset that the implementation of each sub-controls should protect. In detail, we defined: We mapped each primary label with CIS asset type. The resulting mapping is reported in Table 6.

Table 6. Primary Label - CIS Asset Type Mapping.

MACM Primary Label	CIS Asset Type
HW	Devices
Software	Applications
CSC	Users
Network	Network
Data	Data

We denote with: $\mathcal{A}_i$ and $\mathcal{N}$ the ith asset and the total number of assets within the considered MACM model, respectively; $\mathcal{AT}_j$ and $\mathcal{T}$ the jth MACM asset type and the total number of asset types, respectively; $\mathcal{AT}^{CIS}{}_z$ the zth asset type defined by the CIS; $\mathcal{P}_z$ the zth MACM primary label; $\mathcal{S}_m$ and $\mathcal{M}$ the mth sub-control and the total number of CIS sub-controls that has not been implemented within the analyzed profile, respectively; with $i \in \{1, ..., N\}$, $j \in \{1, ..., T\}$, $z \in \{1, ..., 5\}$, $m \in \{1, ..., M\}$; $\mathcal{AT}_j(\mathcal{A}_i)$ the asset type of the asset $\mathcal{A}_i$; $\mathcal{P}_z(\mathcal{AT}_j(\mathcal{A}_i))$ the primary label associated to asset type $\mathcal{AT}_j$ related to asset $\mathcal{A}_i$; $\mathcal{S}_m(\mathcal{AT}^{CIS}{}_z)$ the sub-control $\mathcal{S}_m$ related to $\mathcal{AT}^{CIS}{}_z$.

To determine the *SCR*, our approach involves two phases: (i) selection; and (ii) extraction. The selection phase comprises the following steps: (i) to select the MACM asset type $\mathcal{AT}_j(\mathcal{A}_i)$ for the asset $\mathcal{A}_i$: (ii) to individuate the MACM primary label $\mathcal{P}_z(\mathcal{AT}_j(\mathcal{A}_i))$; (iii) to determine the CIS asset type $\mathcal{AT}^{CIS}{}_z$ associated to $\mathcal{P}_z(\mathcal{AT}_j(\mathcal{A}_i))$; (iv) to collect all sub-controls $\mathcal{S}_m(\mathcal{AT}^{CIS}{}_z)$, linked with the $\mathcal{AT}^{CIS}{}_z$, that have not been implemented within the analyzed profile. So, the set of collected sub-controls represent the starting point from which extract the necessary sub-controls to protect $\mathcal{AT}_j(\mathcal{A}_i)$. Clearly, the asset $\mathcal{A}_i$ will inherit the extracted sub-controls.

In the extraction phase, we manually choose the relevant sub-controls taking account of the specific asset type as well as the typology of threat it may be affected by. In detail, different asset types, with the same primary label, may have different properties and functionalities thus, they may require different sub-controls even if the primary label is the same. As an example, both *HW.PC.LoginNode* and *HW.PC.ComputeNode* have *HW* primary label but, by having different purposes, they will be subjected to distinct sub-controls.

Since the implementation of the sub-controls aims at mitigating the threats, also them must be considered in the sub-controls extraction process: indeed, the countermeasures, which should protect a specific asset type, may mitigate a threat rather than another. For instance, some sub-controls that should be applied to *HW.PC.LoginNode* may mitigate *Authentication Abuse* while others may mitigate *User Session Hijacking*.

On the other hand, it is worth noting that there may be some sub-controls that do not mitigate any threat: this can lead to either missing threats for the asset type or a wrong choice of sub-controls in the selection process.

These considerations justify the choice of considering both asset type and threats in the sub-controls extraction process.

Lastly, to further increase the security level of the analyzed profile, our approach also involves, for each individuated CIS security control, the application of CIS Benchmarks [1], which are secure configuration guidelines for strengthening organizational technologies against cyber attacks that security experts have mapped to the CIS Controls.

8   Case Study

We decided to apply the described methodology to V:HPCCRI: the supercomputer of the University of Campania Luigi Vanvitelli. It is characterized by different hardware assets that may be grouped in: forty-two nodes and three networks. In detail, it involves: two login nodes; two management nodes; two storage nodes; twenty-six compute nodes; 10 GPU nodes; an high-performance communication network (i.e., InfiniBand); two non-high-performance communication networks (i.e., Ethernet and BCM).

An Ethernet network connects all nodes and it has been chosen for its widespread adoption, cost-effectiveness, and compatibility; on the other hand, an InfiniBand network, which also connects all nodes, has been selected for its high performance, low latency, and scalability, especially in the HPC context. A Broadcom (BCM) network offers robust networking solutions with advanced features, scalability, and reliability, ensuring efficient data transmission and effective network management within the system architecture.

Users and administrations may connect to the supercomputer only through the two login nodes, which are the only nodes connected to an external network (i.e., a university public network). The two mentioned nodes have a firewall in front of them. They host authentication and authorization services and a job scheduler (i.e., PBS) to allow the users to run their jobs. One management node hosts various services and three virtual machines that in their turn host: (i) OpenLDAP; (ii) xClarity; (iii) and zChild, respectively. There are two VLANs hosted by the Ethernet network used to connect the virtual machines. The other management node hosts only PBS. All compute nodes and GPU nodes also host PBS and additionally use Singularity as container platform. GPFS is the distributed file system present within the infrastructure hosted by storage nodes.

8.1   V:HPCCRI System Modelling

As specified by the described methodology, we initially modelled the V:HPCCRI architecture through the proposed MACM extension. The MACM model is reported in Fig. 3.

It should be noted that the figure doesn't show all the modeled nodes, but rather focuses on the important ones crucial for providing a clear view of the model. The

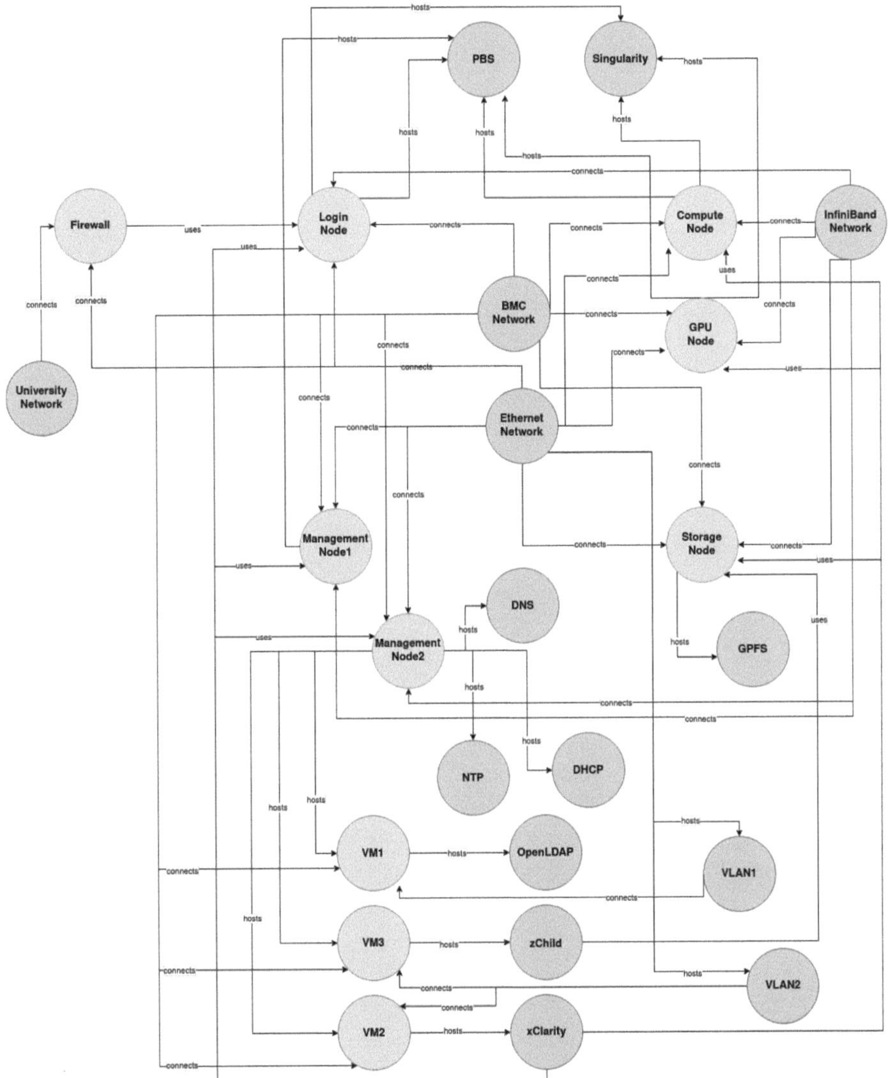

Fig. 3. V:HPCCRI MACM from [3].

complete MACM model comprises 61 nodes, with the nodes' color influenced by their label, while the attributes are not visible. The red nodes indicate the networks including physical networks as well as the two VLANs; the services are denoted by the purple nodes; the green nodes represent the physical-hosting hardware systems involving the firewall since it is a physical device positioned between the supercomputer and the university network; the light blue nodes denotes the virtual machines. Each edge is labelled with the relationship's name between the source node and the target one, consistently with enabled labels. Specifically, three relationships are involved in the

V:HPCCRI MACM model: (i) connects; (ii) uses; and (iii) hosts. To briefly summarize the reported model, we reported some of the relationships involved in Fig. 3 in Table 7. In this regard, we clarify that the notation *Node** denotes that the relationship defined within the table applies to all MACM nodes that fall within a specific class. As an example, *InfiniBand Network connects GPUNode** specifies that InfiniBand network connects all V:HPCCRI GPU nodes.

Table 7. Part of Relations between Components in the Case Study [3].

Start Node	Relation	End Node
InfiniBandNetwork	connects	LoginNode*
EthernetNetwork	connects	LoginNode*
EthernetNetwork	connects	Firewall
InfiniBandNetwork	connects	StorageNode*
InfiniBandNetwork	connects	GPUNode*
StorageNode	hosts	GPFS
ComputeNode	hosts	PBS
ComputeNode	hosts	Singularity
ManagementNode2	hosts	VM*
VM1	hosts	OpenLDAP
VM2	hosts	xClarity
VM3	hosts	zChild
VLAN1	connects	VM1
VLAN2	connects	VM2
VLAN2	connects	VM3
EthernetNetwork	hosts	VLAN*
xClarity	uses	LoginNode*
zChild	uses	StorageNode*

8.2   V:HPCCRI Threat Model

The threat model related to the case study was produced through the threat modelling approach described above and only considering the following criteria:

An asset Ai can be affected by a threat Ti if the Asset Type of Ai is the same of the Asset Type of Ti.

The results (i.e., a list of threats for each asset) are organized in a structured table characterized by six field: (i) *Asset name*, which is the name linked to a particular V:HPCCRI asset; (ii) *Asset type*, which specifies the functional behaviour for each asset; (iii) *Threat*, a label used to define the kind of the threat; (iv) *CIA*, which indicates the CIA requirement that a materialization of a threat may compromise; (v) *STRIDE*, which denotes the STRIDE classification; and (vi) *Behaviour*, a succinct characterization of a threat. Table 8 illustrates part of V:HPCCRI threat model. As already described, it is important to point out that instead of analyzing protocols from a communication point of view, we modeled them by considering the services they support. Accordingly, in our threat model, there are threats related to the services that use the protocols rather than threats that directly affect the protocols themselves.

Key tampering, where an attacker tampers the key used by devices, and Subnet Manager tampering, where an attacker compromises the Subnet Manager (SM) to manipulate InfiniBand network configuration and management information, are two examples of threats specific to the InfiniBand network. Directory enumeration, where an attacker attempts to list user accounts or organizational units within the LDAP directory, is a threat that could affect the LDAP service. Instead, user session hijacking, where an attacker steals or predicts a valid session token to gain unauthorized access to the system, and replay attacks, where an attacker intercepts communication between two endpoints and later retransmits the captured data to impersonate the legitimate sender or gain unauthorized access, are two threats that may affect each node within the Access Zone.

Table 8. Part of Threat Model per Asset [3].

Asset name	Asset type	Threat	CIA	STRIDE	Behaviour
InfiniBand Network	Network. Wired.HPC	Key Tampering	I, A	T	An attacker tampers the key used by devices
InfiniBand Network	Network. Wired.HPC	Subnet Manager Tampering	I, A	T	The attacker compromises the Subnet Manager (SM) to manipulate InfiniBand network configuration and management information
Management Node 1	HW.PC. Scheduler Node	Elevation of privileges	C, I, A	E	An attacker is able to change its privileges in access to the system services and data
Login Node 1	HW.PC. Login Node	User session hijacking	C, I	S	An attacker steals or predicts a valid session token to gain unauthorized access to the system
Login Node 1	HW.PC. Login Node	Authorization Abuse	C, I	S	An adversary is able to circumvent the authorization controls accessing data and services that should be not accessible to him
OpenLDAP	Service. LDAP	Directory Enumeration	C	I	An attacker attempts to list user accounts or organizational units within the LDAP directory
DNS	Service. DNS	NX Domain	C, I, A	D	Attacker floods server with requests, leading to DNS delays and "NXDOMAIN" responses for non-existent records due to overload

Table 9. Some Threats due to Compromised Field [3].

Threat	Post Condition	STRIDE	Asset	Due to
User Session Hijacking	[p, p, n]	S	PBS	Login Node
LDAP Injection	[n, p, n]	T, D	VM1	OpenLDAP
Download Malicious Content	[p, p, n]	S	Each Network	Login Node
Network Partitioning	[n, p, p]	D	Each Node	InfiniBand Network
Container Escape	[p, n, n]	I, E	Each Login Node, Each Compute Node, Each GPU Node	Singularity

Additionally, as previous mentioned, further threats have been identified by means the *Compromised* field. Some of these threats are reported in Table 9. As an example we can consider LDAP Injection threat that affect OpenLDAP service and is characterized by *source(hosts)* in Compromised field; therefore, consistently with what previously stated, its materialization will compromise also the virtual machine that hosts the service. Likewise, user session hijacking, that affect each node within Access Zone and presents *target(hosts)* in Compromised field, will affect all services that these nodes host (e.g., PBS). Additionally, some threats can indirectly affect the network that connects these services: for instance, downloading malicious content from the Login node can impact its communications. Network partitioning targets the network infrastructure, causing partitions that disrupt communication in specific segments, making them temporarily inaccessible. Since it has *target(connects)* in Compromised field, this threat also compromise the integrity of all interconnected nodes within the network.

The results have highlighted that 164 different threats affect the supercomputer, with redundancy not taken into account because of the presence of multiple nodes and virtual machines. Instead, the number of threats goes up to more than 1100 if every node and every service hosted on it is considered.

8.3   V:HPCCRI Security Assessment

To evaluate the security level of the V:HPCCRI and comprehend how to improve it through the definition of a *Security Controls Roadmap*, we followed five steps consistently with [9]: (i) selection of the contextualization; (ii) determination of a current profile; (iii) definition of target profiles; (iv) evaluation of the current profile; (v) definition of a roadmap to reach the target profiles. Each mentioned step is detailed below.

The implementation of the Framework Nazionale per la Cybersecurity e la Data Protection involves the use of security practices: in this work, we opted for CIS Critical Security Controls (CIS Controls) [1]. They constitute a prescriptive, prioritized, and simplified collection of best practices that can be employed to enhance your cybersecurity posture; so, they aim to mitigate the most prevalent cyber-attacks against IT systems and networks. It is worth noting that we chose CIS Security Controls because, on one hand, they are comprehensive and cover a wide range of security areas; on the other hand, they are also specific and actionable, organized into families for better manageability and implementation.

Selection of the Contextualization. It is the initial step required to start the application of the framework. In general, it is possible to choose from the existing contextualizations or create one from scratch. In our work, we used the HPC Contextualization previously defined.

Determination of the Current Profile. This step is based on the selected contextualization. In detail, for each subcategory of the contextualization, the priority and maturity levels must be chosen; furthermore, it is necessary to verify whether the controls (and, therefore, all the sub-controls that make up each control) have been implemented. The selected priority levels align with the contextualization. Meanwhile, maturity levels are established through the following criteria: a subcategory is assigned a specific maturity level if all the security controls associated with that particular maturity level are implemented. Table 10 illustrates an abstract of the V:HPCCRI current profile. It is characterized by six fields: (i) Subcategory, which reports the subcategories of the Framework Nazionale per la Cybersecurity e la Data Protection; (ii) Priority Level, which denotes the priority level for each considered subcategory; (iii) Maturity Level, which indicates the maturity level for each specific subcategory in compliance with what previously described; (iv) Sub-controls, which reports the CIS sub-controls associated with each subcategory; (v) IG, which defines the CIS Implementation Group for each CIS sub-control; and (vi) Implemented, indicating whether a sub-control is implemented in the case study or not.

The subcategory *ID.AM-1*, shown in the table, falls under the category "Asset Management" and the function "Identify". This pertains to the identification and management of data, devices, systems, and so on, in line with the identified security objectives. The subcategory has a medium priority level therefore, it is a relatively straightforward subcategory to implement. The maturity level is *basic*, indicating that only the essential sub-controls (IG1 controls) are implemented for the considered subcategory. The mentioned sub-controls refer to the CIS Control 1, which relates to inventory and control of hardware resources, specifically focusing on device resources. The implementation of these sub-controls is associated with the xClarity software within the infrastructure. The same applies to the subcategory *ID.AM-2* with the difference that the reported sub-controls refer to the CIS Control 2, which focuses on the inventory and control of platforms and software applications. The subcategory *PR.IP-9*, instead, falls under the category "Protect" and the function "Information Protection Processes and Procedures". It has a low priority level, making it a relatively challenging subcategory to implement. The maturity level is *insufficient*, indicating that at least one essential sub-control is not implemented for the considered subcategory. The reported sub-controls refer to the CIS Control 19 which focuses on incident response and management.

It is important to note that, since the subcategories are less specific of a control and they are characterized by an high-level nature, it could be the same control (and sub-controls) in correspondence of different subcategories.

Table 10. Abstract of V:HPCCRI Current Profile.

Subcategory	Priority Level	Maturity Level	Sub-controls	IG	Implemented
ID.AM-1: The systems and physical devices in use within the organization are inventoried or listed.	MEDIUM	BASIC	1.1	IG2	Yes
			1.2	IG3	Yes
			1.3	IG2	No
			1.4	IG1	Yes
			1.5	IG2	Yes
ID.AM-2: The platforms and software applications in use within the organization are inventoried or listed.	MEDIUM	BASIC	2.1	IG1	Yes
			2.2	IG1	Yes
			2.3	IG2	No
			2.4	IG2	No
			2.5	IG3	No
PR.IP-9: Response plans (Incident Response and Business Continuity) and recovery plans (Incident Recovery and Disaster Recovery) are active and managed in case of an incident/disaster.	LOW	INSUFFICIENT	19.1	IG1	No
			19.2	IG2	Yes
			19.3	IG1	Yes
			19.4	IG2	No
			19.5	IG1	Yes
			19.6	IG1	No
			19.7	IG2	No
			19.8	IG3	No

Lastly, it is important to clarify that it was not possible include certain subcategories in the definition of the current profile because: (i) either for the subcategory (present in the contextualization), the Framework Core does not define applicable CIS controls, or

(ii) the Framework Core specifies the CIS controls to consider, but the CIS document does not define sub-controls related to the function to which the considered subcategory refers.

Definition of Target Profiles. The three defined maturity levels previously described lead to the definition of target profiles: therefore, with three different maturity levels defined, there will be three corresponding target profiles: (i) basic; (ii) normal; and (iii) advanced. As previously described, when defining a profile, it is possible to reassign some (or all) of the priority levels and discard the eventual irrelevant subcategories. However, having specifically created an HPC contextualization from scratch, all the required subcategories along with their respective priority levels are already defined. Therefore, each target profile includes subcategories and priority levels that align with the contextualization. Meanwhile, maturity levels are defined consistently with the target profile typology.

Specifically, in accordance with CIS Security Controls, the following applies: the basic profile involves the implementation, for each subcategory, of all IG1 CIS sub-controls; the normal profile involves the implementation, for each subcategory, of all IG2 CIS sub-controls; the advanced profile requires the implementation, for each subcategory, of all CIS sub-controls.

This phase is fundamental for ongoing progress: the target profiles are required to define the gap between the current profile and the desired profile. In particular, they play a key role in establishing a roadmap for improving the security level of the case study.

Profile Evaluation. This step aims at associating an *Overall Maturity Level (OML)* to determine the current profile. It must be defined through a specific algorithm based on the evaluation of the subcategories' maturity levels: in particular, *OML* is equal to the lowest maturity level among the maturity levels associated with individual subcategories (e.g., if the lowest maturity level is insufficient, then *OML* is *insufficient*).

Applying the algorithm to the case study's current profile, resulted *insufficient*. We expected the obtained result because there are multiple subcategories with an insufficient level of maturity. This translates into the fact that some of the essential sub-controls are not implemented within the case study. For confidentiality reasons, we do not disclose the number of sub-controls that are implemented or not implemented, nor which ones they are.

Definition of Security Controls Roadmap. In addition to determine the security level of V:HPCCRI, the previous step allowed us to obtain a list of sub-controls that have not been implemented. Starting from this result, applying the criteria described in Sect. 7, we determined the Security Controls Roadmap. In detail, the selection phase results in 13 sub-controls for the asset types that are characterized by HW as primary label; 10 sub-controls for the asset types that are characterized by Software as primary label; and 16 sub-controls for the asset types that are characterized by Network as primary label. With the extraction phase, the number of sub-controls is reduced taking into account the asset type and the threats it is subjected to. Some results are showed in Table 11.

Table 11. Abstract of V:HPCCRI Security Controls Roadmap.

Asset Type	Asset Name	CIS Sub-Controls	CIS Sub-Controls Title	Mitigated Threats
HW.PC.Login Node	Login Node*	8.1	Utilize Centrally Managed Anti-Malware Software	Malware Compromise
		8.2	Ensure Anti-Malware Software and Signatures Are Updated	Malware Compromise
		8.6	Centralize Anti-Malware Logging	Malware Compromise
		1.8	Utilize Client Certificates to Authenticate Hardware Assets	Authentication Abuse, Authentication Relaxation for services
Service.Job Scheduler	PBS	3.1	Run Automated Vulnerability Scanning Tools	Exploitation of software vulnerabilities
		5.5	Implement Automated Configuration Monitoring Systems	Improper Configuration
		3.2	Perform Authenticated Vulnerability Scanning	Exploitation of software vulnerabilities

We point out that we used the symbol * to denote all assets that fall within a specific category. Accordingly, the expression *Login Node** specifies that the sub-controls defined in the table must to be applied to all login nodes of the analyzed infrastructure to mitigate the reported threats. Readers who are interested to details related to CIS sub-controls or particular threats may consult [1] or contact the authors, respectively.

9   Conclusion

HPC systems are generally considered trusted and secure systems due to their origin in academic and research environments; actually, the truth is quite different. Additionally, the exceptionally powerful computing capacity, the high-bandwidth network connections, and extensive storage that characterize HPC systems, along their employment in research and industry tasks and the heterogeneous resources that they comprise, make them an interesting target for malicious entities.

Accordingly, in this work we defined a three-step methodology aiming at performing a threat analysis and a security assessment of an HPC system. In detail, a threat analysis may be conducted by leveraging on MACM formalism and on the HPC threat catalogue we built using the threats we gathered through a systematic threat search. Additionally, we suggested a possible approach to perform a security assessment of an HPC system by means the Framework Nazionale per la Cybersecurity e la Data Protection using a specific HPC contextualization we defined. Furthermore, we also propose a possible approach to define the Security Controls Roadmap, that represents the set of suitable security controls to improve the security level of an HPC system.

The application of well-defined methodology to V:HPCCRI, the supercomputer of the University of Campania Luigi Vanvitelli, results in 164 different threats that can affect the supercomputer, with redundancy not taken into account because of the presence of multiple nodes and virtual machines. By considering every node and every service hosted on it, the number of threats goes up more than 1100. Instead, the security assessment of V:HPCCRI has highlighted that certain of the fundamental sub-controls are not implemented within the analyzed profile. For confidentiality reasons, we do not disclose the number of sub-controls that are implemented or not implemented, nor which ones they are.

To improve the security level of V:HPCCRI we plan to apply the CIS sub-controls comprised within the Security Controls Roadmap.

As future work, we first plan to completely automate the selection of security controls that must to be applied to improve the security level of an HPC infrastructure. Specifically, our intent is to define a criteria that automatically define which controls are prioritized based on the number of threats that mitigate weighed against the risk value and cost related to the implementation of controls.

Furthermore, since the systematic search has highlighted that there are no fit methodologies aiming at performing an HPC security assessment, we also plan to design and implement a security assessment methodology specific for the HPC domain.

Acknowledgments. This work was partially supported by the UPSIDE project (B63D23000 820004) funded by the Italian MIIMIT and by the IDA "Information Disorder Awareness" project within the framework of the Spoke 2 SERICS (D43C22003050001), funded by the Italian MIUR.

References

1. Center for Internet Security: Cis controls. Technical report, Center for Internet Security (2019)
2. Eicher, B.L., Solomon, S., Hall, S.: High performance computing evaluate and plan. In: Proceedings of the Practice and Experience on Advanced Research Computing, PEARC 2018. Association for Computing Machinery, New York (2018). https://doi.org/10.1145/3219104.3229246
3. Elia, R., Granata, D., Rak, M.: Systematic threat modelling of high-performance computing systems: the v:hpccri case study. In: Proceedings of the 14th International Conference

on Cloud Computing and Services Science, pp. 327–337 (2024). https://doi.org/10.5220/0012733000003711

4. Granata, D., Rak, M., Mallouli, W.: Automated generation of 5g fine-grained threat models: a systematic approach. IEEE Access **11**, 129788–129804 (2023). https://doi.org/10.1109/ACCESS.2023.3333209

5. Granata, D., Rak, M., Salzillo, G.: Risk analysis automation process in it security for cloud applications. In: Ferguson, D., Helfert, M., Pahl, C. (eds.) Cloud Computing and Services Science, pp. 47–68. Springer, Cham (2022)

6. Guo, Y., et al.: NIST Special Publication 800-223. White Paper, NIST (2023)

7. Hou, T., Wang, T., Shen, D., Lu, Z., Liu, Y.: Autonomous security mechanisms for high-performance computing systems: review and analysis. In: Jajodia, S., Cybenko, G., Subrahmanian, V.S., Swarup, V., Wang, C., Wellman, M. (eds.) Adaptive Autonomous Secure Cyber Systems, pp. 109–129. Springer, Cham (2020). https://doi.org/10.1007/978-3-030-33432-1_6

8. Kitchenham, B., Pearl Brereton, O., Budgen, D., Turner, M., Bailey, J., Linkman, S.: Systematic literature reviews in software engineering – a systematic literature review. Inf. Softw. Technol. **51**(1), 7–15 (2009). https://doi.org/10.1016/j.infsof.2008.09.009, special Section - Most Cited Articles in 2002 and Regular Research Papers

9. Angelini, M., et al.: Framework Nazionale per la Cybersecurity e la Data Protection. White Paper, CIS-Sapienza, CINI Cybersecurity National Lab (2019)

10. Malin, A., Van Heule, G.: Continuous monitoring and cyber security for high performance computing. In: Proceedings of the First Workshop on Changing Landscapes in HPC Security, CLHS 2013, pp. 9–14. Association for Computing Machinery, New York (2013). https://doi.org/10.1145/2465808.2465810

11. Mogilevsky, D., Lee, A., Yurcik, W.: Defining a comprehensive threat model for high performance computational clusters (2005)

12. National Institute of Standards and Technology: Framework for improving critical infrastructure cybersecurity. NIST Cybersecurity Framework Version 1.1 NIST CSWP 04162018, National Institute of Standards and Technology (2018). https://nvlpubs.nist.gov/nistpubs/CSWP/NIST.CSWP.04162018.pdf

13. Nowak, M.: Security in HPC centres (2017). https://doi.org/10.5281/zenodo.831509

14. Pleiter, D., Varrette, S., Krishnasamy, E., Özdemir, E., Pilc, M.: Security in an evolving European HPC ecosystem (2021). https://doi.org/10.5281/zenodo.5638456

15. Rak, M., Moretta, F., Granata, D.: Advancing esseca: a step forward in automated penetration testing. In: Proceedings of the 19th International Conference on Availability, Reliability and Security, ARES 2024. Association for Computing Machinery, New York (2024). https://doi.org/10.1145/3664476.3670459

16. Rak, M., Salzillo, G., Granata, D.: Esseca: an automated expert system for threat modelling and penetration testing for IoT ecosystems. Comput. Electr. Eng. **99**, 107721 (2022). https://doi.org/10.1016/j.compeleceng.2022.107721

17. Strohmaier, E., Dongarra, J.J., Meuer, H.W., Simon, H.D.: The marketplace of high-performance computing. Parallel Comput. **25**(13), 1517–1544 (1999). https://doi.org/10.1016/S0167-8191(99)00067-8.   https://www.sciencedirect.com/science/article/pii/S0167819199000678

18. Williams, J.: OWASP Risk Rating Methodology (2020). https://owasp.org/www-community/OWASP_Risk_Rating_Methodology
19. Yang, B., et al.: Research on network security protection of application-oriented supercomputing center based on multi-level defense and moderate principle. In: Journal of Physics: Conference Series, vol. 1828, no. 1, p. 012114 (2021). https://doi.org/10.1088/1742-6596/1828/1/012114

Author Index

C. Pahl and M. van Steen (Eds.): CLOSER 2024, CCIS 2851, p. 177, 2026.
https://doi.org/10.1007/978-3-032-17286-0